The Politics of
International Air
Transport

The Politics of International Air Transport

Betsy Gidwitz
Massachusetts Institute of
Technology

LexingtonBooks
D.C. Heath and Company
Lexington, Massachuestts
Toronto

187441

Library of Congress Cataloging in Publication Data

Gidwitz, Betsy.
 The politics of international air transport.

 Bibliography: p.
 Includes index.
1. Aeronautics, Commercial — Political aspects. 2. Aeronautics, Commer-
cial — Law and legislation. I. Title.
HE9777.G53   341.7'567   79-2706
ISBN 0-669-03234-4

Published simultaneously in Canada

Printed in the United States of America

International Standard Book Number: 0-669-03234-4

Library of Congress Catalog Card Number: 79-2706

Contents

Contents   v

List of Figures and Tables   ix

Preface   xi

Chapter 1   The Structure of International Airlines   1

Schedule Organization   1
Designation of Chosen Instruments   2
Airline Size   3
Load Type   6
Ownership   6
Financing Patterns   14
Political Independence   15
Summary   16

Chapter 2   International Airlines as Government
             Instruments   19

The Airline as Economic Instrument   19
The Airline as Political Instrument   21
The Airline as Military Instrument   26
The Airline as Espionage Instrument   27
Government Reinforcement of Use of Airlines
   as Policy Instruments   28
Summary   32

Chapter 3   Historical Development of International Civil
             Aviation   37

Between the Wars   37
The War Years   43
Planning for Postwar Aviation   46
Postwar Airline Recovery   52
Summary   73

Chapter 4   The International Regulatory Framework: Multi-
             national Regulation in the Worldwide Air-
             Transport Industry   79

The Impact of Diverse Political Systems upon
   Regulation   79

Public International Regulatory Organizations   81
Private International Regulatory Organizations   91
International Aviation Organization of Focused
    Interest   100
Summary   103

Chapter 5   **The International Regulatory Framework: Inter-**
                 nal Regulation of the One Country in the Air-
                 Transport Industry   109

The Role of Government Institutions in Regu-
    lating International Airlines   110
The Role of Nongovernmental Institutions in
    Regulating International Airlines   128
Summary   130

Chapter 6   **The International Regulatory Framework: Bila-**
                 teral Regulation of Air-Transport Relations be-
                 tween Two States   135

Elements of an Air-Transport Policy   135
The Process of Bilateral Negotiations   149
Format of Bilateral Air-Transport Agreements   152
Permits   154
Alternatives to Bilateral Air-Transport
    Agreements   155
Summary   156

Chapter 7   **The International Civil Aviation Route System** 159

The Structure of a Route System   159
The Traffic Base of Air Routes   161
Characteristics of Major International Routes   167
Unconventional International Routes   184
Summary   190

Chapter 8   **The International Transport Aircraft Industry** 193

The International Airframe and Engine In-
    dustries   193
Aircraft Selection and Fleet Planning for Inter-
    national Service   207
Financing Aircraft Purchases in the Interna-
    tional Market   208

Social and Political Problems in the Interna-
    tional Transport Aircraft Industry   212
Summary   214

Chapter 9   **Unlawful Interference with Aircraft**   219

Scope of the Problem   219
Air-Transport Industry Response to the Problem   225
The Political Response to the Problem   227
Summary   235

Biblography   243

Index   247

About the Author   260

List of Figures and Tables

Figures

7-1   Examples of Key Transatlantic Routes   168

7-2   Examples of Key Routes in East Asia and the Pacific   180

7-3   Three Air Routes between Europe and Japan   182

7-4   Berlin Air Corridors   186

Tables

1-1   Estimated Ton-Kilometers Performed (Passengers, Freight and Mail) for 1978 International Scheduled Service   4

1-2   Estimated Passenger-Kilometers Performed for 1978 International Scheduled Service   4

1-3   Estimated Freight Ton-Kilometers Performed for 1978 International Scheduled Service   5

1-4   Variations in Large Airline Ownership   7

1-5   Airline Ownership   8

3-1   Route Expansion of Colonial Airlines   40

3-2   Participants at the International Civil Aviation Conference: Chicago, 1944   47

Preface

The political complexity of the international air-transport industry can be overwhelming to observers and participants alike. The majority of airlines flying international routes are state owned, and many are manipulated by owner-governments for nonaviation purposes, such as implementation of foreign policy. The owner-governments represent more than 130 countries of varying political orientation and different stages of economic development. The air-transport regulatory system is tripartite, subject to the conflicting opinions and demands of multinational organizations, bilateral relationships, and domestic circumstances. The international transport-aircraft industry, expected to supply the airlines with operationally efficient equipment, is buffeted by its own political forces that, through sales and sales efforts, exert some influence on the air-carrier industry. Another outside influence, the phenomenon of air terrorism, illustrates the political weakness of the international air-transport industry—its inability to cope with a defined and obvious threat to the entire civil aviation system.

The purpose of this book is to examine the various political forces influencing the international air-transport industry and to clarify the interaction between these forces and different components of the industry. The first chapter analyzes the structure of international airlines, emphasizing political elements. The second chapter describes how governments use airlines for nonaviation purposes. The third chapter provides historical background to the politicization of international air transport. Chapters 4 and 6 review the regulatory process—multinational, bilateral, and domestic—that governs international civil aviation. Chapter 7 presents an overview of the international air-transport route system, providing both theoretical background and an analysis of many major international routes. Three routes of particular political importance are examined in some detail.

Chapter 8 discusses the strengths and weaknesses of various national aircraft manufacturing industries, fleet planning for international service, financing aircraft purchases in the international market, and several problems affecting the industry. Chapter 9 examines the topic of unlawful interference with aircraft, a crisis so influenced by political factors that a solution seems unattainable.

This book should be of interest to students of international air transportation, airline management personnel, lawyers and government officials concerned with civil aviation, and political and business analysts concerned with the interaction between industry and government, particularly at the international level. Any individual interested in foreign relations, whether associated with transportation or not, should also find the book useful.

The primary impetus for writing this book was provided by graduate students in a course on international air transportation in the Flight Transportation Laboratory at the Massachusetts Institute of Technology. I am indebted to the many foreign students in these classes who contributed insight into air-transport operations in different countries and to faculty and staff colleagues at M.I.T. who provided assistance and encouragement. Many airline industry and government officials in the United States and numerous other countries also provided useful information and advice. Space does not permit listing of individual names, but I am grateful to them all. I alone am responsible for any errors of fact or judgment that may be found in the following pages.

1 The Structure of International Airlines

Airlines of vastly different character, schedule organization, network, purpose, ownership patterns, and financial status fly international routes. No "typical" international carrier exists, but certain patterns may be distinguished among the international airlines.

Schedule Organization

The greater portion of international air service is provided by airlines offering regularly scheduled flights, that is, flights which are listed in published timetables, are available to the general public, and operate at the same time of day over the same general route one or more days each week. Charter carriers (also known as nonscheduled airlines and, in the United States, as supplemental airlines) operate irregularly scheduled special flights, often for established groups, on high-density routes. Charter service constitutes about 15 percent of total world passenger-kilometers flown and, as a component of inclusive tours in the travel industry, has the predominant share of air traffic on routes between Europe and Mediterranean tourist countries.

Two considerations of economics inherent in their operations permit charter airlines to offer substantially lower fares than those charged by scheduled airlines. First, overhead or indirect costs are reduced for the charter carrier because tour agents typically handle commercial procedures, such as promotion and reservations, and traffic management functions, such as passenger service, airport organization, and ground transportation. Second, although scheduled airlines must meet all timetable obligations, even when low passenger loads do not cover expenses, charter carriers typically operate at full or near-full capacity.

American charter airlines usually carry both passengers and freight on specific routes designated by the Civil Aeronautics Board (CAB). Military contracts accounted for as much as 70 percent of the freight traffic on U.S. charter airlines during the 1970s, but less than 20 percent of passenger traffic. In Europe, charter carriers are heavily engaged in inclusive vacation tours packaged by agents specializing in this single type of traffic. The low fares—less than $300 for peak season airfare, two weeks in a three-star hotel, ground transportation, and limited sightseeing—have made sunny

1

Mediteranean sites accessible to northern Europeans of moderate income levels.

Some European scheduled airlines own all or significant interest in subsidiary charter airlines; for example, Lufthansa owns 100 percent of Condor, Swissair owns 62.5 percent of Balair, and KLM owns 25 percent of Martinair. Although U.S. antitrust regulations do not permit American scheduled carriers to own separate charter carriers, the major U.S. international airlines do operate extensive charter services. Best known for its scheduled service, Pan American is, in fact, the largest charter operator in the world.

The charter market caters to the traveler who wants inexpensive air transportation and is willing to travel at the tour operator's convenience. The more traditional passenger is willing to pay for air transportation at his or her own convenience, with more individual service. Markets exist for the service provided by both types of airlines or for airlines that have both scheduled and charter flights.

Designation of Chosen Instruments

Governments, which negotiate bilateral air transport agreements with other governments, make policy decisions on the range or extent of international air service to be provided by home-registered airlines. Domestic and international economic and political factors usually determine both the extent of international air service offered and the number of airlines involved in providing this service.

Many countries in which general governmental authority is highly centralized also have strongly centralized civil aviation sectors in which all civil aviation activity is operated by a single airline. For example, in the Soviet Union and most of the other party-states only one airline exists. Aeroflot and its counterparts operate the entire range of domestic and international civil aviation for their respective countries. In other countries, governments may sanction the development of more than one airline for scheduled service but restrict each to specific and different spheres of operation so that home-based carriers compete only against foreign airlines and not with each other.

Designation of specific routes for multiple carriers usually follows one of several patterns. In some countries, certain airlines are designated to fly international routes and others to operate domestic service. The Australian government, for example, has selected Qantas to fly international service and two other carriers, Ansett and Trans-Australia Airways, to offer domestic routes. Other governments designate one or more carriers to fly longer intercontinental routes and another or others to fly regional international service, the latter perhaps as extensions of domestic service. As examples, one may cite several U.S. airlines that offer essentially domestic service but that also operate flights to Canada: among these are Western, which offers service to western Canada; Republic, which operates service to central Canada; and Eastern and US Air (formerly Allegheny), which operate routes to eastern Canada. Still another pattern is evident in France where one carrier, Air Inter, dominates domestic civil aviation; and two airlines, Air France and UTA (Union de Transports Aériens), operate different international routes. State-owned Air France is the designated French carrier on most international service, but privately owned UTA has exclusive franchise on routes to former French colonies in equatorial Africa, to South Africa, to the South Pacific via Asia, and between French Polynesia and the western United States. Comparable division of intercontinental routes according to regions is also the pattern in Britain with state-owned British Airways and privately owned British Caledonian; and in Canada with state-owned Air Canada and privately held CP Air (Canadian Pacific).

Whichever specific pattern is employed, most governments with more than one international airline adhere to the principle of "chosen instrument" or "exclusive franchise," that is, designation of one airline as official instrument to operate the government franchise on a particular route. Only the United States, with its large traffic base and long-standing philosophy of vigorous free enterprise, encourages competition on individual routes between home-registered airlines, as well as with foreign carriers. In response to deteriorating economic conditions caused in part by the rapid escalation of fuel prices in late 1973 and in 1974, competition between U.S. airlines was eliminated on some service in 1975 by order of the Civil Aeronautics Board. As then-sluggish traffic later resumed growth, dual designation on a portion of this service was restored in 1978. The following may be cited as examples of routes on which two U.S. airlines compete: Pan American and TWA on New York-London and New York-Paris; Pan American and Northwest Orient on New York-Tokyo; and American and Braniff on Dallas-Mexico City.

Airline Size

Airline size can be measured by various indexes, the most common probably being performance-related, such as total ton-kilometers (passengers, freight, and mail) flown, passenger-kilometers flown, and freight-ton kilometers flown. Considerations of kilometers flown can be further divided into domestic and international operations. The top ranking airlines in international scheduled service as measured by three indexes is shown in tables 1-1, 1-2, and 1-3.

Table 1-1

Estimated Ton-Kilometers Performed (Passengers, Freight, and Mail for 1978 International Scheduled Service

County	Ton-Kilometers Performed (millions)
United States	9,400
United Kingdom	5,350
France	3,720
Japan	3,000
West Germany	2,790
Netherlands	1,995
Canada	1,660
Australia	1,530
Italy	1,520
Singapore	1,250
Switzerland	1,335
Scandinavia*	1,250
Spain	1,190
South Korea	1,060
USSR	1,020

Source: "Scheduled Air Traffic Growth in 1978 Was the Highest in Last Decade," *ICAO Bulletin,* 34:6 (June, 1979), p. 27.

*Three states—Denmark, Norway, and Sweden—are partners in Scandinavian Airlines System (SAS), a consortium airline.

Table 1-2

Estimated Passenger-Kilometers Performed for 1978 International Scheduled Service

County	Passenger-Kilometers Performed (millions)
United States	63,200
United Kingdom	43,300
France	25,500
Japan	18,700
West Germany	15,350
Canada	13,800
Netherlands	12,650
Australia	12,600
Italy	11,100
Switzerland	10,150
Singapore	9,750
Spain	9,400
Scandinavia*	8,650
USSR	8,350
South Korea	6,300

Source: "Scheduled Air Traffic Growth in 1978 Was the Highest in Last Decade," *ICAO Bulletin,* 34:6 (June, 1979), p. 27.

*Three states—Denmark, Norway, and Sweden—are partners in Scandinavian Airlines System (SAS), a consortium airline.

Table 1-3
Estimated Freight-Ton Kilometers Performed for 1978 International Scheduled Service

County	Freight-Ton Kilometers Performed (millions)
United States	3,030
France	1,600
West Germany	1,320
United Kingdom	1,220
Japan	1,180
Netherlands	790
Lebanon	505
Italy	500
South Korea	478
Scandinavia*	445
Switzerland	409
Singapore	405
Brazil	390
Belgium	385
Australia	340

Source: "Scheduled Air Traffic Growth in 1978 Was the Highest in Last Decade," *ICAO Bulletin,* 34:6 (June, 1979), p. 28.
*Three states—Denmark, Norway, and Sweden—are partners in Scandinavian Airlines System (SAS), a consortium airline.

Non-performance-related criteria, such as number of aircraft in fleet, can be misleading because differences in operating efficiency can cause two airlines with the same number of aircraft to achieve performance levels so different as to make comparisons meaningless. Similarly, evaluating the size of an airline solely on the number of foreign points in its network does not show that some of its routes may be political with only once-weekly frequency and few passengers. Aeroflot, for example, has a very large network in terms of foreign destinations, but ranks lower in the more important sphere of traffic performance than many airlines with smaller networks (see tables 1-1, 1-2, and 1-3). The explanation lies in the operation by the Soviet carrier of a number of low-frequency routes with poor traffic performance to developing countries.

Pan American and the Beirut-based cargo carrier Trans Mediterranean Airways are the only scheduled airlines to operate around-the-world service. Six carriers—Pan American, Alitalia, KLM, Lufthansa, Japan Air Lines, and Qantas—serve all populated continents as do the combined services of Air Canada/CP Air, British Airways/British Caledonian, and Air France/UTA. Sabena, Swissair, SAS, Aeroflot, and Varig serve all populated continents except Australia; and Air-India and Olympic operate routes to all populated continents except South America.

Load Type

Most international airlines, whether operating scheduled or charter service, transport both passengers and freight.[a] In Europe, as much as 40 percent of the ton-kilometer performance of certain major carriers, such as Lufthansa and Sabena, is derived from freight carriage. JAL shows similar proportions in its international operations. American air carriers, although carrying far more international air freight in ton-kilometers than airlines from any other country, generally transport lower proportions of freight on mixed load international routes. Doubtless this difference is, in large part, due to the operations of several strong American international freight carriers, among them Airlift International (United States—Caribbean) and Flying Tiger (worldwide). No counterparts of these freight airlines exist in Europe or the Far East. Outside the United States, the only strong international freight airline is the the Beirut-based Trans Mediterranean Airways.

Some airlines, while operating scheduled and/or charter service under their own names, also lease out a substantial portion of their equipment to other airlines, frequently to those of developing countries which may lack the capital and experience to purchase and operate large fleets. In a "dry lease," the lessee carrier contracts only for the use of the aircraft itself; in a "wet lease," the more common of the two types, the lessee carrier contracts for the aircraft, crew, fuel, and maintenance. Many airlines least out some of their aircraft; among the most prominent lessors are British Midland Airways, Flying Tiger, and World Airways.

Aeroflot, the Soviet airline, is almost *sui generis*—operating a number of services not normally performed by commercial carriers. Included in its functions are agricultural spraying, iceberg spotting, forest patrolling and fire fighting, oil and gas field support, and medical evacuation. Other party-state airlines, such as Interflug of East Germany, also perform non-commercial work, but most countries assign these responsibilities to more specialized governmental agencies.

Ownership

Privately owned U.S. airlines are the exceptions to the general pattern of total or majority state ownership of international airlines prevailing throughout the world (see table 1-4).

---

[a]The term cargo is usually interpreted to include all types of dead load, including baggage and mail. The term freight specifically excludes baggage and mail. The airlines and different countries often use the two words rather loosely. Specialized all-cargo aircraft generally do not carry baggage or mail and might more accurately be called all-freight aircraft. Freight is often considered to be goods that require an air waybill.

Table 1-4
Variations in Large Airline Ownership

100% Private	Majority Private	Majority State	100% State
Pan American	JAL	KLM	Qantas
TMA	Swissair	Lufthansa	Air Canada
CP Air	Varig	Sabena	British
British		SAS	Airways
Caledonian			Air France
UTA			Aeroflot

Differences in ownership approach can be found within each of these categories as can be seen in brief descriptions of some of the carriers:

1. Pan American and all other U.S. international (and domestic) airlines are owned by thousands of individual stockholders.
2. Trans Mediterranean Airways (TMA) is owned by its president, Munir Abu Hadar.
3. CP Air is owned by Canadian Pacific Railways. Until 1978 Air Canada was owned by the state-owned Canadian National Railway Company; it is now owned by another government body.
4. Fifty-seven percent of JAL is privately held and 43 percent is state-held. JAL itself has total control of Japan Asia Airways, a carrier established specifically to serve Taiwan; it holds minority interest in Japan's two major domestic airlines, All-Nippon Airways (ANA) and TOA Domestic Airlines (TDA).
5. Seventy-five percent of Swissair is privately owned and 25 percent is state-owned. Swissair owns 62.5 percent of Balair, a charter and inclusive tour airline.
6. Employees own 96.11 percent of Varig; the state of Rio Grande do Sul, (in which the airline has its headquarters), owns 3.89 percent.
7. The federal German government owns 74.31 percent of Lufthansa. The Land of North Rhine-Westphalia, (the state in which Lufthansa has its headquarters), owns 2.35 percent; German post office, 1.75 percent; German state railroads, .85 percent; German banks, 3 percent; and private stockholders own 17.84 percent. Lufthansa owns a charter airline, Condor, and German Cargo Services, a cargo carrier.
8. SAS, described later in this chapter, is a multinational airline in which three-sevenths interest is held by the Swedish government and by Swedish private concerns, and two-sevenths interest each held by Danish and Norwegian governments and private concerns.

Most government-owned airlines are organized as semi-autonomous corporate entities. Some are controlled by a specific government ministry, usually a ministry of transportation. Aer Lingus is owned by the Irish Ministry of Finance.

As shown in table 1-5 some governments have authorized both state-owned and privately controlled airlines to operate scheduled international routes. (See table 1-5) In each of the countries listed, the state-owned airline has the larger international network and is usually favored for operation of new routes. The airlines within each country have different route systems and do not compete with one another. In Canada, Mexico, and France, the fleet of one airline is primarily Boeing (CP Air, Mexicana, Air France) and the fleet of the other is primarily Douglas.

Many countries with state-owned international carriers license one or more privately owned carriers to operate charter service and inclusive tours. Privately held airlines operate domestic service in some countries in which international routes are restricted to government-owned airlines.

Airlines as Owners of Other Airlines

Some airlines in developing countries are partially owned by foreign airlines, usually those of the former colonial power. Thus, Air France holds minority interest in Air Madagascar, Air Comores, Tunis Air, Royal Air Maroc, Air Djibouti, and Air Guadeloupe. UTA has minority ownership in Air Afrique, the multinational airline of ten former French African colonies, and the local carriers of six of these countries. British Airways holds minority interest in Cyprus Airways and in CP Air (Cathay Pacific) of Hong Kong. Alitalia owns 49 percent of Somali Airlines. Cultural affinities and British Commonwealth ties have been factors in the minority interests held in Air Panama and Air Jamaica by Iberia and Air Canada respectively. In the latter association, Air Canada's ownership share has been gradually reduced and is due to be sold in its entirety to the Jamaican government as Jamaicans acquire more experience in operating the carrier. In these relationships, the developed country airlines exert varying degrees of influence over the developing country carriers; in almost all instances, the relation-

Table 1-5
Airline Ownership

Country	State-Owned Airline	Privately Owned Airline
Canada	Air Canada	CP Air
Mexico	Aeromexico	Mexicana
Britain	British Airways	British Caledonian
		British Midland
France	Air France	UTA

ship is both tutelary and commercial. The nature of the linkage is clearly evident in the commonality of fleet aircraft types, the equipment in the client airline often consisting wholly or partly of obsolescent or near-obsolescent castoffs of the patron carrier and/or of aircraft manufactured in the patron country.

Shipping Firms as Owners of Airlines

As air transport developed in the 1920s, European shipping firms organized their own airlines to complement their seagoing capabilities. Economic upheavals in the 1930s and the turbulence of World War II terminated some of these relationships, but several shipping/airline associations remain. Dan-Air, a large British charter and inclusive tour operator with some scheduled domestic service, is owned by the shipping brokerage firm of Davies and Newman. Shipping companies also hold significant ownership shares in British Caledonian Airways and British Cargo Airlines. The Dutch NSU shipping firm owns 49 percent of Martinair, an Amsterdam operator of charters, inclusive tours, air taxi service, and aerial photography and advertising services. (KLM owns 25 percent and various Dutch financial institutions hold 26 percent of Martinair.) Hapag-Lloyd Fluggesellschaft, a Hanover-based charter and inclusive tour operator, is owned by the Hapag-Lloyd shipping group. A family-owned shipping firm holds Braathens, the Norwegian domestic airline; and the A.P. Moller Shipping Company of Copenhagen owns Maersk Air, operator of Danish domestic routes, passenger and cargo charters, and inclusive tours.

Multiple Governments as Owners of Airlines

Some small countries desiring to develop an international airline encounter a host of economic problems deriving mainly from insufficient financial backing, lack of management expertise, and an inadequate potential traffic base. Unless political reasons are so overwhelming that an international carrier is founded despite these obstacles, formation of a consortium airline with one or more neighboring states may be a desirable alternative. Governments joining in this venture must be able to submerge nationalism, and should possess a common cultural background and compatible political and economic philosophies. Should any of these factors become a point of dispute, the multinational airline will collapse. Of the multinational airlines formed since World War II — SAS, Air Afrique, Gulf Air, several small carriers in the Caribbean, East African Airways, and MSA (Malaysia-Singapore Airlines) — the last two have failed. A brief description of some of these carriers indicates their strengths and weaknesses.

SAS—Scandinavian Airlines System. The idea of a joint Scandinavian airline for the express purpose of operating North Atlantic service was discussed by representatives of Denmark, Norway, Sweden, and Finland in 1938, but its formation was deterred initially by Swedish reluctance to forego its own individual service and later by World War II. In the postwar period, Finland's exclusion was mandated by its inability to match the capital investment of the other three countries and by its political dependence upon the goodwill of the Soviet Union. The first joint North Atlantic service operated by Denmark, Norway, and Sweden occurred in 1946. In 1947 a holding company controlling the new SAS was incorporated—in New York, to avoid possible legal problems. The shareholders of the carrier were three airlines of the participating countries. Each continued to operate European service until 1951 when SAS took over all international routes. Although none of the three airlines now functions as a carrier, they continue to form the constitutent ownership of SAS with the Swedish member controlling three-sevenths, and the Danish and Norwegian members two-sevenths each. Each of these nonoperating airlines is, in turn, jointly owned by the respective governments and by state-influenced private interests.

Strong efforts are made by the SAS board of directors to distribute equitably among the three owner countries managerial and flight positions, other responsibilities, facilities, and programs. National quotas are maintained in many areas of allocation so as to encourage equality. Even with these measures, charges and countercharges have been made by citizens of each country that citizens of one or both of the others receive preference in appointments, that one or both of the other countries has more than its share of facilities. In 1978 the retiring president of SAS, Knut Hagrup, said, "It would be impossible to form SAS today. The three countries are more national than they were after World War II. They are not in the mood to go together and make one airline."[1]

Although it might be difficult to form SAS today, the airline continues to exist, even to operate a fiscally sound worldwide service that no one of the three countries could offer on its own. The peoples of the three owner-states have much in common, including mutually comprehensible languages, a tradition of hard work, and the common sense to submerge potentially destructive nationalist excesses. The different nationalisms may be partially assuaged by the existence of separate domestic carriers in each of the three countries and, for the Danes, three Copenhagen-based charter operators.

Air Afrique. In 1961 the French carriers UAT (Union Aéromaritime de Transport, one of two predecessor airlines of UTA) and Air France formed a holding company, Sodetraf (Société pour le Dévelopment du Transport

Aérien en Afrique) whose function it was to assist the French West African colonies, then gaining independence, to form a joint international airline. Eleven countries—Cameroon, Central African Republic, Chad, Congo-Brazzaville, Dahomey (Benin), Gabon, Ivory Coast, Mauritania, Niger, Senegal, and Upper Volta—signed the Treaty of Yaounde establishing Air Afrique. Of the remaining French West African countries, Togo joined in 1968, and Guinea and Mali, both under Soviet influence, formed their own international airlines with Soviet and East European assistance. Each of the initial joining states of Air Afriques held 6.54 percent interest in the carrier and Sodetraf retained 28 percent. The airline operates service to more than twenty African countries, to Europe, and to New York. Its headquarters are in Abidjan, capital of the Ivory Coast, one of the richest and most heavily French-influenced of the former French colonies.

As reflected in the predominantly Douglas fleets of both airlines, Air Afrique is a recipient of considerable technical, managerial, and operational assistance from UTA. Even as the carrier approaches its twentieth anniversary, substantial numbers of French citizens hold important posts in management and other sectors of the airline. Their presence connotes not only the actual need of Air Afrique for their expertise, but also the inability of the member African states to agree on apportionment of positions among themselves. From its inception, the carrier has been plagued by intense national rivalries between the constituent countries for employment, service to their own capitals, location of regional headquarters, naming of aircraft after national capitals, and similar issues. It was over such questions that Cameroon left the corporation in 1971, followed by oil-rich Gabon in 1977. Perhaps the major factor insuring the continuation of Air Afrique is the realization by the governments of the remaining member-states, many of them very poor, that few of them could maintain their own intercontinental service.

With international service provided by Air Afrique, most of the member-states possess small airlines for domestic routes and, in a few cases, several routes to adjacent countries. Air Afrique and/or UTA hold minority interest in approximately one-half of these domestic carriers.

Gulf Air. Gulf Aviation was founded in 1950 by a former Royal Air Force pilot. In 1951 British Overseas Airways Corporation (BOAC, now part of British Airways) became a major shareholder. In 1973 the name of the airline was changed to Gulf Air. British Airways relinquished its holdings in 1964 to the governments of the United Arab Emirates, Bahrein, Oman, and Qatar, each of which owns 25 percent of the airline. Headquartered in Bahrein, Gulf Air operates throughout the Middle East, east to Bombay, and west to London. Drawing on oil revenues, the carrier is very well equipped and is heavily staffed in all areas by foreigners, predominantly British.

Many of the long-range routes are operated separately from each capital, regardless of traffic justification, in order to satisfy nationalist demands. Another problem endured by the carrier is frequent disruption of scheduled service resulting from the appropriation of aircraft by heads of state for personal use. Its particular financial resources allow Gulf Air substantial laxity in economic performance.

East African Airways. The joint carrier was founded in 1946 by Kenya, Uganda, Tanganyika, and Zanzibar (the latter two now comprising Tanzania). In 1967 it was placed under the direction of the East African Common Services Organization (EACSO), a body intended to administer a sort of East African common market with jurisdiction over various transport modes, seaports, communications, and other services. Kenya owned 68 percent of the airline, Uganda 23 percent, and Tanzania 9 percent. With headquarters in Nairobi, the hub of its flight operations, East African offered domestic and inter-EACSO service and flights to other African points, Europe, and as far east as Bombay. In January 1977 the airline was dissolved.

East African Airways faltered on the incompatible political and economic philosophies of the owner-countries. The ideology of Kenya is essentially capitalistic and profit-oriented; its government wanted airline routes to be economically viable and international service to be improved (with new long-range aircraft) to boost foreign tourism. Socialist Tanzania insisted that subsidized routes serve remote domestic points as a social service, and downgraded foreign tourism as socially nonproductive. Uganda under the rule of Idi Amin was internally chaotic and outwardly hostile to Kenya and Tanzania, at times claiming parts of the territory of each. Both Uganda and Tanzania resented Kenyan preeminence in the corporation—Kenya's much larger ownership share and its capital's role as major airport. Uganda and Tanzania were also in general financial difficulties and refused to transfer ticket revenues to airline headquarters. A cash flow crisis ensued; inability to pay fuel bills was the immediate cause of collapse.

Uganda had formed a small separate carrier, Uganda Airlines, in 1976 before the dissolution of East African Airways. Establishment of the Ugandan carrier was spurred by Kenyan closing of their mutual land border due to unpaid Ugandan debts in port fees, imports, and other items. With surface transport for its coffee exports thus denied, Uganda obtained two Boeing 707s to fly coffee to London. The exceptionally high coffee prices of the time—and the financial straits of the Ugandan government—made these flights more reasonable than might be initially surmised. On the return flights, the aircraft were loaded with "whiskey, cigarettes and platform shoes," as well as with consumer electronic goods, for Idi Amin's army and secret police.[2]

When East African Airways failed in 1977 both Kenya and Tanzania founded their own carriers, Kenya Airways and Air Tanzania. Each used as the nucleus of its fleet East African aircraft which happened to be in the respective countries at the time of the East African collapse. Kenyan domination of the joint airline enabled it to appropriate the larger portion of the fleet. Reflecting their national differences, the new airline of Kenya operates extensive international service in a network similar to that of East African Airways whereas the carrier of Tanzania, with a small fleet of short-range aircraft, confines service to domestic routes and to the neighboring capitals of Lusaka and Maputo.[3]

Malaysia-Singapore Airlines (MSA). In 1963 the former British colonies of Malaya and Singapore joined to form the Federation of Malaysia. That year a national carrier, Malaysia Airways, was established. In 1965 Singapore withdrew from the federation and, in 1967, the name of the airline, now jointly owned by two separate countries, was appropriately changed to Malaysia-Singapore Airlines (MSA). MSA operated until 1972 when the differences which caused the Federation of Malaysia to collapse also proved too strong to ensure the continuation of a common airline. Singapore is a small island-state with no need for domestic air transport. A prosperous banking and trade center, it desires extensive international airs service. Malaysia's priorities are far different. It is a larger developing country with extensive, relatively primitive rural areas on the mainland and two distant, also primitive, territories located across the South China Sea on the island of Borneo. Malaysia requires substantial domestic air service for elementary economic and social purposes. In addition to this basic insoluable disparity in air transport goals, Malaysia deeply resented Singaporean dominance of MSA because of the location of airline headquarters and major airport on Singapore and the larger Singaporean representation in management.

Two separate carriers, Singapore Airlines and Malaysian Airlines System, were founded in 1972. Both operate long intercontinental service, but the Malaysian carrier also flies numerous short-range domestic routes.

Cooperative Agreements

An alternative to multinational airlines is the formation by different carriers of consortia which fulfill specific functions, such as maintenance and training. Although each airline retains separate ownership, some independence is forfeited through the necessity of reaching agreement on the issues covered by the consortium.

The initial purpose in forming KSSU and Atlas, the two best known international consortia, was the desire by a number of European airlines to economize in maintenance of the Boeing 747 widebody aircraft which each carrier was purchasing in small numbers. KLM, SAS, Swissair, and UTA, all major operators of Douglas narrowbody equipment, formed KSSU in 1968. Air France, Alitalia, Lufthansa, and Sabena formed Atlas in 1969; Iberia joined the group in 1972. The French, German, Belgian, and Spanish airlines were major Boeing narrowbody operators, and Alitalia was beginning to purchase Boeing aircraft. Responsibility for maintenance of different aspects of the Boeing widebody have been assigned to the member airlines within each group. One carrier is designated to perform major maintenance on the airframes of all 747s owned by consortium members; another to handle engines; a third is accountable for another area. Gradually, allocation of specific responsibilities has been expanded to include maintenance of other types of commonly owned aircraft, crew training, and drawing up of common specifications for ordering new equipment. Savings resulting from the common maintenance programs alone are 10 to 20 percent per carrier.

Financing Patterns

Airlines registered in the United States, like other American businesses, are viewed as private financial entities expected to return profits on investments. It is assumed that American carriers will purchase the most efficient aircraft for the routes operated and will fly only those routes for which an adequate traffic base exists. Therefore, financial profit, rather than political rationale, is the key factor in airline management.

The American economic system is imperfect and, in the case of airlines, inconsistent. Since 1958 local-service air carriers (also called regional and feeder air carriers) have been eligible to receive small federal government subsidy for providing economically unjustified service to certain points where the federal government, pressured by local government agencies, considers air transport to be necessary for social reasons. However, American carriers that provide economically unjustified international service on routes considered politically necessary by the U.S. government do not receive subsidies. Pan Am continued flights to Moscow in the hope that its traffic would improve, absorbing losses because the federal government suggested, unofficially, that suspension of service might redound unfavorably to Pan Am when that carrier sought new routes or understanding on another issue.[4]

For Pan American and other U.S. carriers flying international service, the number of economically nonviable routes operated at the request of the federal government is minimal. In U.S. relations with most foreign countries, political and economic ties are mutually and naturally reinforced, and the need for air links usually evolves as an integral component of increased economic interaction. With the Soviet Union, political ties are contrived and forced; economic interaction, including connecting air services, does not evolve in a natural way.

The inconsistencies in American government policy on airline subsidies do not obtain in most other countries. Subsidies, direct or indirect, are commonly given to many airlines whose continued operation, at a certain scale, is perceived as necessary by the government of registry. It should not be surprising that airlines in which majority ownership is held by the government of registry are most often the recipients of subsidy and that need for repeated subsidy of privately owned airlines often leads to airline nationalization.

Forms of subsidy vary widely. The most direct type is a cash payment to meet operating losses. Sabena has received such payments from the Belgian government since the 1950s; in some years the payments have reached more $50 million. In 1978 Air France concluded an agreement with the French government covering three years in which the government agreed to pay the airline $60 million toward the acquisition of new aircraft, $39 million to cover operating costs of inefficient French-manufactured aircraft, and $50 million as compensation for operating, at government insistence, from two different airports near Paris. Other forms of direct government subsidy include provision of equity capital and exemption from payment of dividends.

Among the most important of the many types of indirect subsidy are interest-free or low-interest government loans for equipment and other improvements. Loan guarantees are extended by many governments. A number of governments provide financial assistance for training programs. Various means used to direct and divert traffic to the national carrier can be viewed as forms of subsidy. The requirement that official government traffic be carried exclusively on the national airline is common, even by governments in which airlines are privately owned; when, as in the Soviet Union and other authoritarian states, almost all home-generated traffic is "official," the national carrier has a monopoly on the local market. A monopoly on cargo carriage, including cargo shipped by or to foreign parties, is often achieved by requiring that all cargo be handled by state-owned agencies which then either divert it to the state carrier or so favor the state carrier in handling procedures that shipping by a foreign airline entails substantial time and other penalties. Governments may direct state-owned aircraft industries to sell aircraft to state airlines at reduced prices.[5]

Political Independence

In common with many other economic entities, airlines in which economic power is state-controlled are often subject to substantial political interference in the conduct of normally nonpolitical decisionmaking. For example, a carrier licensed in a country that manufactures transport aircraft may be forced to purchase the home aircraft when foreign-made equipment might be better suited to its transport needs. An airline may be forced to operate an economically nonviable route to specific foreign destinations for foreign policy reasons.

It should not be inferred that all airlines in which majority ownership is government-held are subject to political pressures which impede efficient operation; Lufthansa and SAS, for example, are largely free of government political interference. This subject will be considered in detail in the next chapter.

Summary

Most airlines operating international air routes share some characteristics. Scheduled service predominates among them, although most also operate charter flights or hold significant financial interest in subsidiary charter carriers. Both passengers and cargo are usually carried on the same aircraft; few all-cargo carriers exist. The majority ownership of most scheduled international airlines is held by the government of registry. Governments which register more than one airline generally discourage or even prohibit one carrier from competing against another home airline. Typically, multiple airlines receive government operating certificates for specific, separate regions of the world.

State-controlled airlines are usually managed by semiautonomous state corporations. Many are subject to influence from government agencies responsible for foreign policy, aircraft manufacture, tourism, or other interests concerned with international air transport. The transport function of airlines may be distorted and government subsidies extended to fulfill demands of these agencies.

A significant variation of the state-owned international airline is the multinational carrier — an airline jointly owned by several states. A number of such carriers have been established since World War II, the best known of which is SAS. Governments joining in the formation of multinational airlines should have compatible political and economic philosophies and must be willing to submerge their respective nationalisms.

Although state-owned airlines predominate among the international carriers, American airlines are privately controlled. Their private ownership often represents an outlook on fiscal and political issues that sometimes leads to disagreement with state-owned airlines on various issues.

Notes

1. "Knut Hagrup Expects Closer Cooperation Among European Airlines," *Aviation Daily* 236:12 (March 16, 1978), p.93.

2. See John Darnton, "Coffee Airlift from Uganda to a Thirsty Market is Flying a Route to Instant Riches," *New York Times,* May 25, 1977, p. 3. Copyright by The New York Times Company. Reprinted by permission.

3. At the time of its liquidation East African Airways owed debts totaling $120 million to 7,000 claimants. See "East African Airways Debts Total $120 Million," *Flight* 112:3586 (December 10, 1977), p. 1713.

4. By operating the Moscow service as an extension of a commercially viable route to a west European city, Pan American was able to reduce its losses.

5. Numerous examples of direct and indirect subsidy are cited in *Government Ownership, Subsidy, and Economic Assistance in International Commercial Aviation* (Washington, D.C.: Civil Aeronautics Board, 1975).

2 International Airlines as Government Instruments

It is generally accepted in the United States that civil air carriers exist for the purpose of transporting people and goods according to conventional supply and demand or market conditions. The airline is viewed as an instrument of transportation. In international air transport, where most airlines are controlled by governments, air carriers are viewed not only as instruments of transportation, but also as instruments of economic policy, domestic and foreign political policy, national defense, and, in some instances, espionage.

The Airline as Economic Instrument

Airlines can strengthen a nation's domestic economy and international trade stature. Domestically, airlines provide employment opportunities and may stimulate local industries in such areas as food preparation, fuel management, advertising, and other services. Skills and facilities developed for aircraft maintenance may lead to the creation of aircraft maintenance and construction industries, and to the strengthening of the general national industrial base. In efforts to expand the employment and development benefits of their airlines, some states have intentionally established different sites for concentration of specific airline functions. A prime example of this dispersal effort is in West Germany where the management base of Lufthansa is in Cologne, near the federal capital of Bonn; the operational center is in Frankfurt; and the major maintenance base is in Hamburg.

In the early 1970s the government of Pakistan supported its flag carrier in a course which not only saved the airline from potential disaster, but also has brought it substantial foreign revenue, preserved and improved a strong maintenance and training base, and, not incidentally, earned it goodwill among several oil-rich and other predominantly Moslem developing countries. The 1971 Indo-Pakistani war and subsequent independence of Bangladesh deprived Pakistan International Airlines (PIA) of half of its former domestic network and key services between what had been eastern and western Pakistan. Finding itself with surplus aircraft and staff, PIA leased out some of its excess to other airlines and simultaneously established itself as a maintenance and training base for other airlines. Moslem countries, in particular, have found the PIA training programs attractive. The foreign policy and economic benefits of an airline have proved useful to Pakistan in its difficult postwar experience.

One of the benefits of a national airline perceived by many developing countries is the stimulus to industrialization provided by the necessary training of cadres in both routine and major maintenance skills. Among the reasons listed by these countries for refusing to purchase Soviet-manufactured aircraft is Soviet insistence that major overhauls be performed in the USSR, thus depriving developing nations of acquiring and utilizing mechanical and technical skills that may be applied to other industries.

Economic development of remote regions of a country can be spurred by availability of air transport. In many areas where surface transportation infrastructure is inadequate, implementation of air service may be less expensive than constructing and maintaining roads and railways, especially where the traffic flow is light. The cost of an aviation infrastructure can be very low if service is limited to daytime flights in favorable weather conditions.[1] Several types of modern jet aircraft can be equipped with wheel assemblies suitable for use on primitive runways, and some new propeller aircraft have STOL capability from relatively small clearings. Air service has obvious timesaving advantages for transport of high-value or perishable commodities, such as medicines, fruits and vegetables, and precious stones. The economies of Israel and several African and Latin American countries have been strengthened by using air transport for carrying their agricultural produce to northern markets. Opportunities for foreign tourism and the consequent generation of hard currency revenues are boosted by air transport accessibility to other countries and by internal airlinks between places of tourist interest.

Many governments perceive airlines as earners of hard currency from foreigners and conservers of a state's own foreign exchange. In order to maximize their own foreign currency earnings many countries apply restrictions on foreign airlines.[2]

Although foreign exchange acquisition is perceived by most governments as a major goal for their airlines, all but a few carriers have to spend substantial foreign currency in acquisition of aircraft and other equipment. Many developing countries draw further on foreign currency holdings in hiring qualified foreign managerial personnel, crew members, mechanics, and additional experts to fill gaps in the domestic labor pool and to train local citizens.

States with domestic aircraft industries frequently use their airlines as instruments of support for the manufacturers, forcing them to purchase domestic equipment when foreign-made aircraft may be more suitable to the airline's needs. If both the airline and the aircraft industries are owned by the state, coercion in equipment purchase is facilitated. When British European Airways (BEA, now incorporated into British Airways), on government instructions, purchased British-manufactured Hawker-Siddeley Tridents and British Aircraft Corporation One-Elevens in the 1960s instead of the Boeing 727s which it preferred, it was given $75 million by the British government to cover the higher operating costs of the domestic equipment. Both British Airways and Air France receive substantial subsidies from their governments to operate the commercially nonviable Concorde supersonic transport, a product of the British and French state aircraft industries. In 1974 when Air France sought to purchase Boeing 737s as replacements for its obsolescent French-built Caravelles, the French minister of finance threatened to dismiss the airline's board of directors. It was suggested that Air France purchase French-made Mercures, an aircraft which never went into series production. In 1978 the French government finally agreed to the Air France purchase of modern U.S.-manufactured aircraft—and to French government subsidy for losses accruing from Caravelle operations until that fleet could be replaced.[3]

Should an independent-minded state-owned airline eschew domestic-built aircraft despite government policy, state-owned banks and government import-export institutions can block financing, customs permits, and other measures facilitating purchase of foreign-manufactured aircraft. Even in the United States, where both aircraft industries and airlines are privately owned, Congress, trade unions, and industrial lobby groups can cause discomfort for U.S. airlines purchasing foreign-manufactured aircraft although they cannot legally block the sales.[4]

The Airline as Political Instrument

In a satirical comment, historian Walter Laqueur has written that a viable modern state must have a minimum of four attributes: operation of a television system, a police force of at least 100 men, a budget sufficient to maintain at least one delegate at the United Nations—and a national airline.[5]

Instrument of Prestige

International airlines are often called "flag carriers" because their aircraft carry facsimiles of national flags painted on some part of the fuselage or tail. Airlines are believed by some to carry a less tangible object as well—prestige. Some think of national flags on aircraft to be an image of a presumed level of national technological, economic, and political prowess, or an airborne equivalent of a nation's accumulation of vast numbers of Olympic gold medals. Other observers may scoff that international airline service is no longer likely to confer great prestige on operator-states because it "is simply not the remarkable event that it was in its earlier years."[6] Nonetheless, many countries, particularly among the developing nations and those under control of authoritarian political regimes, perceive their national airlines as instruments conferring prestige upon the homeland.

In 1960, under the rule of Kwame Nkrumah, Ghana embarked upon a plan to establish a major international flag carrier with routes to such places as New York, Rio de Janeiro, New Delhi, and Tokyo. The political leadership obtained six Ilyushin Il-18 propeller aircraft from the Soviet Union and announced their intentions to purchase Western-manufactured jet aircraft. When the British-trained Ghanaian civil aviation establishment advised against such grandiose plans it was overruled. Declaring that Ghana Airways was to be a "prestige instrument," not a commercial carrier, Ghanaian politicians made periodic announcements about impending inauguration of air service to distant points—despite the fact that Ghana had not negotiated air transport agreements with the states involved.[7] By 1963, with none of the proposed longer routes activated and unable to perform necessary maintenance on its aircraft, Ghana scaled down its plans. After Nkrumah was overthrown in 1966 the concept of a global air carrier vanished from Ghanaian political rhetoric. It, along with vast stadiums and large monuments, had become relics of another era.

Instrument of Foreign Policy

No other country has embarked upon a course of international air service as ill-suited to its resources and needs as that of Ghana of the Nkrumah period. It is, though, a question of degree. Numerous other states have directed their airlines to implement specific service which cannot be justified in terms of traffic potential. In most cases, the motivating factor behind the implementation of commercially nonviable international air routes has been promotion of a particular desirable foreign policy objective.

In some ways an international airline is a convenient instrument of foreign policy. It is inherently mobile and has a wide geographic sweep. It is a transporter of people and goods. It is flexible; it can operate a route on a daily or less frequent basis, mount a minimum or maximum exposure promotional campaign.

In the period between the two world wars, the Soviet Union barely operated international air service. Soviet postwar international civil air service to Western countries was inaugurated only in the late 1950s, when the USSR was able to produce aircraft deemed competitive with Western models and when, with the death of Stalin, new policy encouraged the relative toleration of foreigners. In 1958, at the beginning of the first postwar international expansionist period of Aeroflot, the director of the Soviet airline wrote in an article entitled "USSR — Great Aviation Power" that increased Soviet international service was a gesture of Soviet interest in and goodwill toward other countries.

> The appearance in massive ranks on the lines of the civil air fleet of new comfortable multiple-seat aircraft with turbojet and turbo-propeller engines . . . is new convincing evidence that the Communist party and Soviet government, true to the principles of peaceful coexistence with states with different systems of government, devote great attention to the construction of airplanes for peaceful purposes, for the broadening of economic and cultural ties with all states and peoples.[8]

International air service, in itself, can do little to promote peaceful coexistence or expand economic and cultural ties. Other factors, such as freedom of travel and basic economic philosophy, can substantially impede or enhance opportunities for interaction brought about by transportation links. The Soviet statement, however, indicates that the Soviet Union hoped to gain political propaganda advantage from the implementation of new air routes.

Political factors were very important in the conclusion of a bilateral air transport agreement between the Soviet Union and the United States in 1966. Eight years earlier the two countries had included in a cultural exchange agreement a provision stating that both desired to implement direct air service between their nations and would conduct negotiations toward that end. That the agreement required eight years for conclusion was due to a series of political events which disrupted several stages of negotiations: Soviet involvement in the Middle East in 1958; Soviet shooting down of an American reconnaissance aircraft over international waters in 1960; erection of the Berlin Wall in 1961; State Department alarm in 1962 and 1963 over the expansion of commercially nonviable Aeroflot service to developing countries; and tension in general U.S.-Soviet relations in the mid-1960s over support by the two countries of opposing sides in the Vietnam conflict. In mid-1966, the State Department, supported by several other government agencies and to some degree by the U.S. airline industry, urged conclusion of a U.S.-Soviet air agreement for distinctly political reasons. These were understood to be: support for U.S. contentions that an improvement in general bilateral relations was desired; belief that increased Soviet exposure to the United States and U.S. citizens would redound to American advantage; improvement of communications between Washington and the U.S. embassy in Moscow; and demonstration of U.S. technological superiority by use of American-manufactured aircraft more advanced than Soviet aircraft. Soviet recognition of the latter situation was tacitly acknowledged when the USSR delayed implementation of Moscow-New York service until 1968 when the Ilyushin Il-62 jet became available to replace the older Tupolev Tu-114 propeller aircraft. That these political factors were paramount in the American desire to conclude a bilateral air-transport agreement is underlined by the prediction of U.S. government and airline-industry officials that U.S.-Soviet air service was unlikely to be commercially viable. It was, however, politically important to the U.S. government and to Pan American World Airways, a carrier that, having long viewed itself as the world's leading airline and a powerful symbol of the leading superpower, virtually considered Moscow service a patriotic duty and important to its image as a global carrier.[9]

Another instance where foreign policy considerations were paramount occurred in 1976 and 1977 when the State Department and the U.S. Executive branch agreed, over objections of aviation advisors, to issue an operating permit to Jordan and Syria for a joint air service to New York. In a petition to the Civil Aeronautics Board requesting that the permit application be processed without the customary formal hearing, the State Department declared that it had been "determined at the highest levels of the U.S. government that an offer to permit the Syria/Jordan joint operation . . . was advantageous to the foreign policy interests of the United States," and that delay caused by a hearing "would likely be misunderstood and would adversely affect U.S. interests in our relations with Syria and Jordan."[10] Protecting its own power base, the Civil Aeronautics Board denied the request for a hearing exemption, but the case was expedited. Earlier a government source quoted in an aviation publication said that the State Department/Administration action was another example of the "Middle East mystique in that you do not antagonize [the Arabs]" and that it showed how aviation considerations "usually play a secondary role in the total U.S. foreign policy."[11] It was understood that State Department/Administration eagerness to respond positively to the Syrian/Jordanian request was strongly related to ongoing Middle East peace negotiations.

Foreign policy and trade considerations in 1977 motivated the Japanese Ministry of Foreign Affairs to press that country's Ministry of Transport to issue a permit for Iraqi Airways service to Tokyo—ahead of thirty-two other airlines that had submitted applications earlier. A report in a European aviation newsletter stated:

> The reason a permit has been given to Iraq is that Japan procures large quantities of oil from that country. For this reason, the Ministry of Foreign Affairs pressed for Iraq's application to be approved. Despite the continued opposition of the Ministry of Transport, the government is giving priority to oil-producing countries. For this reason, it is widely believed that Saudia will be the next carrier to obtain an operating permit.[12]

For related reasons, the Japanese government has repeatedly denied Tokyo operating rights to El Al despite El Al offers to fly the Lod-Tokyo service alone and share the profits therefrom with Japan Air Lines without the latter's obligation to implement its own Israel service. An operation such as that suggested by the Israelis is not unprecedented. Because El Al is a profit-oriented carrier that does not mount commercially nonviable service for political reasons, it is likely that JAL would realize economic gain from such an arrangement.[13]

In efforts to force Western countries to recognize East Germany (German Democratic Republic) as a sovereign state before they were ready to do so, the Soviet Union proposed, in bilateral negotiations with two Western states, technically unnecessary Aeroflot intermediate stops in East Berlin. In the first case, the Soviet demand was directed at West Germany for a Moscow-East Berlin-Frankfurt route and delayed conclusion of a bilateral Soviet-West German air agreement for more than five years. In response, West Germany requested a Lufthansa intermediate stop in West Berlin — an unacceptable proposal to the Soviet Union which has objected to any strengthening of ties between West Germany and West Berlin.

For a while in 1968, when the ruling conservative Christian Democrats held fast against the Soviet demands for an East Berlin intermediate stop, it seemed that the Soviets would rescind their demand. However a combination of factors caused the Soviet Union to harden its position and eventually gain victory on this issue. First, vigorous objections to the East Berlin stop expressed over several years in the West German press caused the Soviet Union, according to many observers, to maintain its position in order to save face. Second, the election victory of the more moderate Social Democrats and subsequent implementation of Willy Brandt's Ostpolitik led the West Germans to acquiesce to Soviet demands and to drop their own requests for a Lufthansa West Berlin stop. Because the Western allies would not permit Soviet aircraft to enter West German territory directly from East Germany, Aeroflot mounted an extraordinary roundabout service — flying from Moscow over Czechoslovakia, turning north to East Berlin and then back to Czechoslovakian airspace from which it then entered West Germany. Shortly after its implementation, this operational absurdity became clear to the Soviets. They eliminated the East Germany/East Berlin detour and inaugurated nonstop Moscow-Frankfurt service as had Lufthansa.[14] Their political point, however, had been made.

During the last phase of negotiations leading to implementation of Moscow-New York service in 1968 based on the 1966 Soviet-U.S. bilateral agreement, the Soviets insisted that East Berlin be designated as its European intermediate point. The United States refused the Soviet ploy, agreeing to European intermediate stops in Stockholm, Copenhagen, or London, or to an intermediate stop in Montreal.[15]

Another use of airlines as political and political-economic instruments is seen when their governments pressure them to purchase aircraft manufactured by a specific country in order to win favor with that country. That is, even if the equipment is unsuitable for the airline's needs, foreign ministries may force the use of particular aircraft for foreign policy reasons. Ghana's purchase of Soviet-manufactured aircraft, despite disapproval by Ghanaian aviation experts, has already been cited. In 1978 the Japanese foreign policy apparatus, responding to European Economic Community concerns over its large trade deficit with Japan, urged a Japanese carrier to purchase the European-built A300 airbus when the airline, Toa Domestic Airlines (TDA), was known to prefer the American-manufactured McDonnell Douglas DC-10. The United States was also experiencing a large trade deficit with Japan, but several European governments applied greater pressure and the Japanese government responded accordingly.[16]

The Airline as Military Instrument

Civil airlines provide a government with military airlift capability beyond that which may be officially designated as such in a regular military force. Passenger and cargo aircraft can be converted easily into troop and materiel transports. Standing plans exist in many countries for utilization of civil aircraft in national emergencies.[17]

Quite apart from national emergencies—if such emergencies are considered situations evolving from pressing defense needs or natural catastrophes—some civil airlines are frequently utilized in nonemergency military roles. Many military forces regularly charter or requisition civil aircraft to augment air force fleets in peacetime troop and cargo transfers. In Western countries, such use of civil fleets is often a matter of public record; in authoritarian states, impression of civil airline equipment into military service is rarely publicly acknowledged.

Military Control

It is in authoritarian states that ties between a formal military air force and an ostensibly commercial air carrier are most pronounced. A prominent Western military analyst refers to the Soviet civil aviation apparatus as another arm of the Soviet military forces, as are the armored corps, antiaircraft defense units, etc.[18] The administration and management of the Soviet Ministry of Civil Aviation and of Aeroflot are drawn from high-ranking military personnel. Certainly during the 1920s and 1930s and in the immediate postwar period, few persons in the Soviet Union other than air force officers had experience in large-scale aviation operations. But, in recent years, instead of promoting civilian employees of Aeroflot to senior positions, the Soviets have continued to rely on senior military officers to manage Soviet civil aviation. All three men who have headed Soviet civil aviation (as Minister of Civil Aviation or in an equivalent position before civil aviation gained ministry status) in the postwar years have been air force generals and were promoted to the military rank of Marshal of Aviation while director of Soviet civil aviation. In the mid-1970s, at a point when the Soviet civil aviation apparatus had developed several competent middle-level civilian experts, a colonel general in the air force was named first deputy minister of civil aviation.

Effective control of several South American commercial airlines is exercised by military air forces. High-ranking air force officers have also managed several Asian airlines, in a few cases transferring back and forth between airlines and air forces.

Military Airlift

Involvement of civil airlines in troop and materiel transport during military conflicts is widely practiced and, it seems, even accepted procedure. The Dutch ferried troops and materiel in KLM aircraft to Indonesia to quell anticolonial disturbances in the late 1940s. Egypt supported its military action in South Yemen with its civil airline during the Nasser period, and both India and Pakistan used civil aircraft for troop transport during the Indo-Pakistani 1971 war. American troops were ferried to and from Vietnam in chartered civil aircraft.

The Airline as an Espionage Instrument

The international travel industry, with access to remote parts of the world, has long provided opportunities for conduct of espionage operations. For example, Britain's Thomas Cook & Son, a travel agency with worldwide operations, was long rumored to have offered "cover employment" for British spies before World War II. Airlines have, in addition, capabilities for various types of aerial surveillance, though in recent years the use of space satellites and the increased mobility of wider strata of society have diminished the uniqueness of the airline as a cover for espionage activity. No less important in today's fiercely competitive international airline industry, a record of espionage involvement is viewed as detrimental to a civil airline's image. Yet, if published accounts of arrests and expulsion are used as an indication, such activity continues with the Soviet airline as the principal practitioner.[19]

Despite the charges of espionage, Aeroflot is recognized as a scheduled civil airline. Most instances of espionage in which it has been involved have occurred under cover of normal civil airline operations. Acts committed by Aeroflot employees as individuals as well as operations of the airline itself have been used to mask activity of a noncivil airline character. During the 1968 invasion of Czechoslovakia, Aeroflot-marked Antonov An-24 aircraft identified as tourist charter flights running low on fuel appeared over five major Czechoslovakian air fields and requested permission to land for refueling. Once down, the "tourists" emerged as Soviet military and intelligence officers who quickly took control over the facilities. Their Aeroflot-marked aircraft contained complete air traffic control units which guided in tens of additional Soviet aircraft, some Aeroflot-marked, with troops and cargo for the invasion operation.[20] The possibility exists, of course, that the aircraft were not under Aeroflot control and were painted in Aeroflot livery for the purpose of deception. Whatever Soviet agency controlled the aircraft, the use of a scheduled commercial airline name in such activity is unusual conduct in the international civil aviation community. Although Aeroflot is the airline most commonly associated with espionage, the USSR is not the only country to exploit its airline in this manner; an Iraqi employed in the Iraqi Airlines office in London was expelled from Britain in 1978 for espionage.

Other governments have organized separate nominally commercial carriers, usually presented as specialized charter airlines, to conduct intelligence and espionage missions. Most prominent of these was probably the now-defunct Air America, a Taiwan-based airline whose expenses were shared by the U.S. Central Intelligence Agency, the Agency for International Development, and other government organizations. In the last few years of its U.S. government contract work in southeast Asia, its CIA affiliation was scarcely denied. Other airlines reported in the press as CIA proprietary concerns are Air Asia (Taiwan), Evergreen International Airlines (McMinnville, Oregon), Pan African (Miami and Lagos), Southern Air Transport (Miami; not to be confused with Southern Airlines, absorbed by Republic in 1979), Intermountain (Marana, Arizona), and Civil Air Transport (known as CAT; Taiwan). Some of these carriers no longer exist; those still functioning have generally shed CIA ties.[21]

Government Reinforcement of Use
of Airlines as Policy Instruments

So committed are many governments to the survival and strengthening of their national airlines that discriminatory and restrictive measures are often employed to limit the traffic generation potential of foreign airlines. Implementation of these measures is assured through laws and regulations applied to the airlines themselves, handlers, airports, travel agencies, banks, and other institutions. These practices are widely employed throughout the world, as noted in some examples below.

Currency Conversion Delays and Restrictions

Transfers of foreign funds earned by foreign carriers may be delayed or blocked, which leads to cash flow problems and to potential financial loss from currency devaluations and lack of investment opportunities. Some countries engaged in such practices "borrow" the foreign funds from airline bank accounts to bolster their own hard currency reserves. Heavy taxes may be imposed on currency conversions. Egypt, India, and other countries with serious currency convertability problems are most often involved in such actions. The Soviet Union will not accept its own currency as payment for tickets purchased in the Soviet Union by foreigners.

User Charges

Among the fastest growing expenses in airline budgets in recent years are airport and enroute navigation charges. The former includes: landing with surcharge for night landing, parking, and hangar fees; passenger charges; air navigation service fees, fuel nuisance charges, noise levies, and security charges. The latter is concerned with enroute navigation services. Overall, user charges have increased as much as 14 percent on scheduled services in a two-year period in the mid-1970s; in Australia, which levies the heaviest charges in the world, the increase has been as high as 30 percent in a single year. User charges vary substantially from one country to another, sometimes from one airport to another in a single country, and are often reduced or even eliminated for home airlines. In some countries, such as Mexico, user charges are not based on real costs of services provided, but are levied to subsidize airports not used by foreign airlines. In Britain, user charges are highest for aircraft on transatlantic flights, thus placing a disproportionate burden on American carriers.

Ground Handling

Government agencies and/or the national carrier hold monopoly right for passenger check-in, aircraft loading and towing, freight handling, and other ground operations. Preferential treatment in terms of priority and performance is given the national airlines. Among the countries in which monopoly ground handling conditions exist are all communist countries, Argentina, Switzerland, and France.

Cargo Direction

Government freight handlers direct all freight to the national airline, allowing foreign carriers to accept only the backlog. In countries without government freight handling agencies, shippers may be unable to obtain currency for payment of charges due foreign airlines, may be awarded discounts or rebates for using the national airline, and/or may be subjected to questioning about their patriotism if they use a foreign carrier. Communist countries, Brazil, and India are among those states in which cargo direction is most stringently controlled.

Taxation

Home-registered airlines, especially if state-owned, are exempt from taxation, but foreign airlines are taxed on receipts. If the home airline is taxed, it may be liable for net income, and the foreign carrier for gross income. The latter situation is prevalent in some South American countries.

Charter Service

Charter service is either banned or severely limited by the imposition of restrictions designed to impede traffic generation. In Italy, for example, only Italian carriers are permitted to operate charters from the major Rome airport. All other charter airlines must use an alternate airport where a short runway limits takeoff weight, thus not allowing the amount of fuel necessary for nonstop transatlantic flights. Charter companies wholly- or partly-owned by the state are given preferential treatment over foreign charter carriers.

National Carrier Favoritism

Although government employees must use the national carrier in most countries, this requirement is an especially far-reaching means of traffic manipulation in those states in which large sectors of industry are nationalized. Officials and employees in private industry can be directed toward the national carrier by rebates or tax credits and by threats of loss of government contracts. Civic and fraternal groups are urged to use the national airline through appeals to their patriotism. Indian citizens traveling abroad on foreign carriers have more difficulty in obtaining visas and foreign exchange allowances.

Marketing and Sales Restrictions

Foreign carriers are permitted to sell only a specific limited number of tickets, regardless of the capacity of their aircraft. Ticket costs of connecting domestic flights may be absorbed by the national carrier in the Soviet Union and other countries if passengers use its service for international flights. Ticket grades are raised from economy to first class or baggage allowances are increased without additional collection as incentives to fly a particular airline. Free accommodations, meals, and entertainment are provided during discretionary stopovers. El Al controls several major tour wholesalers operating to Israel and thus obtains tour flights. Travel agents are awarded excessive commissions (rebates), free tickets, or other incentives to book clients by many carriers. An automated travel agency reservation system in West Germany shows only the flights of Lufthansa, the German national airline. Governments of most communist states require that their own airlines be used as general sales agents by all foreign carriers—and then prohibit their own airlines from selling tickets for the foreign carriers. States with nationalized media sharply restrict the amount of media advertising allowed foreign airlines.

Special Appeals

Airlines offer special incentives to coincide with particular events or seasons of the year, or to appeal to special groups of people. In the summer of 1974 KLM offered its student passengers fifty dollars for completing a questionnaire in Amsterdam on tourism. Charging the Dutch with attempting to circumvent a ban on discriminatory youth fares, the U.S. Civil Aeronautics Board and several other agencies forced KLM to offer the cash award to all students completing the form regardless of mode of transportation utilized in traveling to Amsterdam.[22]

Such discriminatory measures are most readily effected in those countries in which the national airlines are state-owned. If banks, travel agencies, and other relevant institutions are also state-controlled, implementation of restrictive practices is further facilitated. Although U.S. government officials are required to patronize American carriers, the free enterprise system and decentralized governmental power base renders virtually impossible any policy of restricting the traffic generation ability of foreign airlines in the United States.

Summary

International civil air carriers are widely utilized by their governments of registry as instruments of national policy. Execution of government policy unrelated to air transportation assumes such importance in some countries that the transport function of civil airlines may be limited or distorted.

As economic instruments, airlines are expected to contribute to the expansion of a country's industrial base, spur the development of remote regions, earn foreign currency, and, in some countries, help to support an indigenous aircraft industry. As political instruments, airlines are perceived by some as conferring prestige upon their countries of registry and are used as tools of foreign policy implementation. Inauguration of air service between two historically hostile or even remote states may be viewed as a symbol of détente, desire for expansion of bilateral ties, or some other foreign policy objective. In pursuit of such symbolism government agencies concerned with foreign policy may urge the establishment of specific air routes which have limited commercial viability.

In nearly all countries civil airliners are expected to be utilized for military airlift purposes in times of emergency. In some countries, particularly those with authoritarian political systems, nominally civil airlines are controlled by state military forces. High-ranking military personnel manage the carrier and involve it in military and paramilitary activity, often with attempted clandestineness. Related to this surreptitious use of civil airlines is the employment of carriers for espionage operations. In the United States, intelligence authorities have established separate supplemental airlines to engage in these actions; in the Soviet Union, the nominal commercial carrier, Aeroflot, is engaged in espionage work.

In attempting to build monetary reserves, many governments apply restrictive measures against foreign airlines serving their cities. Measures commonly taken are imposition of discriminatory user charges, and restriction of marketing and sales opportunities of foreign airlines. Most countries implement some restrictive measures against foreign carriers; those with authoritarian political systems and/or those whose own airlines have limited markets appear to be most persistent in application of discriminatory policies.

Notes

1. That most developing countries are in climate zones unaffected by snow or ice is advantageous to air transport growth in these regions.

2. For a study of economic benefits derived from the air transport industry in France, see Victor Chomentovsky, *Impact of Air Transport on the French Economy* (Paris: Institute of Air Transport, 1978).

3. Numerous reports are available for each of the cases cited. A summary article about the British aircraft industry and British airlines is "British Airways Criticized by US Report," *Flight* 111:3561 (June 11, 1977), p. 1691. For reports about France, see: Clyde H. Farnsworth, "Air France Told to Buy French Craft," *New York Times*, February 27, 1975, p. 49; "Official Press on Air France to Buy French," *Interavia Air Letter* 8203 (March 3, 1975), p. 2; Paul Lewis, "Jet Lag at Air France," *New York Times*, (September 18, 1977), Sec. 5, p. 1; "French Government, Air France Sign Compensation Agreement," *Aviation Daily* 235:27 (February 8, 1978), p. 215.

4. See "DOT Seeks $45 Million, Hears Warning on Not 'Buying American,'" *Aviation Daily* 236:31 (April 12, 1978), p. 246; and "Letters to the Editor," *Aviation Week* 108:18 (May 1, 1978), p. 70. In the latter, a reader suggests that all U.S. aerospace personnel "avoid using Eastern Airlines" because of the Eastern purchase of European-manufactured aircraft.

5. Walter Laqueur, "Six Scenarios for 1980," *New York Times Magazine*, December 19, 1971, p. 29.

6. William E. O'Connor, *Economic Regulation of the World's Airlines* (hereafter *Economic Regulation*), (New York: Praeger Publishers, 1971), p. 92.

7. Robert E. Farrell, "Ghana Builds Flag Carrier for 'Prestige,'" *Aviation Week* 73:24 (December 12, 1960), pp. 38-39.

8. Pavel Zhigarev, "SSSR—velikaya aviatsionnaya derzhava," *Izvestiya*, July 20, 1958, p. 2.

9. For details about U.S.-Soviet bilateral air transport agreements, see Hans Heymann, Jr., *The U.S.-Soviet Civil Air Agreement from Inception to Inauguration: A Case Study* (hereafter *U.S.-Soviet Civil Air Agreement*) (Santa Monica: Rand Corp., 1972); and Betsy Gidwitz, *The Political and Economic Implications of the International Routes of Aeroflot* (Cambridge: Massachusetts Institute of Technology, 1976), esp. pp. 376-390.

10. CAB Dockets 30656 and 30657.

11. "Ford Administration Will Okay New Air Sevice by Syria and Jordan," *Aviation Daily* 229:5 (January 7, 1977), p. 34. See also "Airline Observer," *Aviation Week* 105:22 (November 29, 1976), p. 27; and "CAB Refuses to Expedite Royal Jordanian/Syrian Permit Request," *Aviation Daily* 231:12 (May 17, 1977), p. 90.

12. "Japan-Iraq Bilateral," *Interavia Air Letter* 8929 (January 24, 1978), p. 5.

13. Of all the noncommunist industrialized countries, Japan has been the most consistently hostile toward Israel. Israel maintains strong reciprocal air links with the United States and with all West European industrialized states, including several, such as, France, which also have very strong political and economic ties with Arab countries.

14. For an example of the articles in the West German press arguing against an East Berlin stop, see *Frankfurter Allgemeine Zeitung*, March 24, 1971. See also "Frankfurt-Moscow Negotiations," *Interavia Air Letter* 5744 (May 10, 1965), p. 2; "Lufthansa-Aeroflot Agreement," *Interavia Air Letter* 6257 (May 22, 1967), p. 3; and "Moscow-Frankfurt?" *Flight* 94:3119 (December 19, 1968), p. 1017

15. Heyman, *U.S.-Soviet Civil Air Agreement*, pp. 53-54.

16. "Japanese Government Urges TDA to Purchase Airbus," *Interavia Air Letter* 8939 (February 7, 1978), p. 8; "Japan Pressed to Buy European Transports," *Aviation Daily* 236:22 (March 30, 1978), p. 175; "TDA May Still Buy A300," *Flight* 111:3602 (April 1, 1978), p. 905.

17. In the United States the Military Air Transport Service (MATS), under orders from the Department of Defense, administers an aircraft allocation program known as the Civil Reserve Air Fleet (CRAF). Specially equipped aircraft and crews in service with commercial carriers are to be allocated to MATS in three stages according to military need and airline fleet size. See "U.S. Looks to Civil Aircraft from NATO for Airlift Help," and "CRAF Proposal Responses Due in April," both in *Aviation Week* 112:13 (March 31, 1980), pp. 47, 51. The CAB administers War Air Service Program (WASP) fleet which includes all transport aircraft in domestic commercial service after CRAF allocations. Although airlines continue to operate WASP aircraft, the CAB has the authority to reassign routes in order to meet requirements of defense production and transfers on personnel and cargo.

18. John Erickson, "Soviet Military Power," *Strategic Review* 1:1 (Spring, 1973), pp. 13, 19.

19. The expansionist German airline industry of the 1930s, consisting of Luft Hansa and German-related airlines around the world, was probably the first to engage in widespread intelligence operations on behalf of its government. See Melvin Hall and Walter Peck, "Wings for the Trojan Horse," *Foreign Affairs* XIX:2 (January 1941), pp. 347-369; and Oliver Lissitzyn, *International Air Transport and National Policy* (New York: Council on Foreign Relations, 1942), pp. 306-347.

Published accounts of Soviet use of international civil aviation as a shield for espionage activity include the following incidents: expulsion of Aeroflot manager from France in 1965 on charges of industrial espionage regarding Concorde production; diversion of an Aeroflot Moscow-Paris flight to Prague in 1966 so that Czechoslovak authorities could arrest and jail a former Czechoslovak citizen who had left the country, gained U.S. citizenship, and had been a passenger on the flight; expulsion of Aeroflot managers from Belgium, the Netherlands, and Cyprus in 1967 on charges of espionage regarding NATO; expulsion of two Aeroflot employees from Belgium in 1971 on charges of espionage regarding NATO; arrest of a Swiss citizen employed by Aeroflot in Switzerland in 1976 on charges of aiding a Soviet espionage agent employed at Aeroflot (who had left Switzerland); expulsion from Canada in 1978 on charges of espionage of a Soviet citizen employed as a translator at the Montreal headquarters of ICAO; and expulsion of the Aeroflot manager from Madrid in 1980 after being arrested while in possession of "Spanish military material." No other country or civil airline has been so implicated in involvement in espionage under the cover of civil aviation. Additionally, Aeroflot has been charged with committing "navigation errors" which take Soviet aircraft over sensitive areas when on descent/ascent to/from civil airports in foreign countries. See David Owen, "Eye to Eye in the Stratosphere," *The Observer Magazine*, November 14, 1971, p. 33.

20. The An-24 is a twin-engine, propeller-driven, high-wing aircraft in wide use with Aeroflot and several East European airlines—although not with the Czechoslovakian carrier—as a 50-seat, medium-haul, passenger aircraft. Cargo and military transport versions of the aircraft also exist in large numbers. See Colin Chapman, *August 21—The Rape of Czechoslovakia* (Philadelphia: J.B. Lippincott Co., 1968), pp. 1–2; Ansel E. Talbert, "Aeroflot, Soviet Conglomerate Airline, Expands Outside USSR, Eyes SST Routes," *Air Transport World* 6:2 (February 1, 1969), p. 17; Robert Jackson, *The Red Falcons* (London: Clifton Books, 1970), pp. 205–209; Alan Levy, *Rowboat to Prague* (New York: Grossman Publishers, 1972), pp. 247–248, 303–304. Both Aeroflot and the East German carrier Interflug were active in the 1979 invasion of Afghanistan. Aeroflot did have a regular commercial route to Kabul. Interflug had no commercial service there. See Donald E. Fink, "Afghan Invasion Likened to 1968 Action," *Aviation Week* 113:2 (July 14, 1980), pp. 20–23.

21. For information in the general press about CIA proprietary airlines, see the following: *The Evening Star and Daily News* (Washington, D.C.), December 13, 1972; *New York Times*, August 12 and 30, 1973; *Washington Post*, July 11, 1976, and May 12 and 25, 1978; and *Boston Sunday Globe*, April 20, 1980. See also Christopher Robbins, *Air America* (New York: G.P. Putnam's Sons, 1979).

22. IATA regularly publishes accounts of its own investigations of illegal rebating. These accounts are frequently summarized in such publications as *Aviation Daily* and *Aviation Week*. See also promotional material

of individual airlines, such as a 1975 Aeroflot advertisement which invites travelers to fly Aeroflot "more comfortably" because "we don't have to make profits," and a 1977 Air-India brochure stating: "IATA will not let us haggle. Not on paper. But if you, dear passenger, paid the normal fare on any airplane, we shall be glad to pay to have your head examined." Sources listing a variety of discriminatory practices are: *Restrictive Practices Used by Foreign Countries to Favor Their National Carriers* (Washington, D.C.: Civil Aeronautics Board, 1973); Laurence Doty, "U.S. May Harden User-Charge Attitude," *Aviation Week* 108:7 (February 13, 1978), p. 29; *The Critical Role of Government in International Air Transport* (Washington, D.C.: General Accounting Office, 1978), pp. 21–23; "CAB Issues Show Cause on Foreign Charters," *Aviation Week* 112:13 (March 31, 1980), p. 34; and "Threat of U.S. Action Against Foreign Discrimination," *Interavia Air Letter* 9518 (June 10, 1980), pp. 2–3.

3 Historical Development of International Civil Aviation

From the first successful heavier-than-air powered flight in 1903 until the end of World War I, the airplane was seen only as an instrument of sport or war.[1] The end of hostilities spurred the development of aviation for transport purposes — large numbers of surplus bombers were available for conversion to passenger aircraft, pilots had been trained, surface transportation had been disrupted, and postwar conferences generated a market for air transport. Initial services concentrated on the carriage of freight and mail, not passengers. The first known scheduled international air route was initiated in March 1918. It was operated briefly in the waning days of the Austro-Hungarian Empire and terminated a few months later in November 1918 when the monarchy collapsed and, for political reasons, some segments of the route could no longer be flown. The service had been an air mail route between Vienna and Kiev with different aircraft flying individual sectors on the course Vienna-Crakow-Lemberg (now L'vov)-Proskurov-Kiev. From Proskurov a branch route was later operated to Odessa.

Between The Wars

From 1919 through the early 1920s numerous air transport companies sprung up in parts of Europe and the United States — some of them surviving only a few years, others growing to become the major carriers we know today. Several patterns in their organization have become apparent.

The Early Years

Many of the earliest airlines in the more industrialized countries were organized by aircraft manufacturers eager to exploit their manufacturing capabilities and by maritime shipping companies eager to expand their shipping options. Predictably, firms in the two industries sometimes cooperated in organizing an airline with each drawing on its specialized expertise. Deutscher Aero Lloyd, an airline group formed from the merger of small German carriers in 1924, was backed by the Zeppelin and Sablatnig aircraft works and by the Hamburg-Amerika and Lloyd shipping firms. Its largest German rival, Junkers Luftverkehr, had no shipping industry support, but was backed by the Junkers Aircraft Works. The first French airline, Lignes Aériennes Farman, was formed in 1919 by the Farman brothers, owners of an aircraft factory. The second French carrier, Compagnie des Messageries Aériennes (CMA) was established later that year by other aircraft manufacturers. British aircraft and shipping firms also supported air transport companies.

Across the ocean the Boeing Airplane Company purchased an existing airline in 1928 and then operated its own air service along the American west coast. Ford Motor Company, another aircraft manufacturer, also operated air routes as did airlines backed by Curtiss Aeroplane & Motor Company and the Fokker Aircraft Corporation. In 1929 Pratt & Whitney, Hamilton (a propeller manufacturer), Boeing Airplane, and Boeing Air Transport (the airline) merged to form United Aircraft and Transport Corporation, which then purchased the Sikorsky helicopter firm and several small airlines. The conglomerate was short-lived; congressional investigations stemming from controversy over air mail contracts led to the passage of the Air Mail Act of 1934 that, among other provisions, mandated separation of aircraft and equipment manufacturing from airline operations. For reasons of safety, Congress had determined that aircraft builders should not control aircraft users. Boeing Air Transport and the other airlines it absorbed became United Air Lines Transport Company (United Airlines); Pratt & Whitney, Sikorsky, and Hamilton became United Aircraft Corporation; and Boeing once again became Boeing Airplane Company. The Air Mail Act thus rendered illegal any further organizational collaboration between American carriers and American aircraft manufacturers.

In Europe it was not safety concerns but the consolidation of smaller airlines into large state-supported carriers that led to a rapid diminution of the role of aircraft manufacturers in airline activity. Imperial Airways, the predecessor of British Airways, was incorporated in 1924 as a state airline receiving subsidy. The agreement signaling its formation provided that Imperial should assume the assets of existing airlines (Daimler, Handley Page, and others) and should own British aircraft and engines. Although the latter provision was clearly intended to protect the British aircraft industry, it did so without specifying which particular manufacturers were to be patronized. Imperial was able to select its fleet from several different manufacturers.

Junkers Luftverkehr and Deutscher Aero Lloyd merged in 1926 to form Deutsche Luft Hansa (DLH), a predecessor of today's Lufthansa. The move was strongly backed by the German government which held 36 percent of the airline's initial capital; other German-speaking countries held 19 percent, regional airlines 27½ percent, and private interests (mainly shipping companies) 17½ percent.

Air France was founded in 1933 as the successor to five different French airlines, one of which had operated in Asia and another on the South Atlantic between France and Latin America. Twenty-five percent of the stock was held by the French government, which strongly backed formation of the carrier; and the remainder by the constituent airlines (the Farman-backed carrier held 8 percent).

Several factors spurred consolidation of smaller airlines into single carriers wholly- or partly-owned by European governments. Both France and Britain had been subsidizing duplicate operation of single routes operated by different carriers, a practice which was clearly wasteful. At this time France and Britain were both colonial powers whose political objectives could best be served by single strong state-controlled airlines rather than smaller, more independent carriers. Germany, although no longer a colonial power after the Treaty of Versailles, also saw a national airline as an instrument of economic and political policy. Additionally, operation of large state airlines provided guaranteed markets for the aircraft and engine industries in all three countries.

In most of the smaller European countries, privately established airlines quickly attracted government political support. With no domestic aircraft industry demanding assistance, financial structures of these airlines were usually less complex. KLM, the oldest continuous airline in the world, was founded in 1919. Sabena was founded in 1923, Scandinavian and several East European airlines by 1924. Dobrolet, a predecessor of Aeroflot, was established by Soviet government edict in 1923.

It was in the United States, the country which so stands apart from the world pattern today by its commitment to private ownership of airlines, that early air transport received the strongest government support. In 1918 the U.S. Post Office inaugurated its own mail flights between New York and Washington, D.C.; by 1919 the service had been extended to Chicago, and by 1920 to San Francisco. In 1925 the Congress of the United States enacted the first air mail act, known as the Kelly Act, that mandated competitive bidding on transcontinental air mail service by private operators. Contracts were awarded to several airlines in 1927. By 1930 the three carriers which operate the most extensive transcontinental service today — United, American, and Trans World Airlines — were all flying coast-to-coast routes. Other privately owned carriers had inaugurated international routes, albeit of short distance, some years earlier. Hubbard Air Transport began a Seattle–Victoria, British Columbia, air mail service in 1920; and in the same year Aeromarine West Indies Airways commenced contract air mail service between Key West and Havana. By 1930 more than forty airlines were serving in the United States. Later many failed during the Depression.

In the Service of Empires

The imperial powers were quick to realize the value of air transportation in enhancing their positions in far-flung territories. Aircraft provided a means of rapid, privileged communications, and a tangible symbol of colonial presence. Imperial Airways, the predecessor of British Airways, operated scheduled routes to its colony in India by 1929 and an extension to Australia in 1934. Imperial was active on additional routes as were other colonial carriers (see table 3-1).

In addition to operating lengthy routes from mother country to colony, the imperial airlines often established and managed local and regional airlines within the colony. Some of these airlines were so similar in name to the colonial parent carrier that there could be no doubt about their ownership—among others ALM (Antillaanse Luchtvaart Maatschappij) in the Dutch East Indies and SLM (Surinaamse Luchtvaart Maatschappij) in Surinam. Generally after the colonies gained independence, the parent airlines gradually relinquished ownership; some of the old colonial power airlines or their successors, particularly Air France and Union de Transports Aériens (UTA), retain minority ownership in airlines that they once controlled. With many of these new carriers still partially dependent

Table 3-1
Route Expansion of Colonial Airlines

Imperial	KLM	Sabena	Air France (or predecessor French airlines)	Ala Littoria
1926	1930	1935	1926	1928
Cairo	Cairo	the Congo	Morocco	Libya
Gaza		(Zaire)		
Baghdad	1931	via Oron	1931	1936
Basra	Batavia	Niamey	Hanoi	Mogadiscio
Karachi (1929)	(Djakarta)	Ft. Lamy	via Athens	(Mogadishu)
Australia (1934)	via Athens	(Ndjamena)	Beirut	via Cairo
	Cairo	Bangui	Baghdad	Khartoum
1932	Gaza	to	Karachi	
South Africa	Baghdad	Leopoldville	Calcutta	
via Cairo	Karachi	(Kinshasa)	Rangoon	
& East Africa	Calcutta	or	Bangkok	
	Rangoon	Stanleyville	Saigon	
1936	Bangkok	(Kinshasa)	(Kisangani)	
West Africa		Elisabethville	1933	
via Cairo		(Lubumbashi)	French West Africa	
Khartoum			via Tangier	
Ft. Lamy			Casablanca	
(Ndjamena)			Port Etienne	
Kano			(Nouadhibou)	
Lagos			Dakar	
Takoradi			branches down	
			the coast and into	
			the interior	

on their colonial carriers for expertise and cast-off equipment, European powers maintain presence and influence in their former colonies.

Prelude to War

Denied a military role after World War I by the Treaty of Versailles, Germany developed a broad array of ostensibly civilian industries that, initial appearances to the contrary, had substantial military implications. The German airline and aircraft industries were involved in this method of expanding German military potential.

By the end of the 1920s, German-managed airlines, most of them under the control of the powerful DLH, operated far afield in several Latin American countries and in Persia. Vigorous attempts were made to link Germany with the Far East; because access to the traditional "silk route" through the Middle East and southern Asia was impeded for some years by hostile colonial powers, initial efforts to effect a route to China were concentrated on transit through Russia. In 1921 Germany and Soviet Russia created a joint airline, Deruluft (from Deutsche-Russische Luftverkehr Gesellschaft GmbF.), which operated a Berlin-Moscow service from 1922 to 1937. It failed when deteriorating Soviet-German relations and the chaotic political situation inside the Soviet Union rendered its continuation impossible. The route was revived through a joint Aeroflot–Luft Hansa service after the signing of the Ribbentrop-Molotov pact in 1939, and continued until June 21, 1941, the very day that Germany attacked the Soviet Union.

It was the German intention that the Moscow route link up in Alma Ata, Soviet Central Asia, with service operated by Eurasia, an in-China Sino-German airline formed in 1930. Eurasia would then fly on to Shanghai, thus connecting Berlin with China's most populous city and an important port. Germany was destined to be disappointed: the Berlin-Shanghai route never materialized. Three factors prevented its realization: (1) Eurasian aircraft had become targets for Japanese fighter aircraft during the Sino-Japanese war; (2) the Soviet-Chinese transborder sector became impossible to operate in the late 1930s due to deteriorating Soviet-German relations; and (3) unrest in China's Sinkiang province endangered the safety of Eurasian aircraft on both overflights and refueling stops within China.

In the late 1930s, after some decline in postwar anti-German hostility, DLH also tried to effect a China service through the traditional silk, or southern, route. Junkers operations in Persia provided a comfortable intermediate point, but aircraft mechanical problems prevented success before the outbreak of World War II.

German activity in South America was promoted by large German immigrant communities in several countries. In 1919 German settlers in Colombia established SCADTA (Sociedad Colombo-Alemana de Transportes Aeros), the direct predecessor of Avianca, as an air transport company designed to replace the packhorses which until then had been the only means of conveyance in the Colombian mountains. German shipping interests founded separate airlines in Brazil and Bolivia in 1924 and 1925; and DLH established subsidiary carriers in Ecuador and Peru in 1937 and 1938. By linking their DLH South Atlantic service with flights operated by the various German-influenced local carriers, Germany secured access to the South American Pacific coast. Because conditions required that airlines develop their own airfields, the expanded German aviation activity was thought by many to be a possible prelude to the construction of a chain of German military bases in the South Pacific. American suspicions were heightened when the DLH-owned Ecuadorian airline proposed a route to the Galapagos Islands in 1940, a service of no commercial viability but of vast strategic importance in relation to the Panama Canal. On the Atlantic coast, the German-owned Brazilian airline was using its flying boats to supply German naval forces.

In addition to expanding its potential military capability in South America, Germany used civil aviation for military purposes in Europe. German dirigibles on passenger service between Berlin and New York regularly drifted over major British military installations where aerial photographs were taken. Air crews on German civil flights between Germany and Croydon were changed every week in 1938 and 1939 in order to familiarize pilots and navigators with the bomber route to London.[2]

German aviation activities abroad were not limited to use of airlines for military and intelligence purposes. The provisions of the Versailles treaty prohibited German production of armaments, including military aircraft. Military training was also forbidden. To circumvent these edicts Germany sought production and training facilities outside Germany, beyond the jurisdiction of the Military Control Commission. German military aircraft plants were built in Sweden, Italy, and Soviet Russia, the last being the largest of all. Military bases were similarly built abroad, one of the most important being established in Lipetsk, Russia, in 1924. Usually future Luftwaffe pilots and navigators took basic courses at German sport and commercial aviation schools, and then transferred to bases outside Germany for specific military training. Aircraft built in Germany for civil purposes were flown to these bases for military fitting out. Ironically, the Soviet Union, one of the countries to suffer most heavily during World War II, actually assisted in the preparation of the German military machine.[3]

Japanese prewar international aviation operations were far less extensive than those of Germany. Following its occupation of Manchuria in 1932, Japan established an airline, MKKK (Manchu Kokuyuso Kabushiki

Kaisha), which operated both transport service for Japanese troops and civil air service in the area. By 1939 MKKK routes had been extended to most major Chinese cities. Some services of MKKK were competitive with the German-owned Eurasia and/or with CNAC (China National Aviation Corporation), an airline owned jointly by the Chinese government (55 percent) and Pan American Airways (45 percent). As Japanese military forces advanced in China, the route systems of both MKKK and the Japanese national airline NKKK (Nihon Kokuyuso Kabushiki Kaisha) expanded on Chinese territory.

Pan American had been incorporated as Pan American Airways in 1927 and was flying into South America by 1928, its initial routes based on fulfillment of U.S. government air mail contracts. Panagra (Pan American–Grace Airways, Inc.), jointly owned by Pan American and the W.R. Grace Company, was incorporated in 1929; in the same year it received U.S. government air mail contracts for service to Central and South America. By 1931 it was the strongest international airline in Latin America, a factor of some satisfaction to Washington in view of the substantial German (and, to a lesser extent, French) aviation presence there.

As the German-related ostensibly civil aviation activity assumed a quasi military character in Latin America, American government support of the two U.S. airlines increased.[4] Alarmed by German aviation operations on the Pacific coast and by the supply of German naval forces in the Atlantic Ocean from flying boats of the German-owned Brazilian airline, the United States brought enormous pressure upon the involved South American governments to revoke operating permits, nationalize German-owned local fleets, and otherwise destroy the German aviation network on the continent.[5] Pan American and Panagra were well-placed to take over many previously German-operated routes, with Pan American receiving American government funding in support of its efforts to replace German aviation influence. Pan American also was designated contractor for the then-secret Airport Development Program, a U.S. government-financed project which built or improved approximately fifty Latin American airports. Although this contract was signed on November 2, 1940—that is, thirteen months before the Japanese attack on Pearl Harbor and the subsequent entry of the United States into World War II—these airfields were clearly intended to facilitate the transshipment of aircraft and other military materiel to British forces for use in the war.[6]

The War Years

Patterns of civil aviation changed sharply during World War II. In countries occupied by hostile forces, local airlines ceased operations. In non-occupied countries participating in the war effort, civil aircraft were generally requisitioned for military transport; their prewar international civil routes were, in any case, cut off by war action.

The operations of Deutsche Luft Hansa (DLH), Ala Littoria, and the Japanese carriers expanded and contracted as Axis military fortunes prospered and delined. DLH expanded its network into all countries occupied by Germany, reaching as far east as Minsk in 1943. The last known DLH flight lifted off from Berlin on April 21, 1945 for Munich and Madrid—and was never heard from again. The Greater Japan Air Lines Company, which had once operated routes to some of the South Pacific islands occupied by Japanese forces, terminated its flights in August 1945, and was formally dissolved in October 1945.

In most cases airlines of the colonial powers, though some were unable to operate at home, managed to continue a portion of their colonial service with aircraft that had escaped Nazi confiscation. Almost all of these wartime routes were used for military airlift missions rather than customary commercial service. British Overseas Airway Corporation (BOAC) was able to resume service to Lagos in 1941 via Lisbon; and by 1942 was flying to New Zealand on a route through Africa, Basra, Karachi, Singapore, and Australia. A BOAC trans-Africa service that went from Lagos to Uganda and then north through the Sudan and Egypt improved British communications with its military forces in North Africa.

After German occupation and continental military action halted its European operations, KLM transferred the western terminus of its Batavia (Djakarta) route to Tel Aviv. This service ended in 1942 when the Japanese invaded Java. Some Dutch aircraft based in Java escaped to Australia where they were integrated into the American-managed Pacific-area wartime transport fleets. As the war drew to a close, KLM was quick to resume operations in liberated territory. It was the first European airline to resume service to southeast Asia (November 28, 1945) and to New York (May 21, 1946).

In 1942 Air France, forced to cede its domestic operations to Deutsche Luft Hansa, ceased to exist in a formal sense. Where it could be of assistance to Free French forces in the area, French air service was activated in those overseas French territories abutting combat arenas. A subunit of Air France, subsidized by the Free French, operated weekly service between Algiers and Dakar beginning in 1943. During the same year Damascus-based French aircraft began service from that city to Cairo. From the Egyptian capital separate routes developed to North Africa, Khartoum, and beyond Khartoum into both eastern and western Africa. In 1944 these and other French air services were consolidated under the authority of DTA (Directions des Transports Aériens); regional headquarters were established in Algiers, Dakar, Damascus, and, later, London. As the Allied forces liberated more territory, DTA expanded its network. Acquisition of American transport aircraft intended for commercial use commenced in 1945 and, in 1946, Air France was reconstituted.

As Belgium was overtaken by war, the Sabena fleet was flown to London where it, too, became involved in military support operations. Its fleet in the Congo remained active throughout the war, providing useful service between west Africa and Cairo.

Although the United States did not formally join the Allied war effort until after the Japanese attack on Pearl Harbor on December 7, 1941, American carriers were employed by the U.S. government in various ways to give support to the Western allies, particularly Britain. Under government contract, United Air Lines began training American armed forces personnel in aviation specialties in October 1940. In November 1940, Pan American signed the previously noted contract for construction of Latin American airfields which serviced military aircraft en route to British forces. Transcontinental and Western (TWA) began training British flight crews in June 1941 at a newly built base in New Mexico. In the summer of 1941 Pan American contracted with the War Department to ferry lend-lease aircraft and cargo to Cairo and Khartoum in support of British Mediterranean forces. As part of the contract, Pan American constructed or improved airports in a number of enroute African points.

After the Pearl Harbor attack and official U.S. declaration of war, American carriers were mobilized. A number of airlines not previously flying international routes were soon operating transoceanic military support flights. United Air Lines aircraft made 1,700 trips across the Pacific in support of the war effort; and TWA, Eastern, and Northeast flew numerous transatlantic missions. American Airlines operated flights across the Himalayas between India and China, the famous "over the hump" route. Northwest was prominent in flights to Alaska and the Orient.

The decision to assign domestic carriers to international support flights was made by Air Corps Chief of Staff Henry H. "Hap" Arnold who also favored U.S. multiple carrier international service during peacetime. On a military level, Arnold considered reliance on a single American carrier for international service to be unwise. On a personal level, Arnold was envious of Pan Am president Juan Trippe's success and wanted to reduce his prominence. In mid-1943 Arnold encouraged sixteen domestic carriers to petition the CAB for postwar international air routes and to publish a statement calling for an end to monopoly in U.S. flag international air transport.[7]

Neutral countries, such as Switerland and Sweden, were affected by the war as well. Swissair was forced to cease operations because wartime conditions outside its boundaries made it impossible to mount international service. The Swedish airline ABA continued service to London and Berlin throughout the war and approached the Swedish government in 1942 for

financial support of a proposed transatlantic route. The government rejected the request. In 1943 Marcus Wallenberg committed funds of his considerable family fortune to found a new, independent Swedish carrier SILA
(Svensk Interkontinental Lufttrafik) and sought permission to operate a
route to the United States. A token flight on the route was made in June
1945 in a converted B-17 bomber.

Planning for Postwar Aviation

In spring 1944, although several major battles lay ahead, the Allies were
confident of victory and began planning for postwar international civil
aviation. The United States agreed to sponsor a conference in Chicago in
November 1944 which would formulate standards in both technical and
economic spheres and establish the necessary institutions to effect and
maintain them. Robert L. Thornton explains:

> The technical aims concerned setting up international arrangements for
> licensing pilots and mechanics, registering and certifying the airworthiness
> of aircraft, standardization and planning for the development of naviga-
> tional aids, collecting statistics, exchanging technical information, and
> similar essential technical tasks and procedures. The economic objectives
> included: the assignment of air routes to nations and to airlines; the ar-
> rangement for setting air fares, frequencies, schedules, and capacities; and
> methods of facilitating interairline fare transfers, customs arrangements,
> cooperation in servicing and coordination of schedules. An extremely im-
> portant subgroup of aims at the conference concerned the arrangements
> for obtaining authority to overfly another nation's sovereign territory and
> to make stops in foreign territory for technical reasons, that is, for fuel and
> maintenance. The major air nations needed authority from foreign coun-
> tries to take on passengers at intermediate stops to replace those disembark-
> ing prior to the terminus of long-haul flights if the later stages of these
> flights were to be reasonably economic.[8]

Fifty-four countries attended the Chicago conference (see table 3-2).
Although it did not quite meet all of its goals, it did provide much of the
groundwork for the founding in 1947 of the International Civil Aviation
Organization (ICAO), now a United Nations agency. The Soviet Union was
invited to the conference, but did not attend; those countries with which the
Allies were at war — Japan, Germany, Austria, Hungary, Romania, Bulgaria, Italy, and Finland — were not invited and were not represented.[9]

The Soviet decision to forego the conference was sudden and, in fact, a
reversal of an earlier positive response. A Soviet delegation to the meetings
had actually arrived in Canada, en route to Chicago, when it was unex-
pectedly recalled to the USSR. The official Soviet explanation that the
Soviet Union would not attend a conference to which "countries like

Table 3–2
Participants at the International Civil Aviation Conference:
Chicago, 1944

Afghanistan	France	Panama
Australia	Greece	Paraguay
Belgium	Guatemala	Peru
Bolivia	Haiti	Philippine Commonwealth
Brazil	Honduras	Poland
Canada	Iceland	Portugal
Chile	India	Spain
China	Iran	Sweden
Columbia	Iraq	Switzerland
Costa Rica	Ireland	Syria
Cuba	Lebanon	Thailand
Czechoslovakia	Liberia	Turkey
Denmark	Luxembourg	Union of South Africa
Dominican Republic	Mexico	United Kingdom
Ecuador	Netherlands	United States
Egypt	New Zealand	Uruguay
El Salvador	Nicaragua	Venezuela
Ethiopia	Norway	Yugoslavia

Switzerland, Portugal, and Spain, which for many years have conducted a pro-fascist policy hostile to the Soviet Union, have also been invited,"[10] was not convincing. Several other reasons are apparent. First, Soviet authorities considered the planned discussion of the "right of innocent passage" — the right of an airline of one country to overfly the territory of another state — a threat to their national sovereignty. This right became known as the "First Freedom." The "Second Freedom" — the right of civil aircraft of one country to land on the territory of another country for technical purposes — was unacceptable to the Soviets for the same reason. These two "freedoms" were incorporated into Article 5 of the (ICAO) Chicago Convention and were explicitly stated in the International Air Services Transit Agreement (IASTA) presented to the attending states for ratification in December 1944. With several important Allied powers wartime conferences still in the future, the Soviet Union did not want to engage the United States and Britain in a dispute over air rights. If was wiser to boycott the Chicago meetings and thus avoid a confrontation.

The Soviet Union was also concerned that the weaknesses of its war-ravaged economy would be exposed should the much-stronger United States realize all of its goals for the Chicago conference and attain control of the international air transport industry. The United States possessed a large number of transport aircraft readily convertible to civil airline use and was promoting an "open skies" policy in which airlines could fly anywhere in the world with no major restrictions. The Soviet Union was ready neither to undertake such operations itself nor to allow foreign carriers to fly into

Soviet territory. As the conference developed, American desires did not prevail in all spheres, but the United States did dominate the meetings and the postwar international civil aviation arena. The Soviet Union did not want to enter a competitive situation in which American superiority was so obvious. Again it was advisable to avoid exposure of the weak Soviet position.[11]

Another fear which may have kept the Soviets from Chicago was that their participation in discussions might have forced premature disclosure of their plans for Eastern Europe.[12] Czechoslovakia and Poland, two countries which later came under Soviet control, did attend the Chicago Conference and joined ICAO as charter members.

The atmosphere of the conference was one of uncertainty and some anxiety. Uncertainty was prevalent among those delegations whose countries were still occupied by Nazi forces or were so absorbed in the war effort that the postwar period could scarcely be contemplated. Anxiety was felt by nearly all delegations toward U.S. attempts to impose its will on other countries, a will backed by enormous American strength in both aircraft and general economic power.

American advocacy of unrestricted international operating rights with market forces determining frequencies and fares attracted no supporters. The specter of the American colossus, untouched by war devastation and well-supplied with aircraft, dominating international civil aviation, was feared by many countries. Rejecting the American approach, Britain proposed organization of a world regulatory body which would distribute routes and determine frequencies and fares. Because no other government was willing to surrender its sovereignty to an organization likely to be controlled by the major postwar powers (seen as the United States, the Soviet Union, and Britain), this suggestion was rejected.

Australia and New Zealand proposed an even more radical concept — international ownership and management of all long-range international air service by an agency of the United Nations (which had then been discussed but did not yet exist). Such a condominium would assure full service to all of its owner-members, even the remote countries of Australia and New Zealand which, in those days of short-range aircraft, could not be sure of it otherwise. This idea was also rejected.

In a move designed to show its bargaining strength, Britain publicized the possibility of developing an all-Commonwealth airline to be called the "All-Red" line, the color designation deriving from the cartographic practice of showing Britain, the Commonwealth, and British territories in red on maps. The All-Red line would fly around the world, landing only on British-controlled territories to which it would have exclusive traffic rights. The British commonwealth carrier did not materialize, but the publicity surrounding the concept did underscore Britain's great strength in potential landing rights and thus somewhat diminished the apparent overwhelming American advantage.

With its large number of bases, including those at such crucial places as India and Hong Kong, Britain was determined to maintain a system of bilateral route negotiations in which it could extract concessions from every country whose airline wished to serve a British point. Britain was also eager to delay implementation of any economic regulatory policies until its own economic system had recovered from the war years and was better able to withstand American pressure.

The Canadian delegation then proposed a list of four principles as universally applicable working rules for bilateral air transportation relations. These principles, termed "freedoms," are:

1. A civil aircraft has the right to fly over the territory of another country without landing, provided the overflown country is notified in advance and approval is given. This freedom is also called the "right of innocent passage."
2. A civil aircraft of one country has the right to land in another country for technical reasons, such as refueling or maintenance, without offering any commercial service to or from that point. This is often called a "technical stop," as opposed to a "traffic stop."
3. An airline has the right to carry traffic from its country of registry to another country.
4. An airline has the right to carry traffic from another country to its own country of registry.

The Canadian plan called for each state to be allowed to designate one state-registered carrier to operate one weekly round-trip frequency to any point in the world in compliance with the four freedoms. Permission to operate additional frequencies would be granted by a multinational authority according to the traffic carried in the previous twelve months. Known as the "escalator clause," the Canadian proposal suggested that airlines achieving a yearly load factor of at least 65 percent (65 percent of seats filled) on a route be allowed an additional frequency, and airlines failing to reach a load factor of at least 40 percent be deprived of one weekly frequency as long as its frequencies were not reduced below one weekly roundtrip. For operating rights on routes not covered by the four freedoms, that is, on traffic sectors not originating or terminating in the airline's country of registry, the multinational authority would distribute operating certificates according to a state's resources and needs in harmony with safety and economic factors.

The United States opposed granting this authority to a multinational body, preferring that airlines of any country be allowed to fly between any other two countries without regulation by an outside body. To this end, the United States proposed a fifth freedom that:

> An airline has the right to carry traffic between two countries outside its own country of registry as long as the flight originates or terminates in its own country of registry. Such rights may also be called "beyond rights."

The United States clearly perceived this freedom, were it adopted, as enabling American carriers to pick up traffic at intermediate stops on lengthy routes, especially around-the-world routes, and thus gain monopoly or near-monopoly status on major sectors. Cognizant of U.S. hopes, other countries objected to the adoption of the fifth freedom.

Of the various proposals, only the first two freedoms were adopted by the majority of the governments attending the Chicago Conference; they remain in force today as the International Air Services Transit Agreement (IASTA). The full Five Freedoms, or Transport Agreement, was adopted by only sixteen countries and, therefore, never gained acceptance. The United States, one of the few countries to sign the agreement, denounced it in 1946 when it decided that bilateral negotiations should determine capacity and fifth-freedom rights.[13]

The Chicago Conference was unable to formulate an economic policy for international air transport that was acceptable to a majority of governments or even to the two most important civil aviation powers represented there, the United States and Britain. No multinational regulatory policies were established for such questions as the assignment of air routes to specific airlines or the determination of fares and frequencies. The governments could not agree on a common policy and, in any case, were unwilling to surrender their sovereignty to a multinational regulatory body with the power to decide such policy. Although the United States could expect the greatest postwar economic strength of any country, the number of real and potential airbases controlled by Britain around the world greatly enhanced British power. Neither a single country nor a multinational body was able to dictate the economic direction of postwar international civil aviation. Only bilateral negotiations between countries at the opposite ends of proposed routes seemed to provide the proper forum for deciding frequencies and fares.

Although the states represented at Chicago could not reach agreement in 1944 on the economic structure of the postwar international civil aviation industry, they did establish the framework for ICAO. The Provisional International Civil Aviation Organization (PICAO) was formed in 1945 to function along the lines of the proposed ICAO until the latter could be formally constituted upon ratification of the Chicago Convention by the necessary twenty-six states in 1947. Both PICAO and ICAO drafted agreements on economic issues in the early days of the provisional and permanent organizations, but neither attracted sufficient support for enactment. In subsequent years ICAO has failed in its periodic attempts to formulate an international civil aviation economic policy. The organization does serve as the effective body for determining safety and navigation standards and certain measures of facilitation.

The Founding of IATA

The International Air Transport Association (IATA), an international organization of airlines, was founded in April 1945 in Havana. It is the successor of an earlier IATA (International Air Traffic Association) which established many navigational and other technical standards from its formation in 1919 until its demise at the outbreak of World War II. The new IATA has as its main focus the setting of rates at a multinational level for international routes. Certain of the technical functions served by the prewar IATA have been retained by the newer organization, but the latter is best known for its rate-setting authority.

The Bermuda Agreement

The economic issues which the Chicago Conference failed to resolve on a multinational level were left to the United States and Britain to consider binationally. Although not mandated by any international body to establish economic standards, since the United States and Britain were the two major international postwar civil aviation powers their decisions served as models for other countries. Thus the pact on bilateral civil aviation relations concluded by these countries in Bermuda in 1946, known as the "Bermuda Agreement," served as a pattern for bilateral negotiations between other countries.

The most significant feature of the Bermuda plan is its granting of reciprocal rights to the designated carriers of the contracting states to institute at their discretion capacity and fifth-freedom traffic arrangements. The relevant paragraph of the 1946 United States–United Kingdom air transport agreement states that the "primary objective" of a designated airline should be to provide "capacity adequate to the traffic demands between the country of which such air carrier is a national and the country of ultimate destination of the traffic."[14] Should one carrier institute what is deemed by the other to be capacity in excess of traffic demand or fifth-freedom traffic exceeding its combined third- and fourth-freedom traffic, the second can request an ex post facto review by the respective governments. It is the intent of the agreement that the two carriers serving a route refrain from anything "*too unreasonable*, or at least not . . . expect to go on doing it for any great length of time."[15]

The Bermuda agreement also provided that IATA, founded one year earlier, bear primary responsibility for regulating fares and rates—with governments retaining the right to approve or disapprove IATA decisions.[16] When a government disapproves the IATA-established fare, the relevant IATA traffic conference reconvenes and deliberates until a solution acceptable to all parties is reached.

Although the Bermuda agreement has been said to serve as a model for all bilateral agreements, most agreements in which the United States has not been a party do include provisions for some control over capacity. Additionally those countries other than the United States which have multiple points of entry, (as do Great Britain with its remaining colonies and territories, and West Germany with several strong industrial and commercial centers), have often restricted the number of points open to service by foreign airlines.

Postwar Airline Recovery

As the Axis forces were pushed back, prewar civil air carriers resumed service in newly liberated territories. Their efforts were facilitated by the availability of large numbers of easily convertible military transport aircraft and crews skilled in their use. Wartime development of airfields and various technical and support systems offered substantially improved flying conditions.

European Recovery

In most European countries the state airlines of the prewar period were quickly reconstituted. Other than in Switzerland and Holland, where the prewar privately owned airlines prevailed, state ownership was the rule. A European regional network was rapidly established. Notably absent among the European airlines were carriers from Germany, Austria, and Italy; the victorious Allies prohibited their operation for varying periods of time.

Because it was "nonbelligerent" at the end of the war, Italy was permitted to resume airline operations more rapidly than were Germany and Austria. Bilateral air transport agreements with various countries were signed in 1946 and several Italian air carriers began service in early 1947. Although eight different airlines were operating by the end of 1947, financial problems led to mergers and the eventual survival of two carriers—Aerolinee Italiane Internazionale (Alitalia) and Linee Aeree Italiane

(LAI). British European Airways (BEA) owned 30 percent of Alitalia, and Trans World Airlines (TWA) held 40 percent of LAI. Each of the Italian airlines operated both domestic routes and international service, the latter generally in separate areas of the world for longer routes and with duplication on certain European service. Each carrier received financial subsidy from the Italian government and other financial support from private industry, primarily from Italian aircraft manufacturers. By 1957 both government and airline authorities had concluded that the establishment of one large state carrier, rather than the maintenance of two smaller and sometimes competing airlines, would better serve Italian needs. Alitalia took over LAI in August of that year, and a new Alitalia (Alitalia–Linee Aeree Italiane) was formed in September. TWA withdrew its interest upon formation of the new airline, and BEA terminated its holdings in 1961.

Eager to help Austria recover in the postwar period, the three Western allies proposed in 1947 that Austria be allowed to established a civil airline. The Soviet Union, which was still occupying Vienna, failed to concur with the Western suggestion, stating that the Austrians could not be trusted to desist from using ostensibly civil aviation operations as camouflage for illegal military aviation activity. The USSR maintained this position until the conclusion of the Austrian State Treaty in 1955.[17] At that time, each of the two Austrian major political parties established its own carrier. Recognizing that these airlines were unlikely to succeed on such narrow political bases, the two parties conducted protracted negotiations which led to the formation of a joint carrier, Austrian Airlines, in 1957. Although controlling interest has since passed to the government, 72 percent of Austrian Airlines was held by private sources (including 15 percent each by Scandinavian Airlines System and the Fred Olson charter firm) at the time of its formation.

It was the policy of all four occupying powers that Germany be prohibited from operating air service for ten years after the end of the war. The old DLH was formally liquidated by West Germany in 1951. The division of the country into separate states meant that each would establish its own new carrier, a process initiated by both prior to 1955 in anticipation of actual operational capability. In 1953 the West German government authorized formation of a holding company in Cologne to undertake planning for an airline and to purchase equipment. In August 1954 the company evolved into the West German carrier—Deutsche Lufthansa Aktiengesellschaft, Köln—which became known as Lufthansa. Three months earlier the East Germans had established their own airline—Deutsche Lufthansa, Berlin-Schönefeld. Each of the two Germanys had wanted the name of its airline to suggest a relationship with the famed prewar Deutsche Luft Hansa Aktien-Gesellschaft, Berlin—popularly known as DLH—but neither wanted to identify completely with an institution of the Nazi period. Each state thus adopted a name which recalled, yet differed from the earlier German carrier. With assistance from TWA and BEA, West German Lufthansa began domestic, regional European, and transatlantic service in 1955. The development of the East German Lufthansa was much slower due to political constraints imposed by the Soviet Union and the unwillingness of Western countries to receive an East German airline. In 1958 the West German Lufthansa brought legal action in Vienna and Copenhagen against the East German carrier, claiming sole right to use of the Lufthansa name as recognized in an international agreement on trademarks and registered names. The courts found in favor of the West German Lufthansa and ordered East Germany to cease use of that name. The East Germans officially adopted the name of Interflug in 1959 for civil aviation flights to Western countries, and in 1963 began to use the new name for all of its flights.

The new airlines created in Italy, Austria, and Germany stem directly from World War II. The creation of Scandinavian Airlines System (SAS) by Sweden, Denmark, and Norway in 1947 was the culmination of an idea germinated in the 1930s. In both the 1930s and 1940s the major stimulus to the formation of a joint carrier was the desire to mount economically viable transatlantic operations. Each state was aware that it alone could not operate such a route. So rapidly did negotiations between the three states progress after the war that the first SAS service to New York occurred in September 1946. Scheduled SAS service to Buenos Aires was begun before the end of that year. The jointly owned carrier was officially established in 1947, with three-sevenths of the shares held by the national airline of Sweden (ABA) and two-sevenths each by the national carriers of Denmark (DDL) and Norway (DNL). To avoid possible problems of international law, a holding company controlling the airline was incorporated in New York.

In eastern Europe the fairly large and important prewar airlines of Czechoslovakia and Poland, CSA and LOT, were reconstituted shortly after the war and resumed operations along prewar patterns. The 1948 communist coup in Czechoslovakia brought an abrupt halt to CSA's then-extensive international operations. LOT was more fortunate; for various reasons it was allowed to maintain many of its west European routes, thus providing a link between the two parts of divided Europe.

The USSR forced joint-stock airlines upon Bulgaria, Romania, and Hungary in common with the joint-stock companies in these and other Soviet-controlled states in such industries as railroads, mining, banking, insurance, construction, and publishing. In these companies the Soviet Union and the other country owned equal numbers of shares and had equal numerical representation on boards of directors. However, the general manager, who was always a Soviet citizen, held authority to acquire and dispose of company assets as well as arrange mortgages and give credits.

For the joint-stock airlines these practices ensured that Soviet-manufactured equipment was purchased and that management was conducted according to the Soviet model and Soviet needs. After the East Berlin riots of 1953, the Soviets moved to diminish some of the more onerous and most resented economic policies imposed on east European states. The joint stock airlines were dismantled in 1954 and replaced by carriers wholly owned by the relevant states: TABSO in Bulgaria, TAROM in Romania, and Malev in Hungary. Soviet operational policies were, however, retained by these new airlines as well as by CSA and LOT. A joint-stock airline in Yugoslavia had collapsed earlier, in 1948, a casualty of the Soviet-Yugoslav crisis of that time. Jugoslovenski Aerotransport (JAT), a Yugoslav-controlled airline which had operated alongside the joint-stock airline, survived. The East German Lufthansa inaugurated its first international service, to Moscow, in 1955. Until 1957 all East German Lufthansa crew members were Soviet citizens.

The Soviet Union maintained an absolute monopoly on all air service to its territory until 1955. Persons flying between the West and the USSR were forced to transfer from another airline to Aeroflot at an intermediate point, often in Helsinki, Warsaw, or Prague. In 1955, reflecting both a lessening in tension following the death of Stalin and increased self-confidence from the development of domestic-built aircraft considered by the Soviets to be equivalent to Western equipment, the Soviet Union began to sign formal bilateral air transport agreements with the East European countries, Austria, Finland, and the Scandinavian countries, and Afghanistan. CSA, LOT, and JAT began service to Moscow in 1955, followed by most of the other bloc airlines, Finnair, and SAS in 1956. A number of west European countries signed bilateral air transport agreements with the Soviet Union in 1957 and 1958, and reciprocal service by Aeroflot and the relevant European airlines was established between Moscow and Paris, Brussels, and Amsterdam in 1958.

There were two types of extended west European air routes beyond Europe in the postwar period. Service to Africa and Asia by airlines of the colonial countries was usually a conversion of military support flights to commercial airline operations, the transformation occurring without much fanfare. The first noncolonial intercontinental service to be mounted by West European airlines was usually directed toward the North Atlantic—facilitating contact with the United States which was incomparably strong in the postwar period and dispenser of Marshall Plan aid. KLM inaugurated New York service in May 1946, followed in June and July by Air France and BOAC, and in September by SAS. Sabena and Swissair began New York routes in 1947 and 1949.

Aeroflot inaugurated its first intercontinental routes in 1958, mounting service to Egypt and India, two developing countries in which the Soviet

Union had become very active. Reflecting Krushchev's vigorous foreign policy plans, Aeroflot undertook an extraordinarily rapid route expansion in developing nations, initiating service to eight countries in Africa and Asia in 1961 and 1962, and to fifteen more between 1963 and 1965. That few of these routes had real commercial traffic potential did not seem to be a deterrent to their operation.[18]

U.S. Reorganization

Two factors stimulated a major change in U.S. aviation policy after World War II which led to the end of Pan American's monopoly as U.S.-designated airline on international routes. First, a number of American carriers that had operated international flights in support of Allied military forces during the war, in the process earning recognition and developing a service infrastructure overseas, wanted to continue service on a civilian commercial basis. Second, many Americans in positions of influence objected to Pan American's monopoly status as a matter of principle and considered it incongruous in the free enterprise system. Pan American President Juan Trippe, whose vision and political astuteness had created Pan American's vast prewar international route monopoly, vigorously protested to no avail against what he considered an invasion of his own empire.

Even before World War II, procompetition sentiment in the United States had led the then-new Civil Aeronautics Board to award traffic rights between New York and Lisbon to another carrier, American Export Airlines, but the outbreak of war in Europe delayed the inauguration of service. In 1942 American Export began service to Lisbon by flying boat. (American Export Airlines, known as Amex, was founded in 1937 by the American Export Lines shipping company. In 1942 the CAB ordered the shipping company to divest itself of the airline. American Airlines acquired American Export in 1945 and changed the name of its new acquisition to American Overseas Airlines—AOA.)

The First Twenty-five Years: 1945—1969

Following World War II the CAB authorized several different American carriers to operate international flights in specific regions of the world. The first of these authorizations occurred in 1945 in the North Atlantic Route Case [6 CAB 319 (1945)] which defined three specific North Atlantic route areas and authorized a single separate airline to operate service within each area. The northern route area, allocated to American Export, included enroute points in Canada, Greenland, Iceland, Shannon, the United Kingdom, the Netherlands, the Scandinavian countries, Finland, northern Germany, Poland, the Baltic states, Leningrad, and Moscow.[19] The central route area, allocated to Pan American, included London, Belgium, southern Germany, Austria, Hungary, Czechoslovakia, Romania, Bulgaria, Yugoslavia, Turkey, Lebanon, Iraq, Iran, Afghanistan, and northern India. The southern route, awarded to TWA (still known as Transcontinental and Western), included Newfoundland, Ireland other than Shannon, France, Portugal, Spain, Switzerland, Italy, Greece, Algeria, Tunisia, Libya, Egypt, Palestine, Trans-Jordan, Saudi Arabia, Yemen, Oman, southern India, and Ceylon. Pan American's central route operating certificate was later amended to include the Azores, Bermuda, Newfoundland, and Dublin.

In 1948 Pan American initiated efforts to purchase American Overseas Airlines which had proved a drain on its parent company, American Airlines. The attempt was disapproved by the CAB in 1950 after lengthy hearings, but President Truman overrode the board and ordered the approval of Pan American's acquisition of AOA, and the latter's operating rights. In a letter to the CAB declaring his decision, the president wrote that, in the interest of providing better service, such major European points as London, Paris, Frankfurt, and Rome should be served by two competing U.S. carriers. Pan American's absorption of AOA added Paris and Rome to its previously held rights to London and Frankfurt. TWA was then awarded authorization to London and Frankfurt. With its previously granted rights to Paris and Rome, TWA joined Pan American in offering transatlantic flights to the four large European cities.

In addition to authorizing specific service points on the eastern side of the Atlantic, the CAB also designated terminal points in the United States for the American transatlantic flights. Each airline was awarded the same six points: Boston, New York, Philadelphia, Washington, D.C., Detroit, and Chicago.

When the 1945 North Atlantic Route Case authorizations expired in 1952 they were renewed, with some changes, until 1959 [15 CAB 1053 (1952)]. In 1959 they were renewed again until 1966. By 1966 the increasing importance of the American west coast mandated that cities from the western states be included as U.S. terminals; Los Angeles, San Francisco, Portland, and Seattle were designated as U.S. destinations in the third Transatlantic Route Renewal Case [44 CAB 9 (1966)], thus adding a group of western terminals to the original eastern-midwestern points. A freight carrier, Seaboard World Airlines, was authorized by these proceedings to provide service between major west European points and Boston, New York, Philadelphia, and Baltimore.

In 1969, much to the displeasure of Pan American which had applied for the same authority, the CAB awarded National Airlines the right to operate Miami-London service. This decision [51 CAB 1007 (1969)] added a fourth airline to the North Atlantic.

The second major route award case of the postwar period was the Additional Service to Latin America case [6 CAB 857 (1946)] in which Pan American once again lost its monopoly status. The chief architect of the new U.S. design for American carrier service to the southern continent was not the CAB, but President Harry Truman who overrode several CAB suggestions in his efforts to reduce the overwhelming Pan American presence in the southern hemisphere. Although Pan American protested vigorously against the award of Latin American routes to other carriers, it was itself largely to blame for the president's decision. In 1929 Pan American and the W.R. Grace Company jointly founded Panagra (Pan American–Grace Airways), an airline which operated routes between a number of South American countries and as far north as Panama. In Panama and at other points Panagra linked up with Pan American flights for through service to the United States. With the passage of time Panagra built up a very strong traffic base in Latin America and the W.R. Grace Company, a large shipping and trading firm, began pressing for an extension of Panagra routes to a major U.S. point. Pan American objected, preceiving any direct Panagra service to the United States as unwelcome competition to its own routes. The argument between Pan American and W.R. Grace raged on, often in public, and was common knowledge in the countries served by both airlines. Considering the feud between two American partners detrimental to U.S. prestige in Latin America, Truman invoked his presidential powers to institute substantial changes in the patterns of American carrier service to the southern hemisphere.

The chief beneficiary of the route award case was Braniff Airways, which had inaugurated limited Mexico service during World War II and desired to continue and enlarge these international operations. In addition to Mexican points, the 1946 decision authorized Braniff to serve Panama, Bogota, Quito, Lima, La Paz, Buenos Aires, Sao Paulo, Rio de Janeiro, and several other Latin American cities. Its U.S. termini included points in Texas and on both the east and west coasts. More limited route authorizations were granted to American and Eastern (both Mexico) and to Colonial, Chicago and Southern, Trans-Caribbean, and National (all for points in the Caribbean). Pan American retained most of its previous traffic rights, but the presence of other carriers diluted its overall strength.

Over the next two decades four mergers and/or takeovers reduced the number of U.S. airlines in Latin America. In 1953 Delta merged with Chicago and Southern, the surviving airline using the name Delta as it was the stronger partner. Eastern Airlines took over Colonial in 1956. In 1966 Braniff acquired Panagra, further strengthening the Texas carrier's Latin

American position vis-à-vis Pan American. American Airlines, acquired additional Caribbean rights by purchasing Trans Caribbean in 1970.

The third major postwar route case was the Pacific in 1946 [7 CAB 209 (1946)]. Again Pan American lost its monopoly position. Northwest Airlines, which had operated military support flights in the Arctic and Pacific during World War II, was awarded Great Circle transpacific rights via Alaska to Tokyo and other points in the Orient. Pan American retained its prewar routes. Three carriers were authorized to serve China, a destination believed potentially lucrative; Northwest received rights to Shanghai and Harbin, Pan American to Shanghai and Peking, and TWA to Shanghai and Canton. Hawaii, because of its midocean location and status as a territory, was also a consideration in the transpacific case. Pan American's transpacific rights included rights in the islands; United Air Lines was also awarded a Hawaiian route, from San Francisco; and Northwest was granted rights to Hawaii from Portland and Seattle in 1948.

High traffic growth and increasing competition from foreign airlines spurred the CAB to launch an investigation in the late 1950s into the three transpacific routes: U.S. mainland–Hawaii; United States–Orient; and United States–South Pacific. Due to the many destinations involved, the large number of carrier applications for the various routes, and foreign policy considerations in those services beyond Hawaii, the proceedings were complex and protracted. In 1969 important changes were announced on all three routes. American, Braniff, Continental, and Western were authorized to serve Hawaii from their respective traditional bases, thus bringing to seven the number of airlines operating routes between the mainland and Hawaii. TWA, which had received Hong Kong rights from the British in 1966, was authorized to extend its transatlantic route to Hong Kong through Bombay and across the Pacific, via Okinawa and Guam, to the U.S. mainland. TWA thus had an around-the-world route. American Airlines was awarded rights between the United States and the southern Pacific—Australia, New Zealand, Fiji, and Samoa—via Hawaii. Although it was the view of the CAB and White House that traffic potential justified the certification of these new routes, actual experience in the early 1970s proved that expectation incorrect. Several of the carriers involved suffered massive financial losses in their new Pacific operations, thus forcing some changes in route patterns. These alterations will be discussed further.

The fourth major postwar CAB route award case was also decided in 1946—Africa [7 CAB 285 (1946)]. Pan American was authorized to serve African destinations on two routes, one crossing the Central Atlantic to Dakar and down the West African coast and into Leopoldville (now Kinshasa). The second route specified an Atlantic crossing via Natal, Brazil. Although African service was a long-term objective of Pan American, it was not a prime goal of the American carrier's postwar service. Almost all of Africa was still ruled by European colonial powers and little traffic potential could be foreseen for a noncolonial airline. Pan American retained monopoly rights in all of sub-Saharan Africa until 1965 when TWA was awarded competing authorization for East Africa.

The last major international development among American airlines in the postwar period was the inauguration of transatlantic all-cargo service in May 1947. Seaboard and Western (later Seabord World, subsequently merged with Flying Tiger), which was organized only in 1946, began an all-cargo service to Luxembourg in 1947 and expanded into other European destinations as time went on.

The single factor which most differentiated U.S. policy from that of other countries in the postwar period was the firm belief that competition between privately owned U.S.-registered airlines was necessary for the provision of good service to potential air transport consumers. It was this policy that spurred the CAB and the president to authorize several airlines to operate those routes perceived potentially lucrative. In selecting specific carrriers for route authorization, appropriate U.S. regulatory agencies have required that successful applicant airlines be financially sound and fit to undertake and maintain the new route; be able to integrate the new route into their existing route network; and fulfill a demonstrated need for the enhanced service they will provide. Domestic and international political conditions may also play a role in selecting one carrier from several applicants, a factor which is discussed in some detail in a later chapter. In the context of U.S. international route awards in the postwar period, the perceived *economic need* to foster competition and thus authorize additional airlines to operate international routes was supplemented by (1) a *domestic political need* to rebuff Pan American's Juan Trippe whose ambition and aggressiveness had generated substantial resentment, and (2) a perceived *security need* to increase the number of American air carriers operating international routes.

The 1970s — Reevaluation

In the early 1970s even before the doubling of fuel prices following the 1973 Arab-Israeli war, financial returns on a number of international routes began to suggest that expectations of substantial traffic growth were not being fulfilled. The traffic base necessary to support the recently added airlines on already-existing service did not materialize, and some carriers were clearly overextended. A period of retrenchment, expressed by three route exchanges, followed.

In 1973 TWA agreed to suspend its service to East Africa in exchange for Pan American agreement to suspend its traffic rights in Dublin. Each airline thus gained an American carrier monopoly in a specific route area.

The second and third route exchanges, authorized in 1975, were more complex. In the second, involving Pan American and TWA as in the first, both the Atlantic and Pacific routes were covered. On the Pacific, TWA suspended all services beyond Los Angeles, withdrawing from Hawaii, Guam, Okinawa, Hong Kong, Taiwan, Bangkok, and Bombay. Its rights in Bombay, Taiwan, and Okinawa were transferred to Pan American. TWA thus withdrew from Asia and, by extension, from its around-the-world route. TWA also suspended service to Germany and between Washington, D.C. (Dulles) and London. Pan American suspended service between London and several U.S. secondary cities, and between the United States and Austria, France, Portugal, Spain, and Morocco (except on its mid-Atlantic route Miami-San Juan-Lisbon-Madrid-Rome). Its rights at Nice, Barcelona, and Vienna were transferred to TWA; its service to Paris, Madrid, and Casablanca suspended. Some changes were also made in domestic service between the West Coast and Hawaii.

The third route exchange involved American Airlines and Pan American. Implementation of the 1969 transpacific route awards resulted in a loss of almost $30 million for American Airlines during the first three years of Pacific oprations, almost two-thirds of the deficit occurring on its mainland-Hawaii routes which had to be flown as sectors on its South Pacific routes. The lack of turnaround authority in Hawaii, claimed American, impeded their traffic-generating ability. American agreed to transfer all of its South Pacific routes to Pan American in exchange for Pan American transferral to American of its rights in Bermuda and specific New York — Santo Domingo and New York — Barbados routes. Some changes were also made in mainland-Hawaii service. The withdrawal of American from the South Pacific gave Pan American a monopoly there; and the transferral of Pan American Caribbean routes to American, added to American's 1970 acquisition of Trans Caribbean Airways, made American a major Caribbean carrier.

In 1977 the United States and Britain concluded a new bilateral air transport agreement, Bermuda II, which seemed to signal a further consolidation of U.S. international airline service. The British sought a predetermined capacity split, higher fares, and a limitation of U.S. airline beyond rights from British points. It was only their last condition that was fulfilled; the United States agreed to a reduction of U.S. carrier beyond rights service between London and the rest of Europe, and between Hong Kong and a number of Asian points. The United States also agreed to eliminate dual designation of airlines (that is, to limit U.S. representation to one carrier) in all but two American cities. Whereas these restrictions further consolidated existing U.S. international service, other provisions of the agreement permitted London routes for both countries from four additional U.S. points not previously served — Atlanta, Dallas/Fort Worth, Houston, and San Francisco. A British carrier was authorized to operate a

Seattle-London route. Some Pacific routes were also authorized for extensive service. In connection with the Bermuda II agreement and other policy changes of the U.S. government, several airlines were allowed to initiate service on the North Atlantic. Braniff began service between Dallas and London, and Delta inaugurated an Atlanta-London route. National was granted rights to serve London, Paris, Amsterdam, and Frankfurt nonstop from Miami; additional rights, restricted in some cases, were awarded to National for service between Paris and New Orleans and Tampa. Other route awards were given to TWA for service between London and five inland American cities. Pan American received authorization for service on Houston-London and Houston-Frankfurt routes via New York. Northwest took over Pan American's authority on routes between the United States and Iceland, Scotland, Finland, and the Scandinavian countries. Continental Airlines was awarded South Pacific rights similar to those American Airlines had given up—to Auckland and Sydney through Hawaii, Samoa, and Fiji. New routes were also granted to several cargo and supplemental carriers.

Although the Bermuda II agreement was hailed by some as a model for future bilateral agreements throughout the world, it soon faded in significance under the impact of the United States-Israel bilateral agreement and a U.S. statement on "Policy for the Conduct of International Air Transportations Negotiations," both dating from August 1978. The United States-Israel pact, cited by American officials as the type of agreement which the United States would henceforth seek with other countries, permits American carriers to serve any point in Israel from any point in the United States with freedom to serve intermediate and beyond points of their own choosing. Israeli airlines received rights to three U.S. cities in addition to New York. The two countries also agreed to allow liberal charter service and fare-setting practices. Some of the provisions of the United States-Israeli agreement were reflected in the U.S. policy statement issued later the same month in which these U.S. objectives for international air transport were listed:

1. encouragement of price competition;
2. liberalization of charter rules;
3. elimination of restrictions on scheduled service capacity, frequency, and route operating rights;
4. elimination of discrimination and unfair competitive practices faced by U.S. airlines in international transportation;
5. flexibility to authorize multiple U.S. airlines to serve single international markets;
6. improving customer access to international air service through designation of additional cities as international termini; and
7. further development of competitive air cargo service.[20]

So liberal were the practices advocated that American policy was referred to as "open skies," that is, the freedom of airlines to fly to all possible destinations without restrictions.

The importance of the United States in the international civil aviation system means that all airlines serving the United States will have to conform in many ways to American practices. Indeed, subsequent U.S. bilateral air transport agreements with other countries have been much more liberal than would have been deemed possible before 1978. However, the political and economic environment in which American carriers operate is unique to the United States, and many of the policy objectives enumerated in the 1978 statement are rejected by foreign airlines as incompatible with their own requirements.[21] Although the United States has made new route awards (not listed here) consistent with the statement since it was issued, the degree to which U.S. policy can be implemented depends in large part on the reactions of foreign governments and foreign airlines.

Two-Airline Policy in Canada

Climatic factors and the residence of most of its citizenry in a long strip of land adjacent to the southern border impeded the development of large airlines in prewar Canada. Smaller "bush" airlines, however, were abundant. Trans-Canada Air Lines, predecessor of Air Canada, was founded by the Canadian government as late as 1937 and carried its first passengers in 1939. Its expansion to intercontinental service occurred as it was pressed into military support flights during World War II. Until 1978 the official state flag carrier, Air Canada (as it has been known since 1964), was legally owned by the government-held Canadian National Railways. Now owned by a separate state agency, Air Canada is based in Montreal and operates an extensive domestic network and international service to the United States, Caribbean, eastern South America, Europe, sub-Saharan Africa, Middle East, and Indian subcontinent.

Canada's second large scheduled airline, CP Air (Canadian Pacific Air Lines) was established in 1942 when the privately owned Canadian Pacific Railways acquired and merged ten bush airlines. Its international service began in 1949. Based in Vancouver and still owned by Canadian Pacific Railways, CP Air's greatest network concentration is logically in the western Americas and the Pacific. Its domestic routes are concentrated in western Canada. Its international service emphasis is in the western United States, Central America, western South America, and Pacific and Asian countries east of India. CP Air also serves certain European countries not served by Air Canada. It is Canadian government policy that the two airlines not compete against each other on the same route. In addition to the two major carriers, several smaller Canadian airlines operate regional domestic service and charter flights.

Far East and Pacific Reemergence

Among the more interesting features of Australian international civil aviation in the postwar period was its inauguration of flying boat service to London in 1946. The journey usually required seven days. By the end of 1947 the Qantas London service was flown in Lockheed Constellations, an aircraft which cut travel time to four days. Qantas expanded its Asian service in the late 1940s and inaugurated transpacific service to San Francisco, via Hawaii, in 1954. In 1958 the Australian carrier began an around-the-world service through San Francisco, New York, and London, but this route was later suspended due to the intense competition on the North Atlantic sector. Qantas has no natural market on the North Atlantic, and could not generate sufficient traffic to sustain the route. The great distance of Australia from many potential traffic points has caused its government to be conservative in concluding air transport agreements with other countries, a policy which surely is at odds with the 1978 U.S. government liberal international civil aviation statment.

New Zealand also maintains a conservative international civil aviation policy, confining its operations to the Pacific area. In 1978 Air New Zealand, the state-owned international airline, merged with and absorbed the state-owned domestic carrier.

As an Axis power, Japan, like Germany, faced restrictions in rebuilding civil aviation in the postwar period. Japanese Air Lines was formed as a private concern in 1951 and was initially confined under the Allied Peace Treaty to domestic routes and employment of non-Japanese pilots only. In 1953 the company gained full operating independence and reorganized as Japan Air Lines (JAL) with 50 percent government ownership. JAL inaugurated Tokyo-San Francisco service in 1954, regional Pacific routes between 1956 and 1958, and a polar route to London in 1961. Its expansion continued rapidly throughout the 1960s — so rapidly that its support capabilities were overextended. After a series of accidents, a review committee determined in 1972-1973 that serious deficiencies existed in logistics, pilot experience, and maintenance programs. JAL reduced its expansion rate while implementing various measures designed to correct shortcomings. The airline has since resumed a high growth rate.

Korean Air Lines, owned by a conglomerate industrial group, was founded in 1962 to replace a government-owned South Korean airline founded in 1947. Korean flies domestic routes and international service to Honolulu, Los Angeles, and New York, various Asian points, the Middle

East, and several European cities. As in eastern Europe, the Soviet Union forced a joint-stock airline in North Korea, establishing SOKAO (Sovietsko-Koreyskoye Aviatsionnoye Obshchestvo) in 1950. Along with other joint-stock companies, SOKAO was dissolved in 1954. The current North Korean airline, Chosonminhang, has developed very slowly, doubtless due to the political isolation of the country. Its only international routes are to Khabarovsk in the Soviet Union and to Peking.

The prewar airlines of China were transferred to Taiwan by the Kuomingtang after the communists took power on the mainland in 1949. SKOGA, a Soviet-Chinese joint-stock company, was formed in 1952 to operate routes in northern China and transborder routes between China and Soviet Central Asia. Another Chinese airline, CCAC (Chinese Civil Aviation Corporation), was wholly owned by the Chinese government and operated in southern China. In 1962 the two airlines were merged to form CAAC (Civil Aviation Administration of China). Organized in a pattern similar to that of Aeroflot, CAAC is responsible for all civil aviation activity in China, including such nontransport functions as crop dusting and forest patrolling. As a domestic transport service, CAAC is poorly developed, flying only to about 100 points. Until the last years of Mao Tse-tung, CAAC operated a limited international network—to Pyongyang, Irkutsk in Siberia, Ulan Bator in Mongolia, Hanoi, and Rangoon. In the mid- and late-1970s, reflecting China's changing foreign policy, CAAC expanded its international network, adding Karachi, Addis Ababa, a numbr of destinations in Europe, and several daily flights to points in Japan. A Hong Kong-Guangzhou (Canton) service was inaugurated in 1978—the twenty five-minute Trident flight between the British Crown Colony and the large southern mainland port city an alternative to a four-hour train ride. Perhaps these new route implementations were at least partly foreshadowed by China's first purchase in 1970 of western-manufactured aircraft—in this case, Hawker-Siddeley Tridents from Pakistan International Airlines (PIA). Additional purchases of Tridents followed, including twenty-nine new ones. In 1972 and 1978 CAAC purchased ten Boeing 707s and three Boeing 747s respectively, aircraft suitable for the airline's long international routes.

Cathay Pacific Airways was organized in Hong Kong in 1946 by a group of former pilots from one of the prewar mainland airlines. Majority control is held by the Swire Group, a London conglomerate with extensive Far East and Australian interests. The airline, often known as CP Air, operates extensive Asian service.

China Airlines, the flag carrier of Taiwan (Republic of China) was founded in 1959 as a charter carrier by a group of retired Chinese air force officers. In 1965 it was designated the national airline. CAL operates service throughout Asia, west to the Middle East, and east to San Franciso and Los

Angeles. Taiwan was eased out of ICAO in 1971 in favor of the People's Republic of China (PRC), which joined the UN aviation agency in 1974. CAL resigned from IATA in 1974 in expectation of a membership application by CAAC (not yet submitted) which would cause a negative response to CAL. Despite Taiwan's political isolation, CAL is financially sound and enjoys a good growth record. The island is a popular Asian vacation site and among the airline's frequent foreign passengers are tourists as well as prosperous ethnic Chinese from the large Southeast Asia Chinese diaspora of 15 million people.

Perhaps the most rapid growth rate achieved by a southeast Asian airline is that of Singapore Airlines (SIA), another carrier drawing on ethnic Chinese diaspora traffic. SIA was formed in 1972 after the collapse of Malaysia-Singapore Airlines, a carrier jointly owned by Malaysia and Singapore. A prosperous, strategically located free-trade island, Singapore is the banking and commercial center of Southeast Asia. Its population is 95 percent Chinese and maintains strong relations with other Chinese diaspora communities. SIA fulfills the diverse needs of the Singapore economy with an extensive international network stretching from Europe to San Francisco. Non-Chinese foreigners are drawn to the airline by the excellent service it provides.

Latin American Independence

Controlling interest in most Latin American airlines was held by foreigners prior to World Was II. During the war and the immediate postwar period the large German influence in these carriers, usually exerted through local German emigré communities, was replaced by American interest, often through partial Pan American ownership. A combination of forceful U.S. government pressure and aggressive Pan American leadership brought the American airline a prominent role in Latin American civil aviation. In efforts to reduce the Yankee presence and strengthen state control over important industries, a number of governments began buying out or nationalizing Pan American and other foreign shareholders in the late 1940s. Efforts to completely eliminate foreign ownership continue today, impeded in a few Central American and Caribbean nations by local need to retain the foreigners for technical or managerial assistance. Several state airlines, such as Aero Peru, LAP of Paraguay, and PLUNA of Uruguay, are operated by the military air forces of their countries.

Brazil's VARIG (Viacas Aerea Rio-Grandense) is Latin America's largest single airline, maintaining a fleet of approximately seventy aircraft and operating international routes to numerous foreign countries, including points in Africa and Asia. Its domestic service is also extensive, as is that of three other Brazilian carriers which try to fulfill the transportation needs of a large country poorly served by surface transport. Colombia also has a strong aviation infrastructure, motivated in part by a pioneering prewar tradition and by topographical conditions rendering ground transportation difficult. Avianca, Colombia's privately controlled major carrier, is the oldest airline in the Americas. Among the youngest are Aero Peru and Ecuatoriana; their emergence in the mid-1970s, with strong protectionist support of their governments, disturbed a sort of status quo which had existed in northwestern South America for many years in which foreign-owned airlines held prominent roles.

Air service was inaugurated in Mexico in the 1920s by Americans. Initially operations were limited to carrying payrolls to oil fields and silver mines and silver from the mines. The largest of the carriers, CMA (Compañia Mexicana de Aviación) was purchased by Pan American in 1929. It grew rapidly, extending northward into the United States and southward into Guatemala where it connected with Pan American's other Latin American airlines. Pan American acquired 40 percent of Aeronaves de Mexico, another local airline in 1940. United Air Lines purchased 75 percent of a regional Mexican carrier in 1942 and expanded that airline's network into Texas in 1944. In the mid-1940s the Mexican government enacted laws forcing foreigners to reduce their holdings in Mexican airlines. Aeronaves, in which the Mexican government held controlling interest, took over several regional carriers, including the one owned by United, and in 1959 nationalized the minority shares held by Pan American. By 1968 private Mexican sources gained complete control of CMA-Mexicana. Today Mexicana operates a large domestic route system and international routes to the Caribbean and the United States. Aeronaves has become known as Aeromexico-AMSA and, as the state-owned official flag carrier, serves nearly sixty domestic points, destinations throughout the hemisphere, and several European points.

Fitting Cuba's role in the Caribbean, Cubana stands apart from other Caribbean airlines. The carrier was founded in 1929 by Curtiss Aircraft and taken over by Pan American in 1932. Pan American reduced its shareholding in 1945 and withdrew completely in 1953. The Cuban government under Castro nationalized the airline in 1959. Although Cuban officials express a preference for U.S.-manufactured equipment, Soviet aircraft have come to dominate the Cubana fleet. In addition to domestic routes, Cubana operates international service to Montreal, Mexico City, Lima, and several Caribbean points in the Western hemisphere; Madrid, Prague, and East Berlin; and several points in African countries where the Cuban presence is large.

African Beginnings

As the colonial powers prepared to grant independence to their African possessions in the 1950s and 1960s, European aviation specialists sought to create a permanent African aviation infrastructure or at least persuade the Africans to create one along European lines. In most countries the European efforts were successful, if only because the emerging states required European expertise, equipment, and financial assistance. This encouraged the continuation of European influence in the newly independent nations.

Of the two major departing colonial powers, France and Britain, French participation in African aviation has been more extensive. France possessed more colonies, each of which was contiguous to at least one other French territory. This alone facilitated French involvement and the operation of joint services. British colonies were fewer in number and several were distant from one another, some on each coast of the African continent. Further, the inhabitants of the British colonies were generally better educated and better prepared for independence than were those of the French territories, thus lessening the need for intensive British participation in the airline operations of former British colonies. These factors, plus the above-noted desire of colonial powers to maintain influence, stimulated French support of a multinational African airline to fulfill the needs of its former colonies for Africa-based longer in-Africa and intercontinental air service. In 1961 the two French airlines serving Africa formed a holding company designed to assist the former French African colonies to establish a joint carrier. Eleven of these fourteen countries formed a new airline, Air Afrique, each owning 6.54 percent and the holding company owning the remainder. The airline fulfills its mandate to operate international service. French involvement in the carrier remains substantial.

The member-states of Air Afrique maintain very small airlines for domestic routes. Small, limited-network carriers exist in most other West African countries, except for oil-rich Gabon (a member of Air Afrique until 1977) and oil-rich and populous Nigeria, both of which operate larger airlines with intercontinental routes.

On the other side of the continent, those involved in East African Airways—Kenya, Tanzania, and Uganda—split apart in 1977 as a result of political and economic differences. Each of these countries formed its own airline to serve its particular needs. Kenya Airways, for example, stresses regional and intercontinental routes serving its tourist industry.

The best established carrier in East Africa is Ethiopian Airlines, founded in 1945 and beneficiary of postwar technical assistance from Trans World Airlines (TWA).[22] Both intercontinental and domestic service—the latter of great importance in a country with Ethiopia's topography—grew in sophistication with TWA direction and gave the country a sophisticated aviation system in an essentially backward economy. Domestic political upheavals beginning in the mid-1970s have impeded the continued progress of the airline.

In southern Africa the largest air carrier is South African Airways, founded in 1934. South African operates domestic routes and intercontinental service to Europe, North and South America, Australia, and Hong Kong. A privately-owned cargo carrier, Safair, operates semi-clandestine service to more than a dozen black-governed African countries partially dependent on South African food, medical, technical, industrial or financial assistance.

Middle East Expansion

The leading country in Arab civil aviation has been Lebanon, home base of two sophisticated intercontinental air carriers, Middle East Airlines (MEA) and Trans Mediterranean Airways (TMA). MEA was founded in 1945 and thrived on traffic generated by Lebanon's role as banking and entertainment center of the Arab world. Both Pan American and BOAC once held substantial portions of the airline's stock, but have since withdrawn. Majority ownership of MEA is now controlled by a Beirut investment company, a minority share by Air France. TMA was established in 1953 and is the only large allcargo carrier outside the United States. Operating worldwide service, TMA is owned by its president. The overwhelming importance of both airlines in the Arab Middle East has been reduced in recent years by the growth of air carriers from oil-rich states and by the internal unrest in Lebanon which has sharply diminished that country's commercial role in the Middle East. Almost all airlines of Arab countries have expanded rapidly during the 1970s.

Royal Air Maroc maintains the largest route network of the three Maghreb carriers, its operations including service to New York, Montreal, and Rio de Janeiro. Consistent with its emphasis on a pan-Arab political ideology, Libyan Arab Airlines has stressed Arab destinations in its network. The fleet and route system of Egyptair have reflected Egypt's changing political alliances; when Egypt was under Soviet influence, the airline had numerous Soviet-manufactured aircraft and maintained service to various east European capitals. The Egyptians never denied their dissatisfaction with Soviet equipment and returned eight almost-new Tupolev TU-154s to the USSR in 1974.

Alia Royal Jordanian Airways and Syrianair inaugurated a joint service to New York in 1977. Alia expanded rapidly during the 1970s as one element in a government policy to strengthen the role of Jordanian civil aviation in the Arab world. Motivated in part by a desire that Jordan replace strife-torn Lebanon as the Arab commercial center in the eastern Mediterranean area, Alia's route network was expanded and Arab Wings, the first executive jet charter service in the Middle East, was established in Amman by Alia to serve the entire Arab world. An aviation academy training pilots, mechanics, and other personnel also operates in Jordan. ArabAir Services Corporation, a consulting firm founded and chaired by former Pan American President Najeeb Halaby, has its headquarters in Amman.

Israel's El Al Airlines was established in 1948, six months after the founding of the state. It has long operated service to Europe and North America, and is the most sophisticated carrier in the Middle East. Route expansion of El Al to Asia has been impeded by the refusal of Arab states to grant it overflight rights. Freight service of El Al and Israeli cargo carriers has been vital in airlifting Israeli agricultural produce to Europe during winter months.

Although never a large airline, Cyprus Airways has provided an important transport link between Arab countries, particularly Lebanon, and Israel. Schedules of flights between Cyprus and Israel and Cyprus and Lebanon are coordinated to provide transit service where political differences prevent a direct route. The efficiency of this and other Cyprus air service has been compromised by the 1974 Turkish invasion of the island which forced Cyprus Airways to relocate from Nicosia to Larnaca. Cyprus Airways is, and has been, operated by the Greek Cypriot community. Following the invasion, the Turkish national carrier THY and Turkish Cypriot interests established Cyprus Turkish Airlines to fly between Ercan, an airport near Nicosia in Turkish-held territory, and several cities in Turkey.

THY (Turk Hava Yollari) was founded in 1933 and is owned by the Turkish government. It operates domestic service and routes in the Middle East and to European countries. The approximately one million Turkish citizens who work in Europe constitute an important market for the national carrier.

Iranair was established in 1962 as a government-owned successor to two privately held carriers, Iranian Airways (widely reported to have had ties to the U.S. Central Intelligence Agency, perhaps through minority shares owned by TWA)[23] and Persian Air Services (a company with connections to a British firm). Iranair operates domestic service and an extensive international network stretching from New York in the west to Peking and Tokyo in the east. After the fall of the Shah in 1979, a new Iranian management signaled the consolidation of the carrier's international network by suspending previously agreed-upon purchases of new aircraft, cancelling plans for new routes, and announcing the termination of existing uneconomic service.[24]

Among the airlines with extremely poor safety records by world standards are several Middle east carriers — Alia, Egyptair, and THY. Conversely, El Al, Cyprus Airways, and Iraqi Airways all have excellent safety records.

South Asian Contrasts

Civil aviation in India developed in the late 1920s and early 1930s, initially as extensions of the British Imperial Airways route through Asia, and later through separate efforts of local Indians and some Britons. The major carrier, Tata Air Lines, continued to operate through World War II and managed to acquire twelve U.S. war-surplus DC-3s as hostilities drew to a close. In 1946 the airline became a public company and its name was changed to Air-India. J.R.D. Tata, the airline's founder, continued as manager. Air-India operates an extensive international route system. Some service is directed toward Indian diaspora groups in east Africa and elsewhere; other routes, such as a successful North Atlantic run between London or Paris and New York, are aimed primarily at non-Indian traffic. A second major carrier, Indian Airlines, was formed in 1953 from the nationalization of eight smaller airlines, all but one of which had been privately owned. Indian Airlines operates domestic service and regional international routes to such countries as Afghanistan, Burma, and Sri Lanka.

Prior to Partition in 1949, Pakistani terrritory was served by some of the same airlines that served preindependent India. Several of these airlines were Moslem-owned and continued operations in the new Pakistan, but various problems restricted their ability to provide service required by the new state, particularly service between the eastern and western sections of the country. In 1951 Pakistan International Airlines (PIA) was founded as a government department to provide these air transport capabilities. Modern aircraft were acquired — shorter range for regional domestic operations and longer range for longer domestic and for international service. PIA was the first jet operator in Asia. After East Pakistan became Bangladesh in 1971, a number of PIA staff and aircraft became surplus and subsequently were made available to other airlines, particularly those in other developing Moslem countries. Some staff were assigned to a PIA maintenance base and training facility often used by other carriers. The Pakistani airline serves a number of domestic points and international destinations stretching from New York to Peking and Tokyo. Similar to Air-India, the PIA network reflects their common British colonial experience and need to serve a farflung ethnic diaspora.

Bangladesh Biman, carrier of Bangladesh, was established in 1972 and mounts domestic service, regional Asian routes, and service to London. Its emergence and early operations were facilitated by the availability of PIA-trained Bengali staff and provision of equipment by India and the Netherlands.

To the north and west, the government of Afghanistan has two airlines. Ariana is the international flag carrier, operating service to Europe, Moscow, and regional Asian destinations. Pan American holds minority ownership in the airline and provides it with substantial technical and managerial assistance. The second airline, Bakhtiar, serves several domestic points. Its fleet is small and its operations irregular.

Civil aviation operations in Sri Lanka (Ceylon) have also been irregular; air transport in that country suffers from mismanagement and imprecise articulation of goals. In Burma, the inward-looking government of that country has fostered an airline compatible with its general political orientation. Burma Airways Corporation operates an extensive domestic system and an international service limited to a small number of regional Asian points.

Thai Airways International was established as a national flag carrier in 1959 with 30 percent ownership held by SAS and considerable assistance provided by the Scandinavian airline. The Thai government has since bought out the SAS interest, but the SAS assistance program continues. Thai International operates service in Asia and the Pacific and to the Middle East and Europe. A smaller airline serves Thai domestic needs.

Garuda (name of a legendary Indonesian bird) was founded in 1949 by the Indonesian government and by KLM, the airline of the former colonial power. Garuda flies to thirty domestic points and to Europe, Asian destinations, Honolulu, and San Francisco. Almost entirely owned by the Indonesian state, Garuda receives substantial assistance from KLM.

More Airlines, More Routes, More Conflict

As the international route structure has grown and the number of airlines operating international routes has proliferated, conflict in the international air transport industry has intensified. Issues of contention — especially the degree of regulation in the industry — stem from the diverse nature of the more than one hundred carriers involved in international air transport.

American airlines are privately owned, responsible to individual stockholders who expect a return on their investment. American carrriers seek out the most economic aircraft available and the broadest possible passenger market. If routes are not economically viable, U.S. airlines decline to operate them. U.S. carriers are generally independent corporations free from government interference, notwithstanding occasional government requests for operation of commercially nonviable international routes.

Most foreign carriers are state-owned and state-controlled. In addition to providing air transport, they may be mandated by the state to: earn specific amounts of convertible currency; maintain a level of employment in excess of real needs; support a domestic aircraft-manufacturing industry or a certain foreign aircraft industry for political or economic reasons; or operate commercially unsound routes consistent with a particular foreign policy. Intervention by the government on behalf of such objectives usually reduces airline efficiency and may encourage the adoption of protectionist policies regarding competition with foreign airlines. Protectionist, non-competitive policies may also be adopted by authoritarian states as one means of enforcing restrictions on citizen travel. Many small or underdeveloped countries employ protectionist procedures to create a market unattainable by conventional nonpressure commercial practices.

It is inevitable that the civil aviation policy of the United States — based on vigorous free enterprise and competition, minimum regulation, a large and advanced industrial base, and a broad passenger market — should be at variance with the policies of countries practicing state-control. Although the principle of reciprocity of operating conditions is stipulated in almost all bilateral air transport agreements, such reciprocity is impossible to achieve on routes where carriers originate in countries supporting radically different aviation policies, such as the United States and the Soviet Union, or France and a small, poor, former French colony. In the first case, the American carrier finds itself unable to maintain commercially viable service and suspends its flights; in the second case, the French carrier maintains service but in a patronizing, often tutelary manner that hardly suggests reciprocity.

The evolution of international air transport is less a function of aviation technology or conventional commercial traffic than an expression of political forces in specific historical periods. It has been the politics of expansionism, war preparation, diplomacy, economic doctrine, or other conditions not intrinsically related to air transport itself that have defined the development of international civil avialtion. Doubtless these forces will continue to influence the future of international air transport more than the nature of available aircraft or the amount of traffic actually carried on world airlines. The size and scope of a particular airline's network do not always accurately reflect the commercial strength of that airline's individual routes or of its entire route network.

Summary

The use of aviation for civil transport is a product of the period immediately following World War I. Surplus aircraft were available and a demand for air transport was created by wartime disruption of surface transport and the convening of postwar international conferences. In industrialized Europe and in the United States, much of the material support for the establishment of civil aviation companies was provided by aircraft manufacturers wishing to exploit their production capabilities and by maritime shipping firms eager to expand their transport options. In the 1920s a number of European governments nationalized the existing privately owned airlines in their countries, each establishing one or two large consolidated carriers. The route systems implemented by the new government-backed airlines closely reflected their government's foreign policies, that is, each carrier of an imperial power was directed to extend its routes to the most distant colonial possession. The route networks activated by several European airlines in this effort stretched into Africa, the Middle East, and Asia.

Though deprived of its colonial possessions after the Great War, Germany also established an extensive international aviation presence. In some places it did this through implementation of air service by German airlines, and in other areas through creation of separate carriers by quasi-independent friendly sources. The German civil aviation presence in Latin America, in particular, so alarmed the U.S. government in the late 1930s that Pan American, already active in the southern hemisphere, was accorded various means of U.S. government support to expand the American aviation presence there. The government itself used its considerable influence on several South American governments to force a reduction in German aviation operations — all before the Japanese attack on Pearl Harbor and formal U.S. entry into World War II.

German and Japanese airlines expanded and reduced their route systems during World War II as Axis military fortunes rose and fell. In those countries occupied by German troops, local airlines were compelled to suspend operations or confine their flights to military support efforts in unoccupied colonies and unoccupied friendly states. Airlines in the United States were mobilized for military support operations, many carriers with no prior international experience flying to Africa, India, or the Far East.

As the Allies grew confident of victory in 1944, a conference was called to establish a postwar international civil aviation regulatory scheme. Policies advocated by the participating governments differed so strongly that no multinational regulatory system controlling commercial aspects of international civil aviation could be effected, but the foundation was laid for the creation of the International Civil Aviation Organization, a body regulating international technical standards. Later, another organization, the International Air Transport Association, was formed by airlines to consider commercial questions.

The availability of convertible military transport aircraft, the advances made in aviation technology during hostilities, and the demobilization of thousands of military-trained aviation personnel spurred a rapid growth of commercial air transport in the immediate postwar period. Airlines of European colonial powers reactivated their large international networks. A new international civil aviation policy was instituted in the United States when Pan American lost its monopoly to serve foreign destinations and a number of other American carriers were designated by their government to operate specific international routes. By the late 1950s the familiar Western airlines were joined in foreign airports by aircraft of lesser-known carriers, among them Aeroflot of the Soviet Union and airlines of other east European states. As colonies in Africa and Asia gained independence, even more airlines were created. In the late 1970s the airline of the People's Republic of China, the most populous nation on earth, entered the ranks of international carriers.

Airlines from more than one hundred countries now fly international routes. Perceptions of airline objectives vary widely among the governments that regulate the industry; satisfaction of commercial traffic demand, widely viewed in the United States as the most important civil aviation goal, is considered only one of a number of legitimate objectives by many other governments. The operation of particular international routes by a carrier should not be cited as proof that the routes are commercially viable.

Notes

1. The following is not intended to be a conventional historical treatment of world airlines, but rather a review emphasizing economic and political factors that shaped the development of international civil aviation. A good general history is R.E.G. Davies, *A History of the World's Airlines* (hereafter *History*) (London: Oxford University Press, 1967).

2. E.H. Cookridge, *Spy Trade* (New York: Walker & Co., 1971), p. 39.

3. Gerald Freund, *The Unholy Alliance* (New York: Harcourt, Brace & Co., 1957), pp. 93, 209-211.

4. For a detailed account of Pan Am operations in Latin America during this period, see Robert Daley, *An American Saga* (New York: Random House, 1980), Part IV.

5. See Davies, *History,* pp. 151-160.

6. Frederick C. Thayer, Jr., *Air Transport Policy and National Security* (Chapel Hill: University of North Carolina Press, 1965), pp. 35-36.

7. A much more detailed account of American civil airline support participation in World War II can be found in Davies, *Airlines of the United States Since 1914* (London: Putnam, 1972), pp. 264-292. See also Daley, *An American Saga*, Part IV; and Ronald W. Jackson, *China Clipper* (New York: Everest House, 1980).

8. Robert L. Thornton, *International Airlines and Politics* (Ann Arbor:

Bureau of Business Research, Graduate School of Business Administration, The University of Michigan, 1970), p. 20.

9. Don Cook, *The Chicago Aviation Agreements: An Approach to World Policy* (New York: American Enterprise Association, Inc., 1945), pp. 10-16.

10. "Russia to Boycott Civil Aviation Talk," *New York Times,* October 30, 1944, p. 1. Copyright 1944 by The New York Times Company. Reprinted by permission.

11. The following Soviet sources may be consulted for expression of these views: Lazar Sh. Gordonov, *Vozdushnye puti zarubezhnykh stran* (Moscow: Gosudarstvennoye Izdatel'stvo Geograficheskoy literatury, 1961), pp. 102-104; Andrey N. Vereshchagin, *Mezhdunarodnoye vozdushnoye pravo* (Moscow: Izdatel'stvo Mezhdunarodnoye otnoshenye, 1966), p. 75; and A. Stromov, "SSSR - Chlen ICAO," *Grazhdanskaya aviatsiya* 6 (June 1971), p. 8.

12. Thornton, *International Airlines and Politics*, p. 23.

13. Ibid., pp. 19-34; O'Connor, *Economic Regulation*, pp. 16-45.

14. U.S., Department of State, *Agreement between the United States of America and the United Kingdom of Great Britain and Northern Ireland and Final Act of the Civil Aviation Conference*, (hereafter *Agreement*) 1946, Paragraph 6 of the Final Act.

15. O'Connor, *Economic Regulation*, p. 46.

16. U.S., Department of State, *Agreement*, Annex 11.

17. This information was provided to the author by reliable persons familiar with postwar Austria. The Austrian State Treaty pledged Austria to permanent neutrality, a condition demanded by the Soviet Union in return for the withdrawal of its troops.

18. Additional information about the development of Soviet and east European civil aviation can be found in the author's *The Political and Economic Implications of the International Routes of Aeroflot, op. cit.*

19. The Baltic states are Estonia, Latvia, and Lithuania. These three countries were overrun and annexed by the Soviet Union in 1940. The United States considers their incorporation into the USSR illegal.

20. "United States Policy for the Conduct of International Air Transportation Negotiations," *Aviation Daily* 237:19 (May 25, 1978), pp. 147-150.

21. See, for example, the editorial, "Somebody Please Stand Up to Uncle Sam," *Interavia* (Geneva) XXXIII:10 (October, 1978), p. 893, and Carole Shifrin, "Air Deregulation Fears," *Washington Post,* February 18, 1979, p. F1.

22. One recent publication claims involvement by the U.S. Central Inteligence Agency in early Ethiopian Airlines operations. See Robbins, *Air America,* p. 68.

23. Allegations of CIA involvement in Iranian Airways are widespread and long-standing. See Robbins, *Air America,* p.68.

24. Iranair's long-term chairman and managing director, Lt. Gen. Ali M. Khademi, was shot and killed by Iranian revolutionaires prior to the fall of the Shah. Lt. Gen. Khademi was an adherent of the Baha'i religion, a faith claimed heretic by fundamentalist Moslems.

4

The International Regulatory Framework: Multinationial Regulation in the Worldwide Air-Transport Industry

Three levels of regulation or control exist and interact with each other in the international air-transport industry: (1) the internal air-transport regulatory system in an individual country; (2) bilateral regulation of air-transport relations between two countries; and (3) multinational regulation of the worldwide industry or of that part of the worldwide industry that is concerned with international operations. This chapter considers the multinational — or, perhaps, supranational — aspects of international civil aviation regulation; subsequent chapters are concerned with bilateral civil air-transport relations between states and with those aspects of the air-transport regulatory system of a single state that impinge upon international air-transport regulation.

The Impact of Diverse Political Systems upon Regulation

Gabriel Almond and G. Bingham Powell, in their volume on comparative politics, have included regulation as one of five basic capabilites of political systems.[1] According to the authors:

> The regulative capability refers to the political system's exercise of control over behavior of individuals and groups. By common definition, this is the distinguishing capability of political systems, the employment of legitimate coercion to control behavior. In characterizing regulative performance one must consider what individuals and groups are being subjected to regulation, what areas of individual and collective life are affected, and what frequency or intensity of intervention is exercised.[2]

Application of regulation differs between systems in its style — whether it is "legal rather than customary or arbitrary"[3] — and in its intensity and comprehensiveness. In cases of very strong regulative capability, political systems attempt to control all aspects of behavior of individuals and groups within their boundaries. Regulation in these systems might be limited only by the complexities of information flow, concentration, cost, and problems of regulating the regulators.[4] In recent decades various totalitarian governments have provided examples of extreme control, most of them one-party states of communist or nationalist orientation.

The level of regulation in the air transport industry varies from country to country and generally reflects the nature of the political system of which the industry is a component. In highly regulated states almost all civil aviation functions are concentrated in an air transport ministry which both operates and regulates airlines and airports. Regulatory intervention from outside the ministry appears to be exercised by representatives of political, security, and defense sectors. Such regulatory systems are inherently secretive and thus difficult to analyze; however, intervention by these sectors appears to be both customary and arbitrary.

In decentralized political systems, civil aviation functions are exercised by separate operational and regulatory bodies. Regulatory intervention is usually exercised within defined boundaries and is subject to public review, the latter occurring through juridical procedures and, unofficially, in the public press. Even among politically decentralized states, however, the level of aviation regulation may be intrusive. For example, airlines owned by Western governments may be mandated by these governments to maintain levels of employment in excess of actual needs, to purchase particular types of aircraft less suited to actual needs than other available models, or to operate commercially nonviable routes for political reasons. Although common in such European countries as France and Great Britain, regulatory intervention of this type is by no means standard in other Western countries and, if attempted in the United States, cannot be enforced.[5]

Strain and controversy are inevitable in an international regulatory framework including political systems as diverse as the United States and Gabon, and the Soviet Union and Belgium. The major international aviation regulatory agencies and institutions were established in the mid- and late-1940s by governments and airlines that were representative of lightly regulated systems. Governments and airlines from more heavily regulated political systems—one-party and non-party, industrialized and developing—joined the agencies in later years, bringing with them political and economic philosophies not always consistent with the goals of the founding states and carriers.

International agencies and institutions are of two types, public and private. Members of public international organizations are states or governments that have authorized the organization to represent them in specified spheres of activities. This legal authorization extended by separate states provides the agency with an international legal personality, privileges and immunities, and the capacity to conclude treaties and conventions. Theoretically the public international agency also has the ability to bring international claims, but the realities of international politics render such claims very difficult to enforce. Private or nongovernmental international agencies have none of these capabilities. Their members are private or nongovernmental organizations. In various countries they are recognized, usually informally, as representing a particular private entity. Again, the realities of international politics distort the meaning of "private" as that term is understood in the United States. Many "private" organizations in Soviet bloc and developing countries are controlled by their respective governments or by ruling political parties and their ability to act independently is severely limited.

Public International Regulatory Organizations

International Civil Aviation Organization

The International Civil Aviation Organization (ICAO) was established on April 4, 1947 as an outgrowth of the International Civil Aviation Conference held in Chicago from November 1 to December 7, 1944. On May 13, 1947 ICAO concluded an agreement with the United Nations whereby ICAO became a specialized agency of the United Nations, similar in status to FAO (Food and Agriculture Organization) and WHO (World Health Organization).

Membership in ICAO is open to sovereign states, admission procedures differing for those governments invited to the Chicago Conference and those that were not invited (because they fought on the side of the Axis powers during World War II) or did not yet exist at that time.[6] In the late 1970s members included over 140 states.

The aims and objectives of ICAO are outlined in article 44 of the Chicago Convention:

1. Insure the safe and orderly growth of international civil aviation throughout the world;
2. Encourage the arts of aircraft design and operation for peaceful purposes;
3. Encourage the development of airways, airports, and air navigation facilities for international civil aviation;
4. Meet the needs of the peoples of the world for safe, regular, efficient and economical air transport;
5. Prevent economic waste caused by unreasonable competition;
6. Insure that the rights of contracting States are fully respected and that every contracting State has a fair opportunity to operate international airlines;
7. Avoid discrimination between contracting States
8. Promote safety of flight in international air navigation;
9. Promote generally the development of all aspects of international civil aeronautics.[7]

In practice, ICAO work has centered on the technical aspects of civil aviation. The International Air Transport Association (IATA) has dominated economic issues, although some members of ICAO favor the agency playing a greater role in establishing an air transport economics policy.

ICAO attempts to meet its goals and objectives through work undertaken by an assembly, a council, and a number of commissions and standing committees. All member states are represented in the assembly which meets at least once every three years to debate general policy for the agency and review agency work in technical, economic, and legal spheres. The assembly also votes to establish subsidiary commissions, determine financial arrangements, undertake technical and financial assistance programs for member states, and to elect the council.

The ICAO Council consists of 30 contracting states, each serving three-year terms. In electing states to council membership, the assembly is asked to apportion representation equally to three groups: (1) states of great importance in air transport; (2) states not otherwise included which make the largest contribution to the provision of international air transport navigation facilities; and (3) states not otherwise included whose membership assures that all geographic areas of the world are represented on the council.[8] In practice, this membership allotment provides for the permanent membership (through reelection) of the major powers (as in the permanent members of the Security Council of the United Nations) and rotating membership of one or two countries each from the remaining NATO and Warsaw Pact groups, and from other countries representing various geographic areas. The council elects its own president and one or more vice-presidents. Unlike the Security Council of the larger United Nations in which the presidency is rotated every two months among the council members, the presidency of the ICAO Council has been a long-term position; only three men have held the office since ICAO was founded in 1947. In both prestige and responsibility, the position of ICAO Council president is closer to that of the UN secretary-general than to the UN Security Council president. In addition to differences in the status and application of presidential power, the ICAO Council and UN Security Council differ in voting procedures; unlike the Security Council, no state on the ICAO Council can veto a proposal before the council. Decisions are reached by a majority vote, and no member can vote in consideration of a dispute to which it is a party.

The ICAO Council has legislative, judicial, and administrative functions. In exercising its legislative responsibility, the council adopts international technical aviation standards which become binding on ICAO members. Judicially, it is empowered to adjudicate disputes between members relating to interpretation and application of the governing convention. Its administrative functions include appointment of the secretary-general and members of various committees and commissions.

Six standing committees or commissions undertake much of the research and planning for the council. The Air Navigation Commission develops international air navigation standards and is concerned with all related practices, including telecommunications, navigational aids, meteorology, and other facilities and services. The Committee on Joint Support of Air Navigation Services assists the council on matters of technical and financial support of air navigation facilities and operations servicing international routes. It maintains fixed telecommunications facilities in Iceland and Greenland for use on North Atlantic routes.

The Air Transport Committee is concerned with the economic aspects of international civil aviation, facilitation of air transport, problems of multiple taxation and insurance requirements, and compilation of statistical studies on various aspects of air transport. Its economic interests include general development of air transport, airport financing, defining the role of charter services, and fares and rates. Air travel facilitation deals with minimizing and standardizing documentary requirements related to air transportation (regarding customs, immigration, public health, and other formalities); provision of adequate facilities at airports to meet passenger and shipper needs; and simplifying handling and clearance procedures for cargo, mail, and baggage.

The Legal Committee evaluates international air law and drafts relevant air law conventions. Its major work has concerned legal liability and unlawful interference with aircraft. A separate body, the Committee on Unlawful Interference with Aircraft, was established in 1961 to deal with this problem in a comprehensive way, but its freedom to recommend effective multinational measures against air terrorism is severely limited by the cooperation of some ICAO member states with various terrorist groups and the intimidation of other states by the groups and their supporters. The sixth ICAO committee, the Finance Committee, administers ICAO financial policy.

The staff work of ICAO is performed by a secretariat of approximately 700 international civil servants headed by the secretary-general as chief executive officer. ICAO headquarters are located in Montreal and regional offices are maintained in Mexico City, Lima, Paris, Dakar, Cairo, and Bangkok. The secretariat itself is organized in bureaus which implement the decisions of the various committees and undertake other ICAO responsibilities.

The Technical Assistance Bureau, a division of the secretariat, arranges aviation assistance for developing countries. In most cases funds for specific projects are provided by the United Nations Development Program

(UNDP) upon request by individual countries. A few oil-rich developing nations have provided their own funding for ICAO assistance projects; and certain aid-rendering countries have established their own programs that are administered with ICAO cooperation. The Netherlands, for example, offers scholarships to aviation law courses at a Dutch university; and Denmark, Sweden, and Finland provide experts for assistance in the aid-receiving countries. The Soviet Union donates nonconvertible funds that are used for fellowships in Soviet aviation courses by students from Soviet client states. In programs administered by ICAO itself, a variety of projects are undertaken, among them training courses for aircraft crews, mechanics, air traffic controllers, and other personnel; fellowships for study in appropriate foreign institutions; airport planning and construction; provision of telecommunications and other equipment; and on-site advisory assistance. ICAO also supports several regional aviation training centers, such as the African School for Meteorology and Civil Aviation which offers courses in both English and French to students from a number of African countries.

ICAO collaborates with other UN specialized agencies whose areas of focus are related to civil aviation, such as the International Telecommunications Union, the World Meteorological Organization, the World Health Organization, the Universal Postal Union, and the International Labour Organization. Additional aviation-related groups not formally affiliated with the United Nations frequently attend ICAO meetings as observers. Among these organizations are the International Air Transport Association and the International Civil Airports Association.

The realities of restrictions placed on economic assistance extended by individual countries—as noted in the instances of the Netherlands and the Soviet Union—provide some evidence that legal, economic and technological issues before ICAO are not always considered in a disinterested manner. Advocacy of policies or standards is often encouraged not only in terms of the inherent worth of a proposal, but also in terms of economic or political advantage perceived as accruing to a specific country if the proposal is adopted. Debate within the ICAO Air Navigation Commission of proposals for standardization of new aviation technology should be viewed with this motivation in mind.

In the mid- and late-1970s, to cite one example, the Air Navigation Commission considered the adoption of one of several proposed microwave landing systems (MLS) as a world standard. According to authorized procedure, each ICAO member-state is allowed to participate in commission conferences and later to comment on commission proposals. The commission may then alter the proposals before submitting a final draft to the ICAO Council which must approve the measure by a two-thirds majority for it to be adopted as an "International Standard." In this instance, competing proposals for ICAO consideration were developed by firms in Britain, France, and West Germany, and by a joint U.S./Australian team.

Each commercial effort was strongly backed by its government which perceived three principal dividends resulting from the selection of "their" system: financial gain to the companies (and, eventually, to the governments) involved in development of the system; domestic support for future outlays of funds for technology development; and national prestige.

The French proposal attracted little support and was withdrawn. A number of developing countries perceived the West German system to have certain cost advantages and indicated their preference for it on that basis. However, consultations between the American and German delegations to the Air Navigation Commission meetings led to a German decision to back the American/Australian system in return for American/Australian support of development of the German technique for other purposes. After this bargaining had been completed, only the American/Australian and British systems remained in contention. These two competing proposals had been favored from the beginning. The British charged the U.S. Federal Aviation Administration (FAA) with providing the ICAO expert panel with inaccurate data designed to discredit the British system. American officials answered with accusations that British interests had engaged in "vicious lobbying" in an effort to impugn FAA integrity by distorting FAA technical data. The Government Operations Committee of the U.S. House of Representatives criticized both countries, chastizing the British for employing a lobbyist to reverse support in the United States for the American system and accusing the Massachusetts Institute of Technology Lincoln Laboratory of improper conduct in a conflict of interest situation. The laboratory, noted the Government Operations Committee, was serving as a general contractor to the FAA and backing the U.S. system while simultaneously analyzing competing systems for ICAO. Under the circumstances, the Laboratory's reports could hardly be considered impartial and unbiased.[9]

The rancor notwithstanding, the final ICAO vote was taken in April 1978. Both sides did their best to round up all possible support. On the American/Australian side, the Australians presented Papua New Guinea which had gained independence only a short time earlier and whose civil aviation services were operated by Australia. The new state cast its vote for its mentor. The Soviet Union also backed the American/Australian-proposal and did its best to secure the votes of all the bloc countries. Even North Korea, not previously known for participation in ICAO affairs, was persuaded to appear. The French, thought by some to be in collusion with the British, proposed a secret ballot to encourage free expression of preferences "without concern for possible political repercussions or prior commitments." The French suggestion was backed by supporters of the British system who feared that in an open vote U.S. pressure could be employed to American/Australian advantage. A secret ballot was used and, despite the French efforts to advance a majority for the British system, the

American/Australian proposal won by a large margin. The British accepted their defeat with grace, and subsequent expression of ill will has been minimal, despite the intense, often harsh campaigning by both sides. It is, perhaps, ironic that the secret balloting prevented the contestants from determining which countries supported them and which did not.[10]

Another subject of conflict in ICAO is the development by the organization of an economic policy. Because participants in the 1944 Chicago Conference could not agree on the nature of an economic role for ICAO, none was formulated and the task was left, almost by default, to other entities to establish the economic rules of the international air transport industry. In 1945 airlines from thirty one countries met in Havana to found the International Air Transport Association (IATA), an organization charged with resolving the economic issues left unsettled in Chicago. Economic regulation has indeed accounted for a major share of IATA activity, but the Association has long been dominated by the large North Atlantic carriers and thus mistrusted by others. A second form of international regulation has been exercised by individual states that implement their own regulatory systems; if strong enough in a political or economic sense or located in a sufficiently strategic position on international air routes, individual countries can exert substantial influence on international air transport regulation. Countries lacking these attributes, primarily developing nations, claim such a de facto regulatory framework is inherently unjust and ignores their needs. To counter what they perceive as inequities in international regulation caused by the power realities of IATA and the advantages of political, economic, or geographic strength, a number of developing countries have sought to involve ICAO in establishing an international air transport regulatory system. Relying on their numerical majority in UN agencies, the developing states hope to institue a different economic policy through the ballot box.

The first serious attempt to introduce economic regulatory issues in ICAO proceedings was made during 1963 sessions of the ICAO Air Transport Committee. A working paper on possible ICAO tariff action was discussed and dismissed within six hours, the committee concluding by a vote of sixteen to eight that ICAO involvement in airline tariff matters was unjustified. At the 1965 ICAO Assembly a group of developing states proposed ICAO support of a plan to institute special fares promoting tourism to their own countries. Most of the other states opposed ICAO intervention in any tariff matters, saying that governments would be incapable of dealing with the complexities of tariff-setting and that IATA was discharging its responsibilities in this area quite responsibily. Tourism promotion was a worthwhile endeavor, they agreed, but ICAO involvement in it should not impinge on the tariff-establishment work of IATA.

Additional efforts to enlist ICAO in tariff-setting were undertaken in late 1976 at an ICAO Council meeting, and in 1977 and 1980 at ICAO Air

Transport Committee meetings. In support of their views, proponents, primarily developing countries, enumerated many IATA weaknesses, such as domination of the association by a small number of airlines and inadequate procedures for enforcement of IATA policies.[11] If ICAO did not replace IATA in its economic regulatory role, some governments state, it should at least participate in IATA decision making.

Although developing countries voting in a bloc may succeed in obtaining a nominal economic role for ICAO, Western states will probably retain real economic power for some time. Their airlines are by far the most important in international service, their airports (such as, New York, Miami, London, and Paris) of vital importance to the developing countries – and certainly of far greater importance to the developing states than is, for example, Nairobi or any other African city to the industrialized nations – and their traffic-generating capabilities far stronger than those of the developing countries.[12]Attempts to involve ICAO in economic regulation will not alter these realities.[13]

Whereas issues of microwave landing systems or international regulation entail substantive economic questions, other divisive issues before ICAO have been wholly political and have, in fact, been introduced in ICAO for no purpose other than to underline a political point. That ICAO should become heavily politicized is not surprising; several other UN agencies, such as the UN Educational, Social and Cultural Organization (UNESCO) and the International Labour Organization (ILO) have been exploited by their members for irrelevant political issues for some years. Because ICAO is concerned with issues of fundamental safety, its abuse may be viewed with greater concern.

The major political issues injected into ICAO proceedings have been those which have plagued other UN proceedings: the Arab-Israeli dispute, South Africa's apartheid policy, the division of Korea and the role of the United Nations in South Korea, and competing membership claims by the People's Republic of China and Taiwan. Throughout the 1950s and most of the 1960s charges and countercharges exchanged on these issues were fairly petty. In the late 1960s and throughout the 1970s politicization of ICAO intensified dramatically, perhaps reflecting Arab frustration at the outcome of the 1967 Middle East war, a perceived need by some Arab and other states to justify Palestinian terror attacks against airlines and aircraft; anti-Americanism generated by the Vietnam conflict; and resentment of many developing countries against Western domination of international civil aviation. So strong was the politicization of the 1971 ICAO Assembly that Secor Browne, CAB chairman and head of the American delegation to the assembly, led the delegation in unprecedented walkouts from two general meetings. American representatives claimed that a coalition of developing countries, Arab states, and communist governments voted against the United States, regardless of the issues involved, simply to express general political opposition to the United States. It was noted by the American delegation that many foreign representatives were political figures, rather than aviation experts. One U.S. participant commented, "It's absolutely unacceptable to have a delegate who doesn't know what an airplane looks like, telling us what to do to upgrade navigational aide somewhere.[14]

Politicization of ICAO is also expressed in conflicts over membership status. In late 1971 the People's Republic of China was recognized as the only legitimate representative of China to ICAO, thus displacing Taiwan. However, the ICAO Far East and Pacific regional office in Bangkok is permitted to retain an "unofficial" aggreement with Taiwan to assure continued operation of an ICAO flight information/air traffic control center on Taiwan which links Korea and Japan with Hong Kong and southeast Asia. Although extension of the Taiwan station service agreement may be viewed as hypocritical, it reflects the reality of Taiwan's location and the extraordinary expense of trying to duplicate the ICAO station in another, less suitable, location.

In 1974 the ICAO Assembly withdrew the voting rights of South Africa, a move without much substantive meaning because South Africa had ceased paying its dues in protest of earlier action taken against it. South Africa operates the largest and most sophisticated international airline on the African continent; its exclusion from the ICAO safety framework could prove just as harmful to other countries as to its own aviation interests.

By far the most controversial membership issue before ICAO was its 1974 assembly resolution authorizing the ICAO Council to extend invitations

> . . . through the organization of African Unity or the Arab League, to representatives of liberation movements recognized by both of these organization to attend, as observers, ICAO meetings dealing with matters pertaining to their respective territories.[15]

The only "liberation movement" recognized by the Arab League is the Palestine Liberation Organization (PLO). The resolution passed 68-4, with 34 abstentions. Voting against the proposal were the United States, Israel, Ecuador, and Nicaragua. Most of the other Western countries, as is their custom on issues concerning Arab terrorism, abstained. Some of the developing countries voting in favor of the resolution opposed it in principle, but were standing for reelection to various ICAO bodies and supported the measure in exchange for support by radical Arab states of their own candidacies. As an umbrella organization, the PLO includes a number of Palestinian terror groups that, together, committed approximately thirty terrorist actions agains civil aircraft or airline-related targets before being granted observer status by ICAO in late 1974.[16]

Observer status is not equivalent to full membership; it does, however, permit the PLO to send representatives to ICAO meetings and discussions on means of preventing unlawful interference with aircraft. It seems improbable that the presence of PLO observers enhances the quality of work completed at these sessions or contributes to greater safety in air transportation.

The economic realities of the international air transport system and the increasing politicization of UN bodies in general suggest that developing countries will continue to press for a strong ICAO economic role and that politicization of ICAO will continue to threaten the integrity of the agency. It would not be the first UN organization to deny reality in response to partisan political action initiated by some of its member states.[17]

Regional International Regulatory Organizations

Government air transport regulatory agencies have joined together in several regional bodies in pursuit of coordinated and standardized regional development, efficient use of regional facilities, and institution of common regional regulatory procedures. One of the youngest of such bodies is LACAC, the Latin American Civil Aviation Commission. Established in 1973 with ICAO encouragement, LACAC aims to function as a regional ICAO and foster implementation of ICAO standards in Latin America.

CACAS, the Civil Aviation Council of Arab States dates from 1967 and has been perceived by its member-states as a regional ICAO. Additionally, it has been advanced as a supranational single Arab voice representing all Arab states in international civil aviation matters and as an organizer of a unified Arab aircraft manufacturing industry.[18] Such plans have not been fulfilled; their realization has been thwarted by persistent political differences between a number of Arab states, incompatible economic policies of member states, insufficiently developed industrial base to support an aircraft industry, and the existence of a functioning Arab airline association that has diluted CACAS authority.

Several regional aviation regulatory bodies exist in noncommunist Europe. Among these is the Commission (secretariat) of the Common Market, active in air transport only since the late 1970s; it is concerned with intra-European fares and other commercial issues. ECAC (European Civil Aviation Conference) has more than twenty member states from Portugal to Turkey and has made only modest progress since its creation in 1954 toward joint development and coordination of technical procedures, facilitation, and economic policy. Difficulties stem from differing national perceptions of the role to be played by charter service, for example, or by discount fares or scheduled service. Eurocontrol, a more specialized organization, was established in 1961 to provide a unified air traffic control system for its member-states. Although this objective remains official policy, effective Eurocontrol jurisdiction is limited to a fairly small territory of its multistate mandate. Several member governments are unwilling to surrender their air sovereignty to an international organization. Other countries have decided that the particular traffic patterns over their territories are better served by national authorities or that national air traffic control systems are less expensive.

AFCAC (African Civil Aviation Commission), whose membership includes forty two African countries, is a specialized agency of the Organization of African Unity. Its status within the OAU is similar to that of ICAO within the United Nations. Its mandate is relatively broader than the charge of ICAO, including, for example, work on tariffs and fares. AFCAC considers the training of flight and technical personnel to be among its major tasks and has sought assistance from ICAO and various non-African sources in operating training centers. Another task of particular relevance to Africa is the AFCAC aviation medicine study of the effect of sickle cell anemia on flight personnel. AFCAC work is conducted in English and French, the two major transnational languages of Africa. Headquarters of the organization are in Dakar, capital of Senegal, a state of francophone Africa.

Another type of regional regulatory body is maintained by the Council for Mutual Economic Assistance (CMEA) whose member-states are the Soviet Union, the East European countries, Mongolia, Vietnam, and Cuba. In 1962 CMEA established a standing Commission on Transport which was concerned with both air and surface transport. A 1975 reorganization brought about a separate Standing Commission on Civil Aviation which has among it goals: standardization of communications techniques, tariffs, cargo handling procedures, airport mechanization, and agricultural aviation; coordination of aviation research; and operation of a joint personnel training center.[19]

Evaluating the work of the CMEA commission presents the observer with two complex tasks. First, in most CMEA countries it is very difficult to discern the difference between the authority of the relevant government aviation body, that is, a Ministry of Transport and the airline itself. Some CMEA commission functions are performed by nominal ministry authorities and others by nominal airline authorities (not to mention party authorities and security authorities). Given these uncertainties as to the actual controlling powers, comparison of CMEA commission activity with that of other regional bodies whose operations are clearly conducted by constituent member states is difficult. Second, in common with other joint undertakings of Soviet bloc countries, it is likely that at least some ventures of the CMEA commission are more coercive than cooperative. Certainly a number of commission decisions have been more beneficial to the Soviet Union than to the other member-states, among the most obvious of which is standardization of aircraft purchases on inferior Soviet aircraft when various east European airlines are known to have preferred western equipment.[20]

Private International Regulatory Organizations

International Air Transport Association

The International Air Transport Association (IATA) was established in April 1945 by a special act of the Canadian Parliament. Its predecessor was another IATA—the International Air Traffic Association, usually referred to as "prewar" or "old IATA". The prewar organization was founded in 1919 at The Hague by six European airlines; by 1939, when the outbreak of hostilities in Europe forced suspension of its activites, its membership consisted of twenty nine carriers, most of them European. Pan American, the single North American member, had joined only in 1938 and was unable to actively participate in association affairs prior to the outbreak of World Was II.

The old IATA was basically a European organization; due to the limited geographic concentration of its membership and the limited level of competition on intercontinental air routes in the prewar years, it did not function on a global scale. The major work of prewar IATA was in cooperative navigation efforts and in establishing standards for the rapidly growing aircraft industry in airport construction and operation, and in flight procedures In the context of current technology, some prewar IATA standards appear unsophisticated, even primitive. In 1932, for example, prewar IATA determined that throttles should move forward to accelerate power and backward to reduce power. This decision was passed on to the aircraft manufacturers in the hope that it would be incorporated into standardized aircraft design and construction.[21] Prewar IATA was not formally empowered to establish fares and rates, but some tariffs were discussed and settled at association meetings called "Timetable and Accountancy Conferences."

Although most IATA activity was suspended during World War II, executives of several airlines were able to meet and plan for a new, worldwide association of scheduled airlines in the early postwar period. After this new IATA was founded, members of the old IATA agreed to transfer their organization's authority to the new group. Linkage between the two associations, however, has no legal significance.[22]

Whereas ICAO is an organization of governments, IATA is an organization of airlines. It is a private international trade association of approximately 100 scheduled international carriers. Private though it may be in a technical sense, it is also influenced by state interests because the majority of its member airlines are state-controlled. Although American carriers are privately owned, they too are subject to a degree of state influence because the U.S. Civil Aeronautics Board, should it disagree with positions supported by the carriers, is able to act against them on such issues as route awards and tariff approval. Factors motivating a government to prefer a particular international aviation policy vary among governments, airlines, and specific circumstances, but governments can and do exert influence on IATA through the airlines. This state influence imparts to IATA a "quasi-public" or "semigovernmental" character.[23]

Membership in IATA is open to any airline licensed by an ICAO-eligible government to provide scheduled air service. Carriers operating international service are active members, and those providing only domestic service may join as associate members. Each active member airline has one vote in the IATA Annual General Meeting, the body which decides the general direction of the organization. An elected Executive Committee, consisting of high-level executives of twenty-five airlines (representing both power and geographic distribution), provides year-round direction. IATA administration is headed by a director-general and five assistant directors-general.

IATA designates its offices in both Montreal and Geneva as "head" offices. Regional technical offices are located in Rio de Janeiro, London, Geneva, Nairobi, and Bangkok, and traffic service offices are located in New York, Montreal, and Singapore.

The largest portion of the IATA budget is provided from dues or assessments made of member airlines according to international ton-kilometers flown, subject to established minimum and maximum amounts. A few IATA activities, to be noted later, generate funds applied to the budget.

Four standing committees conduct much of the routine work of the organization. The Financial Committee is concerned with the standardization of accounting procedures and the settlement of accounts between airlines covering business they do with or for one another. Its various provisions allow the customer using several different airlines, whether passenger or shipper, to book complex routes on one ticket against a single charge payable in a single currency. Its Clearing House accepts claims from member airlines against other member airlines (for passage provided a customer but booked by the claimed-against airline) and matches the claims with payments due them according to the same procedures. Claims must be submitted to the Clearing House in Geneva one month after the end of the business month being processed; within one week accounting is completed and member carriers notified of their net credit or debit position. Regulations obligate debtors to settle accounts, in dollars or sterling, with creditor airlines within the next seven days. This system assures each airline of regular and prompt settlement of accounts; minimizes correspondence and documentation; saves foreign exchange expense; and provides some protection from foreign currency devaluations.[24] In 1979 the Clearing House handled more than $20 billion in two-way transactions involving one hundred international airlines, additional U.S. airlines (through a similar organization for American carriers), and five special accounts. Since the mid-1970s the cost of the Clearing House operation has been offset by interest from investment management of short-term settlement funds. The interest accruing above costs provides income for IATA.[25] The Financial Committee also has sub-committees on currency, taxation, insurance, and other subjects related to finances.

The IATA Legal Committee, whose membership is limited to lawyers associated with member airlines, is concerned with all legal issues related to international civil aviation. Among its concerns is worldwide standardization of traffic documentation, such as passenger tickets and cargo waybills. It also deals with the legal relationship between airlines and travel agents, with liability laws enacted by various governments and expressed in international conventions, with security standards, with airline-related crime (such as stolen tickets and theft of cargo, mail, and baggage), with the carriage of hazardous materials, and with other legal issues of an international industry.

The primary objective of the IATA Technical Committee is the international standardization of technical facilities and procedures as a means of enhancing the safety and efficiency of airline operations. IATA sponsors various programs to encourage implementation of international standards in airport planning and operation, air traffic control, navigation procedures, and so on. It is recognized by ICAO as the representative of the airline industry and, as such, works with ICAO in drafting aviation standards. IATA also works with other relevant organizations, such as the World Meteorological Organization and the International Telecommunications Union. The IATA Medical Advisory Committee, under the general direction of the Technical Committee, works on problems of health of air and ground crews and passengers. It reviews information from member carriers about cardiovascular diseases among pilots, medical causes of pilot grounding, and other medical issues. It is also concerned with health-related aircraft equipment (such as galleys), aircraft systems (such as sewage disposal, and disinfection), quarantine, and immunization.

The fourth major IATA committee is the Traffic Committee, a group concerned with international traffic and sales issues. This committee has established a number of conferences to deal with administrative and procedural matters. Among these agencies are the Passenger Agency Conference, Cargo Agency Conference, Passenger Services Conference, and Cargo Service Conference. The first two of these conferences work with the agents who sell passenger tickets and cargo space, endeavoring to maintain international standards in relations between consumers and agents. IATA endorsement of a particular agent guarantees the financial integrity of that agent, thus protecting the consumer. The Traffic Committee also serves as a steering committee to the Tariff Conferences and advises them of IATA procedures regarding the establishment of tariffs, conditions of carriage, and other pertinent issues.

IATA bylaws specify the size of each committee, the number of members varying from eighteen to twenty-four. Members are appointed by the Executive Committee for two-year terms and confirmed by the annual general meeting. Decisions of all committees other than the Traffic Advisory Committee must be approved by the Executive Committee prior to implementation.

The function with which IATA is most widely identified is the negotiation of international passenger fares and cargo rates. Although participants in the 1945 Chicago conference could not agree on a system for determining fares and rates, they did conclude that a system of uniform tariffs should be established and that tariffs for similar distances should be comparable. In 1946 the United States and Britain accepted in the Bermuda agreement a provision that IATA be designated as the agency to set international tariffs, its decisions subject to approval by the U.S. and British governments. Most bilateral air transport agreements written subsequent to the Bermuda model similarly delegate the ratemaking authority to IATA.

The Bermuda decision of the two principal postwar aviation powers conferred recognition upon the establishment by IATA in 1945 of regional Tariff conferences. These conferences are authorized to study and act upon regional international air transport issues related to: analysis of operating costs; fares, rates, and charges for passengers and cargo; schedules; and approval of travel agencies and their management.

Three Tariff Conferences—known as TC1, TC2, and TC3—meet individually at least once every two years. TC1 encompasses the North and South American continents and adjacent islands, including the Hawaiian Islands, Palmyra, and Midway. TC2 encompasses Europe, including the European USSR, adjacent European islands, Africa and adjacent islands, Ascension Island, and Asia west of and including Iran. TC3 encompasses Asia and the adjacent islands, excluding territories in TC2, and Australia and the Pacific islands, excluding those in TC1. Any airline operating routes within a traffic area is a member of that Tariff Conference. In addition to the individual conferences, joint meetings of Tariff Conferences are held to consider issues arising in traffic between a point in one Tariff Conference and a point in another Tariff Conference. The Joint Tariff Conferences— JT 12 (TC1 and TC2), JT 13 (TC1 and TC3), JT 23 (TC2 and TC3), and JT 123 (TC1, TC2 and TC3)—usually meet at the same time and place as one of the individual Tariff Conferences.

All conference meetings are closed to the public, conducted in secrecy, and empowered to act only upon unanimous affirmative vote of members present. The unanimity rule necessarily provides every conference airline with a veto and encourages intense bargaining in order to achieve the necessary compromise. If a conference fails to achieve a compromise on a given issue or if a government rejects a conference decision, an open fare or open rate situation develops in which case fares or rates are determined according to existing bilateral agreements. In most instances of discord, however, the conference agrees to maintain current fares or rates until a compromise can be reached; few airlines or governments have been willing to embark upon an open fare or open rate situation.

Over the years IATA Tariff Conferences have experienced recurrent crises over tariffs and other issues. More efficient airlines generally support lower fares and rates, less efficient carriers favor higher tariffs to cover their greater costs. Airlines slow to purchase new equipment have tried to force more modern, aggressive carriers to add compensatory surcharges to tariffs in order to reduce the attraction of the new aircraft. Disputes have arisen over uniformity of passenger services provided under various fares; a controversy later known as the "sandwich war" erupted when SAS began serving a sandwich described by its competitors as more than a sandwich and therefore improper under existing regulations. SAS countered that its sandwiches were of the larger Scandinavian variety and that surely airlines should be permitted to serve food according to national tradition. If Scandinavian sandwiches differed from other nations' sandwiches, SAS should not be penalized and forced to conform to non-Scandinavian standards. The Czechoslovakian government has similarly stated that, because it is customary in Czechoslovakia to serve beer with meals, the Czechoslovakian national airline will serve free beer with meals in tourist class. In more serious crises, governments have threatened to detain foreign aircraft if their airlines did not accept various proposals.[26]

To ensure that member airlines and accredited travel agencies adhere to IATA policies on tariffs, commissions, and other issues, the Compliance Office is mandated to check for malpractices. Representatives of the office investigate specific charges brought against one carrier by another and also initiate independent probes. The Breaches Commission evaluates circumstances of complaints and assesses fines to those found guilty of contravening IATA regulations. Among the most common malpractices are the offering of illegally discounted tariffs to customers by airlines and travel agencies, and the awarding of excessive commissions to travel agencies by airlines. Because IATA operates on a worldwide basis in numerous countries with distinctive and not wholly compatible commercial traditions, it is inevitable that enforcement procedures are unevenly applied. In some major air hubs, IATA supervision is far more effective with airlines issuing their own tickets than with travel agents. Illegal rebating by airlines to agencies in other cities is widespread and agencies routinely offer unauthorized discounts to retain customers. The entire IATA enforcement apparatus has broken down in several countries, occasionally encouraged by the intimidation of IATA officers by agents of offending airlines. Even in cities where IATA enforcement procedures function well, some carriers continue to flaunt regulations, knowing that the heavy fines levied against them will be less than the profits accruing from their illegal practices.

Perhaps because the established Western airlines continue to dominate

IATA, politicization is much less pronounced in the association than in ICAO. However, state-owned airlines from some Arab and African countries have periodically inserted measures directed against El Al or South African or Portuguese member carriers into IATA proceedings. Although such actions have had some impact on regional and local IATA affairs, their real effect on IATA functions has been limited.

To evaluate IATA two questions must be considered. The first, whether or not it is an international cartel and therefore in violation of U.S. and/or European Economic Community antitrust laws, has been debated almost since the founding of IATA. The second question concerns the long-term viability of the organization in view of a number of very visible problems affecting it in the late 1970s and early 1980s.

Determining whether IATA is a cartel is impeded by the absence of widely accepted explicit definition of the term "cartel." Key elements in most definitions of the term include: a closed organization of producers or traders, allotment and limitation of output or sales, and controlled prices. An international cartel, perhaps well expressed by the Organization of Petroleum Exporting Countries (OPEC), is a closed organization of two or more countries (or industries in two or more countries) aiming to control an international market by restricting or eliminating competition (through regulation of supply and prices) between the participating members. IATA does not conform to this characterization of a cartel in all of its aspects. Its membership is not closed, but open to all scheduled airlines whose governments are members of ICAO, the latter a broadly based organization. It does not divide the international air transport market; the allocation of scheduled international air service is regulated by bilateral agreements between countries. On the other hand, IATA does exhibit cartelistic characteristics in its price-fixing and its secretive negotiations. It might be called an "imperfect cartel"—incomplete and irregular.

Antitrust legislation of the European Economic Community (Common Market) specifically exempts transport from its regulation.[27] Antitrust legislation in the United States (Sherman Act of 1890 and Clayton Act of 1914) would doubtless find several IATA activities illegal—for example, price-fixing and common agency selling. However, until 1978 Section 412 (b) and Section 414 of the Federal Aviation Act of 1958 exempted airlines from antitrust provisions concerning cooperative agreements when these agreements are not "adverse to the public interest or in violation of the [Federal Aviation] Act."[28] Over the years, the Civil Aeronautics Board evaluated the various IATA resolutions and found them eligible for antitrust immunity; in 1978, in a major change of policy discussed later, the CAB issued a different interpretation of the relevant legislation and thus intensified a crisis already brewing in IATA.

Several serious problems, some immediate and others long-term and cumulative, have cast doubt on the continued viability of IATA. Among the cumulative difficulties is the poor public image of the association in the United States where it is widely perceived simply as a cartel striving to fix airfares at unreasonably high levels.[29] Another problem is its lack of global representation; several important airlines — important commercially or important because of their countries of registry — have never joined IATA or have terminated their memberships. Singapore Airlines, the rapidly expanding carrier of an important trade center, is one of several Asian flag airlines whose nonadherence to IATA regulations has complicated air transport marketing in southeast Asia. Although of lesser commercial importance, the absence of Aeroflot and the Chinese carrier CAAC from IATA activity has contributed to the operational backwardness of these carriers and their general isolation from the international air transport community. Northwest Airlines, an American carrier with routes across the Pacific and the North Atlantic, and Delta Air Lines with routes between the southern United States and several European points, withdrew from IATA in the 1970s, both citing ineffectiveness of traffic conferences as a decisive factor in their actions. Far more important than the withdrawal of these two airlines was the pull out in 1979 of Pan American. The president of the U.S. global carrier stated that his airline had no interest in "participating in rate and fare setting conferences" and desired to operate in a manner it deemed more consistent with the new U.S. policy fostering greater competition.[30]

A third cumulative problem facing IATA is the growing conflict between the airlines of developing countries, which dominate the association in numbers, and the airlines of the industrialized states, which continue to dominate IATA in real power and therefore in the ability to set policy. Officials in developing country airlines perceive their needs to differ significantly from those of more established carriers. They are often inefficient, serve no mass travel markets, encounter no competition from charter carriers, face no demand for innovative fares, lack ability to offer high level inflight service, and have a strong need to show their national flags and to fly routes for political reasons. They are frequently highly protectionist. The nature of their operations disposes their leadership to seek higher tariffs to counter their greater costs. Although some carriers of industrialized countries are also inefficient, few would support protectionist measures as extreme as those promoted by a number of developing country airlines. Many airlines of industrialized countries operate service on the North Atlantic and other routes where they face intense competition from low-fare charter or supplemental carriers as well as from other scheduled airlines. They desire sufficient flexibility to adjust tariff and service levels to meet these market needs.

The unease within IATA was exacerbated in 1977 by the conclusion of a new bilateral air transport agreement between the United States and Britain. Known as "Bermuda II," the agreement significantly downgraded the role of IATA in its tariff clause and, instead, advocated a stronger role for bilateral American-British dialogue over fares and rates.[31] At the time, the United States declared Bermuda II a model for future agreements, a statement of importance to all carriers on the North Atlantic.

Reacting to the problems facing the organization, IATA proposed a number of reforms in 1978 which *inter alia*, divided its functions into two categories: (1) those of a trade association, concerning such matters as technical work, legal work, ticketing, debt clearing house, and safety and (2) tariff-setting through traffic conferences. Airlines could elect to participate in both categories of functions, or to join in only the trade association activity and engage in tariff-related affairs outside IATA on a bilateral basis. Two levels or "tiers" of membership were foreseen. It was also recommended that regulations pertaining to the nature of meal and bar service and inflight entertainment be minimized, thus averting another sandwich war. Further, even an airline accepting the tariff-setting functions of the Tariff Conferences would be allowed to introduce innovative fares and rates between its own country of registry and another country in response to market changes *after* a new tariff was effected without rescinding the tariff agreement.

These reforms notwithstanding, the U.S. Civil Aeronautics Board issued a "show cause order" in June 1978 announcing a tentative finding that the IATA Tariff Conference procedures and related agreements were not in the public interest. The CAB questioned whether American airlines should continue to receive antitrust immunity allowing them participation in IATA Tariff Conference fare-setting. It also questioned whether foreign airlines flying to the United States should be immune from antitrust prosecution if they conferred to set tariffs on U.S.-bound routes. IATA was required to show cause why the CAB should not finalize its tentative findings. Other governments and interested parties were invited to comment. Approximately forty-five governments, through their foreign ministries or civil aviation authorities, made formal submissions on the issue to the U.S. government, the overwhelming majority of them opposed to the CAB position. A similar number of international airlines made submissions of protest to the CAB or statements in support of IATA. Position papers in support of IATA were also presented by regional government aviation organizations and airline associations and by associations of travel agencies, freight forwarders, and other affected groups. Submitted comments by consumer associations favored the CAB tentative findings. IATA's own response stressed that the CAB was ignoring basic differences between domestic and international air service and was attempting to force the United States antitrust free competition policy on the rest of the world. The IATA submission also claimed that multilateral coordination and standardization of many civil aviation issues was required for convenient and economical international air transport. By rescinding the antitrust immunity of American airlines regarding participation in IATA activity, the CAB would be ignoring the public interest which it claimed to advance.

The U.S. Transportation and State departments were reported to be distressed by "the vehemence of reaction by other governments and foreign airlines" to the show cause order and urged the CAB to act cautiously and permit IATA to function under its proposed new rules with interim approval.[32] The Justice Department, firmly opposed to the antitrust immunity granted the airlines, supported the CAB show-cause order. In mid-1979, after considering the submissions pertaining to the order and the views advanced by other government agencies, the CAB took several measures to reduce the scope of the show-cause order. However, the issue is not permanently resolved.

International Air Carrier Association

The International Air Carrier Association (IACA) is a trade association of charter or supplemental airlines. Its membership is small, consisting of approximately fourteen European and North American charter carriers plus Pan American and TWA as associate members. Politicization of IACA has been minimized by limitation of its mandate to trade association activity and by the absence of charter airlines in countries that customarily exploit international arenas for political purposes.

Regional International Airline Organizations

Regional trade associations of airlines have been organized in several areas of the world. None is empowered to establish tariffs. Five major organizations of this type exist: Association of European Airlines (AEA), Arab Air Carriers Organization (AACO), Association of African Airlines (AAFRA), Orient Airlines Association (OAA), and International Association of Latin American Air Transport (AITAL).

These associations are concerned with traffic, economic, technical, and legal matters specific to their airlines. They may operate common training programs for personnel in specific positions, such as, reservations clerks, mechanics, or computer programmers. Another multicarrier activity undertaken by several regional associations is the operation of technical pools for certain aircraft types at regional airports, thus obviating the need for each airline to maintain its own spare parts stock and mechanics at every airport.

The Soviet-bloc airlines also operate several joint programs, although as noted earlier with regard to regional governmental aviation organizations, it is difficult to determine how independent these programs are in relation to the individual governments and parties on a national basis and to the Soviet Union on a supranational basis. The bloc airlines signed a cooperative pact, the Berlin Agreement, in 1965 which calls for joint programs in maintenance and commercial and financial matters. Maintenance and spare parts pools for member airlines are operated at some airports outside the bloc. A clearing house handles financial transactions between member airlines, using "convertible rubles," the bloc currency. Citizens and institutions of member states are guaranteed a 50-percent price reduction on fares and rates on bloc airlines; whether this tariff discrimination was mandated by the airlines themselves, the Council for Mutual Economic Assistance (CMEA), or some other body is not known to outsiders, but it seems unlikely that these airlines could implement such a policy without substantial input from other agencies.

International Aviation Organizations of Focused Interest

Whereas ICAO and IATA are comprehensive in their concern with international air transport, a number of other organizations and institutions exert influence on particular aspects of international civil aviation. These may be categorized as: (1) specialized function organizations; (2) air-transport-related organizations; (3) air-transport professional associations and unions; and (4) research and educational institutions.

Specialized Function-Organizations

One of the better known specialized function organizations is SITA — Société Internationale de Télécommunications Aéronautiques. Founded in 1949 and with headquarters in Brussels, SITA operates a worldwide telecommunications network on behalf of its more than 150 member airlines. The nonprofit organization is funded by user carriers on the basis of their participation.

The International Civil Airports Association (ICAA) is an organization representing approximately 250 airports in seventy-two countries. Membership is open to airport authorities, some of which operate more than one facility. Organizations other than airlines that conduct research or other programs specifically related to airports may join as associate members. ICAA aims to: develop good relations and collaboration among civil-airport authorities in different parts of the world; formulate common positions on issues of common interest; and advance the level of airport operations. The organization has established commissions on various topics of interest to airport authorities—such as personnel management and training, airport data processing, and airport commercial activities—which produce appropriate manuals, catalogues, and other resource materials. It organizes annual congresses, exhibitions of airport equipment, seminars on specific topics, study tours, and regional activity. It also publishes several periodicals. ICAA holds consultative status with the United Nations and participates with the United Nations and its specialized agencies in activities related to airports. In conjunction with several regional international airport associations, ICAA established the Airport Associations Co-Ordinating Council (AACC) to represent these organizations in dealing with ICAO, IATA, and other organizations and commercial firms. It is the task of AACC to present a unified airport view. ICAA maintains headquarters in Paris, AACC in Geneva (where ICAO, IATA, and several other organizations also maintain offices).

Air-Transport-Related Organizations

The interdependence of the tourism and air-transport industries is particularly important in international markets. Almost all international airlines sell vacation tours and some very large international carriers—among them Pan American, TWA, British Airways, and Air France—own hotel chains with facility locations keyed to their route networks. Many airlines work closely with national tourist authorities in promoting travel programs.

The World Tourism Organization (WTO), known until 1975 as the International Union of Official Travel Organizations, is an association representing approximately one hundred national tourist authorities and has ad hoc consultative status with the Economic and Social Council (ECOSOC) of the United Nations. In addition to promoting tourism, WTO works for the standardization of tourism terminology, encourages the elimination or reduction of governmental procedures controlling tourists (such as visas, police registration), conducts research, and offers technical assistance to developing countries. The organization sends representatives to some ICAO meetings and is recognized by ICAO, additional UN agencies, and other organizations as the world authority on tourism; however, it has no legal policy-making impact on them.

Regional international tourism councils, generally focus their efforts on the promotion of tourism to their regions by foreigners. Because each of the countries involved in such a council may have its own airline competing with other regional carriers, formal ties between regional tourism associations and airlines are often difficult.

Air-Transport Professional Associations and Unions

Most unions of air transport personnel are national in scope and have little direct international significance. The leading international association is the International Federation of Airline Pilots Associations (IFALPA), founded in 1948 on the basis of existing contacts between American, Canadian, and British pilots' organizations. In approximately sixty countries, it is financed by member associations according to the number of their individual pilot members. IFALPA maintains standing committees on such issues as accident investigation, airworthiness standards, medical standards, personnel training, and other matters deemed useful in establishing good conditions of service for pilots. It is accredited in ICAO as the forum of international pilot opinion.

Although its membership rolls include pilot associations from countries with vastly different political and economic systems, pilots from western states dominate the organization. Two key differences which separate some member associations from others are (1) the legal inability of pilots of some state-owned airlines to strike, and (2) the approval of political aerial hijacking by some states which exert substantial control over their pilots associations. In the latter controversy, pilots from some countries that actively or passively support terrorism have simply failed to attend IFALPA conferences on relevant topics and have thus allowed IFALPA to adopt a strong position against unlawful interference with aircraft. Its outspokenness on the issue is in sharp contrast with the softer stand taken by ICAO, which is so sharply politicized that firm action against political terrorism is nearly impossible.

Research and Educational Institutions, Media

Various research and educational institutions and aviation publications influence the international regulatory system by evaluating existing procedures and proposing and studying new alternatives. The Institut du Transport Aérien (ITA), with headquarters in Paris, studies economic, technical, and policy aspects of air transport and tourism. It publishes a weekly bulletin, conducts and publishes studies on air transport and tourism topics, undertakes private contract studies, maintains a computerized data bank of information related to many aspects of civil aviation, and sponsors various symposia and training courses. ITA is financed by fees from its membership which includes airlines, aircraft manufacturers, airports, private and governmental aviation associations, and universities. It frequently publishes partisan policy statements by western aviation officials and airline executives and has produced a study on civil aviation in the People's Republic of China, but it has refrained from establishing its own position on a number of sensitive topics, such as operation of noncommercial political routes by nominally commercial airlines and politicization of the hijacking problem.

Several universities preparing students for careers in air transport have exerted some influence in international civil aviation through their graduates and through leadership and scholarship of their faculty members. Among the most significant are the Institute of Air and Space Law at McGill University in Montreal, the Flight Transportation Laboratory at the Massachusetts Institute of Technology, Embry-Riddle Aeronautical University in Miami, the complex at the Cranfield Institute of Technology and the Loughborough University of Technology in England.

Professional aviation publications present analyses of civil aviation policies and problems. Although the more important periodicals are independent, some nonetheless reflect the policies of the countries in which they are published and their editorial writing, not always formally identified as such, may sometimes be polemic in support of the home country and in opposition to other states. In this category are *Aviation Week and Space Technology* of the United States and *Flight International* of Britain which reflect their respective national viewpoints. Aviation publications of communist-governed states frequently contain an abundance of ideological material irrelevant to air transport. This diversion notwithstanding, Soviet publications such as the monthly *Grazhdanskaya aviatsiya* (Civil Aviation) and the thrice-weekly *Vozdushniy transport* (Air Transport) do publish articles critical of specific aspects of Soviet civil aviation, although broader policy issues — political routes, Soviet support of groups that have hijacked aircraft — are not discussed. The *Journal of Air Law and Commerce*, published by the School of Law at Southern Methodist University in Dallas, Texas, and *The Journal of the Royal Aeronautical Society*, London, are important scholarly publications.

Summary

Regulation of international air transport is pursued on several different levels by public and private international organizations. The International Civil Aviation Organization (ICAO), a specialized agency of the United Nations, is recognized as the authority on technical and safety questions. It sets standards for aircraft manufacturers and operators that are recognized around the world. It is a public association, its membership consisting of sovereign states accepting the mandate of ICAO on specific issues. In some areas of the world, regional associations of states pursue aviation goals of particular relevance to their regions, often drawing upon ICAO as a model for organization.

An association of scheduled airlines – the International Air Transport Association (IATA) – has regulated fares and rates charged on international routes. Its future role is somewhat cloudy because of adverse public reaction to its cartel characteristics, possible action by the U.S. government rescinding the antitrust immunity allowing American carriers to participate in it, its failure to represent all airlines, and its plans for reorganization whose outcome and impact upon the industry cannot be foreseen.

Regulatory influence on a multinational level is also exercised by specialized organizations concerned with telecommunications and airports, and with professionals working in the industry. Some influence is also enjoyed by several educational institutions offering courses in air transport and by several air-transport publications.

The international air-transport regulatory system is largely a product of American and British domination of the postwar civil-aviation arena. Numerous other countries, additional international conflicts, and increasingly more sophisticated aviation technology have all exerted influence on multinational air-transport regulatory agencies since then, and the existing regulatory framework has not always proved capable of absorbing these changes.

In general terms, regulatory agencies have adapted well to changing technology and have established new standards reflecting advances made. They have done less well in accommodating the needs of many developing countries, needs which are sometimes perceived as unrealistic, unjustified, or threatening by officials of traditional aviation powers. Even when considered justified, the sheer scope of weakness in the aviation infrastructure of many developing countries suggests that the existing regulatory system faces a possibly insurmountable challenge in extending a common level of air transport standards throughout the world.

Conduct and evolution of international air transport regulation is made more difficult by the injection of irrelevant political issues into various regulatory agency proceedings. That this phenomenon is common in many international organizations renders it no less inauspicious for civil aviation. Distortion of several U.N. agencies for narrow political purposes portends difficulty for ICAO if partisan abuse continues.

The very diversity of political systems represented among states operating or supervising the operation of civil air transport suggests that conflict and lack of unanimity will continue to characterize the international air-transport regulatory system. Large and small, industrialized and developing, centralized and decentralized countries are all likely to endorse similar standards for narrow issues of technology and safety. Agreement is far less likely on questions related to economic and political policy.

Notes

1. Gabriel A. Almond and G. Bingham Powell, Jr., *Comparative Politics* (Boston: Little, Brown and Co., 1966), p. 196. The other four capabilities delineated by Almond and Powell are extractive, distributive, symbolic, and responsive.

2. Ibid., p. 197.

3. Ibid.

4. Ibid.

5. The question of international route authorization for American airlines is decided by a federal agency, but no U.S. carrier can be forced to operate a specific route. As an example, one can cite the 1978 Pan American decision to suspend service to Moscow although it is the only American airline authorized to serve the Soviet Union and the Department of State would have preferred continuation of the service.

6. For a detailed discussion of this issue see Thomas Buergenthal, *Law-Making in the International Civil Aviation Organization* (Syracuse, N.Y.: Syracuse University Press, 1969), Part 1.

7. U.S. Civil Aeronautics Board, *Aeronautical Statutes and Related Materials*, revised ed. (June 1, 1970), "Convention on International Civil Aviation," December 7, 1944, Chapter VII, Article 44, p. 446.

8. Ibid., Chapter IX, Article 50, p. 448.

9. The American/Australian proposal was based on a time-reference scanning beam, the British on a Doppler system. For further reference to debate on this issue, see the following: Richard Witkin, "Hearings on Plane Landing Devices to Study British and U.S. Rivals," *New York Times*, January 30, 1978, p. D1; Klass, "Landing System Battle Detailed," *Aviation Week* 108:7 (February 13, 1978), pp. 12–14; Klass, " 'Secrecy' Issue Aired at MLS Hearings," *Aviation Week* 108:9 (February 27, 1978), pp. 54–57; *Interavia Air Letter* 8984 (April 13, 1978), pp. 1–2; Witkin, "Ex-FAA Head Assails Agency on New Landing System Choice," *New York Times*, April 13, 1978, p. 61; *Aviation Daily* 236:33 (April 14, 1978), p. 259; *Aviation Daily* 236:34 (April 17, 1978), p. 271; *Aviation Daily* 236:36 (April 19, 1978), p. 284; *Aviation Daily* 236:38 (April 21, 1978), p. 302; Klass, "Deadlock Looms at ICAO Talks" and "ICAO Group Picks U.S. Landing System," *Aviation Week* 108:16 (April 17, 1978), pp. 28–30; Witkin, "Air-Landing Plan of Americans Wins Over British Concept," *New York Times*, April 20, 1978, p. 53.

10. Philip J. Klass, "ICAO Group Picks U.S. Landing System," *Aviation Week* 108:17 (April 24, 1978), p. 23.

11. See Rosalind K. Ellingsworth, "Expanded Economic Role for ICAO Recommended," *Aviation Week* 106:2 (January 10, 1979), pp. 24–25; Ellingsworth, "ICAO Parley Isolates Problems," *Aviation Week* 106:18 (May 2, 1977), pp. 32–33; and Joan Feldman, "Montreal: More Control is the Message," *Flight International* 3556 (May 10, 1977), p. 1237.

12. See Tables 1–1, 1–2, and 1–3.

13. Issues in the economic regulation controversy are discussed by K.G.J. Pillai, *The Air Net* (New York: Grossman Publishers, 1969).

14. "U.S. Reassesses Role in ICAO After Vienna Assembly Walkout," *Aviation Daily* 196:21 (July 30, 1971), p. 164.

15. Quoted in Ellingsworth, "Politics Clouds ICAOs Mission," *Aviation Week* 101:21 (November 25, 1974), p. 28.

16. That the number of Arab terrorists acts against aircraft and airline-related targets reached approximately thirty by late 1974 has been ascertained by the author on the basis of published news accounts. The problem of air terrorism is discussed in Chapter 9.

17. Several such actions occurred within UNESCO during the 1970s. In 1974 and again in 1978, UNESCO condemned Israel and voted economic sanctions against her because of archeological excavations alleged to encroach on Islamic sites in Jerusalem—ignoring the report of a UNESCO delegation to the site that found the Arab allegations unjustified. Also in 1978 the UNESCO Director-General refused to submit to its general conference a UNESCO delegation report absolving Israel of earlier charges of "cultural aggression" in occupied territories. ILO (International Labor Organization) has frequently ignored violations of worker rights in the Soviet bloc states and many developing countries.

18. Laurence Doty, "Arabs Plan Own Air Code and Industry," *Aviation Week* 103:21 (November 24, 1979), pp. 28–29.

19. See the following on activities of the CMEA Commission: N. Oprishko, "Sodruzhestvo aviatorov bratskikh stran," *Grazhdanskaya aviatisia* (May 1966), pp. 30–31; V. Morozov, "Transport—An Important Link in Integration," *Foreign Trade* (Moscow) 11 (November, 1975), pp. 18–24; and B.P. Bugayev, *K novym vysotam*, Izdatel'stvo (Znanye, 1976), pp. 28–30.

20. Romania has a mixed fleet of Soviet and western aircraft; her participation in CMEA Commission work is at a low level. Poland, Czechoslovakia, and Hungary have all admitted preference for Western equipment and political inability to purchase it. For an account of Hungarian puchase desires, see "Hungary Seeks Aircraft, Airport Equipment," *Aviation Week* 110:18 (April 30, 1979), p. 62. See also chapter 8.

21. *50 Years of World Airline Cooperation* (Montreal: International Air Transport Association, 1969), p. 4.

22. See Peter P.C. Haanappel, *Ratemaking in International Air Transport* (hereafter *Ratemaking*) (Deventer, The Netherlands: Kluwer B.V., 1978), pp. 1–4.

23. The terms "quasi-public" and "semigovernmental" are from Haanappel, *Ratemaking*, p. 33.

24. See *World Airline Cooperation* (Montreal: International Air Transport Association, n.d.), pp. 6 and 7; "Passing the Bucks," *IATA Review* 14:2 (March–April, 1979), p. 7; and "Topping 20 Billion Dollars," *IATA Review*, 15:2 (March–April, 1980), pp. 2–3.

25. "Topping 20 Billion Dollars," IATA Review.

26. For a dicsussion of two serious IATA crises, see Nawal K. Taneja, *The Commercial Airline Industry* (Lexington, Mass.: Lexington Books, 1976), pp. 265–268.

27. Haanappel, *Ratemaking*, p. 45.

28. *Federal Aviation Act of 1958*, 72 Stat. 731, as amended.

29. This situation is recognized by IATA. See, for example, "The Other Side of IATA," *IATA Review* 13:4 (June–July 1978), pp. 5–16.

30. "Pan Am Withdraws from IATA," *Interavia Air Letter* 9815 (February 2, 1979), pp. 1–2.

31. U.S., Department of Transportation, *Air Services Agreement Between the Government of the United States of America and The Government of the United Kingdom of Great Britain and Northern Ireland*, 1977, Article 12.

32. Carole Shifrin, "IATA Struggles for Survival as Cartel Role is Diminished," *Washington Post*, April 8, 1979, p. M4.

5

The International Regulatory Framework: Internal Regulation of One Country in the Worldwide Air-Transport Industry

Operation of a worldwide air-transport regulatory system must necessarily respect the systems of individual states or at least those systems of the most influential states within the international framework. As noted in the previous chapter, application of regulation — "the employment of legitimate coercion to control behavior"[1] — differs among systems in its style, intensity, and comprehensiveness.

Air-transport regulatory authority in a sovereign state exercises "legitimate coercion" to control air-transport policy in two central spheres: (1) technical and (2) political-economic. In the technical arena, the regulatory authority develops and enforces standards and certification procedures in such areas as airspace control, meteorological services, aircraft airworthiness and noise suppression, personnel training, maintenance and repair criteria, aircraft accident investigations, and airport design and construction.

Development of political and economic regulation must reflect established national policy on the basic political and economic status of air transport. Fundamental issues impinging upon regulation are: airline ownership (whether by state or private sources); permissible competition (whether two or more home-registered carriers can compete on a single route, the role of charter service); financial structure (whether air service should be profitable or operate social and political routes for which state subsidies are granted); and aircraft purchase policy (whether carriers may purchase whatever equipment deemed most suitable for their operations or whether they are restricted to aircraft of a specific manufacturer for political/economic reasons; if aircraft purchase is restricted, whether carrier receives state compensation for resulting operating diseconomies). Once these fundamental issues are resolved and implemented, decisions to alter them will usually be made by a government administration, rather than by air transport officials, as part of a larger and general policy change. In 1979, for example, a decision to sell a minority shareholding of state-owned British Airways was made by a new Conservative government in consonance with its overall economic philosophy. Aviation officials had been informed, but not consulted, prior to the public announcement by the Secretary for Trade in the House of Commons.

The specific aviation regulatory authority usually concentrates its political and economic decisions on such issues as route development and tariffs. In debating route development, the authority will consider the demonstrated and potential need for service; the impact of service on the existing route system and overall operations of the relevant carrier; restrictions about intermediate stops and other matters; and, in situations where competing home-based airlines are under the authority's jurisdiction, designation of one or more carriers as operators. Other government agencies, such as a ministry of foreign relations in the case of international routes or local authorities in the instance of domestic service, may contribute to the debate.

The politics of air-transport regulation within a single country are often complex and competitive, each of a number of agencies and interest groups pursuing separate policies in encouraging particular decisions. Depending on custom and on governmental systems, efforts to advance a cause may be quite public or may be conducted quietly. In some countries, one or another interest group is so dominant that debate, whether open or closed, rarely occurs. In other countries, the relative strength of various interest groups changes with time and policies develop and change accordingly. This chapter identifies and considers the major interest groups, both governmental and private, within a country that may affect its international air-transport policy.

The Role of Governmental Institutions in Regulating International Airlines

Governmental agencies regulating international airlines are of two types, those whose mandate is centered on, perhaps limited to, transportation, and those whose mandate is in a nontransport sphere impinging in some way on international air transport. In the first category are such agencies in the United States (and their counterparts in other countries) as the Civil Aeronautics Board, the National Transportation Safety Board, and local airport authorities. Nontransport government agencies whose competence nonetheless extends to certain areas of international air transport include foreign ministries, parliaments, tourism offices, defense interests, and a number of other authorities.

Transportation Agencies and Institutions

The Controlling Corporation

Most state-owned airlines are controlled by a formally autonomous public corporation created by statute. The designation of autonomy ostensibly reflects an intention to preserve the independent nature of the corporation, protecting it from the intrusion of politics; as will be noted, this intention is often observed in the breach. The corporation is directed for a fixed term by a board appointed by a government minister (such as the minister of transport). In some countries, board membership is restricted to persons not serving in the government in any other capacity. In other countries, a number of directorships may be reserved for representatives of transport, defense, or other agencies; in these instances, it would seem, the independence of the corporation is compromised simply by the presence of delegates from additional state institutions.

Autonomous corporations are usually responsible to parliament. They derive revenue from the sale of their products or service, and may receive capital funds by parliamentary appropriation or by sale of government-backed bonds. If truly autonomous, they hire and fire personnel independently and buy and sell property in their own name. They can sue or be sued.

Theoretically, an autonomous corporation makes independent decisions that are implemented by managers appointed by the corporation. In reality, the corporation may be influenced by government policy in such areas as equipment purchase (a recommendation to support a domestic aircraft industry or a particular foreign concern for foreign policy reasons) or route structure (a requirement to serve certain points for foreign policy considerations). Full-time managers appointed by the corporation board — as well as the board members — usually perceive themselves as air-transport experts and resent the intrusion of nonaviation interests. The nonaviation interest groups may well be considered intruders; they may also be seen as representing an element in the "checks and balances" system in democracies that evaluates and regulates priorities, theoretically preventing any single institution from accumulating power at the expense of others. Intervention in international air transport by nonaviation government agencies is defended in both democratic and nondemocratic societies as being in the "public interest," a term of manipulative definition.

The issue of checks and balances is essentially one of power determination, of recognizing how subsystems of a polity react to events and interact with each other. It cannot be denied that independent decisions of an airline may lead to difficulties in nontransport areas of society; it is possible, for example, that hiring and firing practices of a carrier may contribute to unemployment or exacerbate ethnic tensions at levels deemed unacceptable to other government authorities. Purchase of certain aircraft or suspension of service to a particular country may lead to foreign relations complications. In other situations, mandated nonaviation policies and customs may seriously impede the efficient functioning of the carrier; SAS and Sabena, to cite two cases, are affected by decisions of higher government authorities to maintain certain ethnic proportions in staffing their companies. SAS has managed to preserve an employment balance between the three countries it serves that, although satisfying none completely, has been accepted by all and does not adversely affect the efficiency of the airline. The continuing conflict in Belgium between that country's two major ethnic groups, the Flemings and Walloons, is reflected in Sabena in a far less satisfactory manner. Duplicate staffing and other problems arising from tense Fleming-Walloon relations have contributed to Sabena's very substantial economic difficulties. In Austria and several other countries, airline personnel decisions have been tied to political affiliations of applicants. In some countries, political affiliations of executive personnel must match in proportion the balance in a coalition government.

Air France may be cited as an example of a state-owned airline subject to large-scale state intervention. The French government holds 98.9 percent of the carrier's capital. An additional 1 percent is held by the Caisse des Dépôts et Consignations, a public state institution. The airline is run by a board of sixteen members (appointed by the Cabinet), including five civil servants.[2] In recent years, Air France has suffered large operating losses which have had to be offset by substantial government subsidy. The government itself has been responsible for a large proportion of the deficit, forcing the carrier to undertake such uneconomic policies as:

transferring most of its operations to a new Paris airport while maintaining some service at another;

operating the Concorde which, although "spectacular" and "prestigious," is commercially nonviable;

maintaining and operating a large subsonic fleet of obsolescent and uneconomic French-manufactured aircraft (Caravelle) rather than purchasing more efficient equipment because it was made abroad; and

operating low-fare service to overseas French territories.

In 1978 the French government signed a contract with Air France granting the carrier financial compensation for the obligations imposed upon it. The airline was also authorized to purchase efficient foreign-made aircraft to replace the Caravelles. As long as the government continues to subsidize Air France (said to amount to $900 per passenger on the Concorde alone), the carrier cannot be independent. Without subsidy, it would collapse.

It is unlikely that any designated autonomous public airline corporation is truly autonomous. Each is subject to a degree of external intervention, the amount and nature of which varies markedly from country to country even within fairly compact areas. In Western Europe, for example, Air

France and Sabena can be characterized as heavily dependent airlines, and Lufthansa and SAS as lightly dependent carriers.

The Economic Regulatory Agency

Economic and technical air-transport regulation are the responsibility of a single agency in many countries. In the United States, the two regulatory areas are assigned to different government institutions. The Civil Aeronautics Board (CAB) regulates economic and commercial aspects of air transport, and other agencies regulate technical aspects.

The CAB was established (as the Civil Aeronautics Authority) by the Civil Aeronautics Act of 1938. It was reorganized as the CAB in 1940, having then, as it had in 1938, responsibility for technical and safety issues as well as economic policy. The Federal Aviation Administration and National Transportation Safety Board assumed authority for technical and safety regulation in later years.

The major functions of the CAB may be summarized as follows:

1. It authorizes U.S. companies to operate interstate and international air service;
2. It decides which airlines can operate which specific routes within the United States and between the United States and foreign countries;
3. It authorizes and pays government subsidies to certain airlines for the operation of domestic public service routes;
4. It regulates fares and rates charged the public for air transport;
5. It determines air mail rates;
6. It promotes and maintains a competitive airline environment, judging questions of mergers, acquisition of air carrier control, and interlocking relationships between carriers and between carriers and other transport industries;
7. It promotes and maintains a fair and competitive environment among carriers and agents selling air transport;
8. It regulates accounting practices of airlines and requires carriers to submit regular financial and operational data;
9. It publishes financial and operational data filed by the airlines; and
10. It advises and assists the Department of State in negotiating bilateral air transport agreements with foreign governments and issues operating permits to foreign carriers authorized to serve U.S. points.[3]

The tasks of the CAB are performed by five offices — Administrative

Support Operations, Community and Congressional Relations, Consumer Advocate, Comptroller, and General Counsel; and six bureaus—Enforcement, International Aviation, Accounts and Statistics, Pricing and Domestic Aviation, Economic Analysis, and Administrative Law Judges. Five persons serve as Board members, each appointed for a six-year term by the President with the advice and consent of the Senate. The Civil Aeronautics Act provides that no more than three Board members may belong to the same political party and that no member can own stock in any civil aviation enterprise. One member is designated by the President of the United States as President and Chairman of the Civil Aeronautics Board; another member is appointed Vice-President. All five Board positions are considered full-time positions.

CAB legal decisions may be challenged in court, but neither the President nor Congress can veto Board decisions. The CAB is subject to lobbying and CAB hearings are open to arguments from various interested parties. One observer has written that the CAB handles its problems in "an atmosphere of political controversy generated by conflicting interest groups. The result has been policies openly made and openly criticized".[4]

The impact of conflicting interest groups is felt particularly strongly in international service cases. By law, international route cases are resolved in executive agreements subject to Presidential approval. The President usually responds to political advice from the Department of State—which may conflict with economic advice offered by the Board. Advice from the Board is based on its own expertise in the air transport industry and is provided by the CAB Bureau of International Aviation (BIA). The BIA has four major divisions: Negotiations, which provides country and regional information; Regulatory Affairs, which does the economic staff work required for processing route certificates for U.S. carriers and permits for foreign airlines; Legal, which administrates legal functions for the Bureau; and Economic and Systems Analysis, which provides economic forecasting and analysis relevant to cases under study. In the event of disagreement between the President and the CAB or another agency regarding specific route awards, the Interagency Group on International Aviation, a continuing group of representatives from concerned agencies, is convened to resolve the differences. The Interagency Group will be discussed below.

The CAB and counterpart agencies in other countries that, like the United States, have multiple airlines face special problems in that route awards may be contested by several airlines. In the United States, all contesting airlines are privately owned and compete for route designations on a more-or-less equal basis. Pressure groups—frequently from congressional delegations and political forces in the area in which an airline is based—support one or another airline and attempt to influence the Board. In Britain, Canada, and France, CAB counterparts must contend with competition for specific route awards between private and state airlines. In all three countries, route designations are usually determined on the basis of a pre-existing policy of regional franchise allocated to different carriers. Although a regional policy may well be established — usually favoring the state-owned airlines — domestic political factors may suggest a change in actual practice for specific route awards at specific times. In Japan, Israel, and several other countries, predominantly domestic carriers have been awarded regional international routes and subsequently have pressed for these regional capabilities to be extended to more distant destinations at the expense of designated long-haul airlines. In each case, the regulatory agency is buffeted by competing interest groups and, on occasion, may be forced to relinquish its authority to the Executive Branch in response to political conditions.

In 1978, as a component in a general administration policy to reduce government involvement in and regulation over commercial activity, the United States enacted a law providing for the dissolution of the CAB by 1985. Those CAB functions determined vital will be transferred to existing government agencies, such as the departments of State, Justice, and Transportation.

The Technical Regulatory Agency

Technical and safety regulation of civil aviation at the national level in the United States is within the scope of the Department of Transportation (DOT) and is the special focus of a DOT subagency, the Federal Aviation Administration (FAA), and an independent DOT affiliate, the National Transportation Safety Board (NTSB). Although the FAA and NTSB are U.S. government institutions, their influence extends well beyond U.S. borders. American carriers flying international routes must conform to American standards worldwide. Foreign airlines flying to and from the United States must meet U.S. regulations on U.S.-involved routes. American-manufactured civil aircraft, the most widely used transport aircraft in the world, are designed and constructed according to U.S. certification standards. Non-American manufacturers wishing to sell aircraft in the United States must satisfy the same certification requirements. Even foreign-manufactured aircraft operated by foreign carriers must meet some U.S. standards in order to receive a permit to fly into American airspace. The strength of the American aviation industries and market — in air transportation and in aircraft — establish the importance of U.S. regulations far beyond American borders.

In addition to satisfying international standards, whether "official" international standards established by recognized international agencies such as the International Civil Aviation Organization (ICAO) or standards that are simply accepted as international criteria, regulatory agencies must be sufficiently flexible to adjust to rapidly developing aviation technology. Over fairly short periods of time the range and passenger capacity of aircraft have increased dramatically, creating a need for new standards reflecting these developments. Changes in economic and political conditions may also require rapid adaptations and alterations of existing standards: airports may suddenly become excessively crowded; labor unrest may lead to deterioration in operating conditions; political instability may bring on a closure of airspace or airports; and any one or combination of additional circumstances may compel a sudden (and perhaps temporary) deviation in standards. Regulatory authorities must have the power and flexibility to effect such changes as required.

In 1966 the Department of Transportation (DOT), one of the newer U.S. government ministries, was founded to achieve the following:

1. Assure the coordinated, effective administration of the transportation programs of the federal government;
2. Facilitate the development and improvement of coordinated transportation service, to be provided by private enterprise to the maximum extent feasible;
3. Encourage cooperation of federal, state, and local governments, carriers, labor, and other interested parties toward the achievement of national transportation objectives;
4. Stimulate technological advances in transportation;
5. Provide general leadership in the identification and solution of transportation problems; and
6. Develop and recommend to the President and the Congress for approval national transportation policies and programs to accomplish these objectives with full and appropriate consideration of the needs of the public, users, carriers, industry, labor, and the national defense.[5]

To accomplish these goals DOT brought together under its aegis several separate government bodies concerned with different modes of transportation. Today seven such agencies constitute DOT "operating administrations": U.S. Coast Guard, Federal Aviation Administration, Urban Mass Transportation Administration, Federal Highway Administration, Federal Railroad Administration, National Highway Traffic Safety Administration, and St. Lawrence Seaway Development Corporation. The National Transportation Safety Board is an independent affiliate of DOT, a status that will be discussed below. Although general transportation and some specific aviation policy statements are issued from time to time by DOT (through the office of its Secretary for Policy and International Affairs or its Air Transportation Policy Staff), DOT is not an effective participant in political and economic aspects of international air transport policy making. Those areas of air transport have long been dominated by the

CAB, Department of State, and Executive Branch; accordingly, occasional DOT pronouncements on international political and economic issues do not attract much attention.

The Federal Aviation Administration (FAA), one of the seven DOT "operating administrations," is itself organized in six separate units or services. An Administration Service includes separate offices for management, budget, logistics, personnel and training, labor relations, investigations and security, and accounting and audit. The Engineering and Development Service is concerned with systems engineering management and systems research and development. An Air Traffic and Airways Facilities Service concentrates on management of air traffic, both civilian and military, in the nation's airspace. Its work includes development of national programs and standards for: (1) air navigation and communications systems and facilities; (2) air-traffic control; (3) coordination of civilian air-traffic control with national defense requirements; and (4) operation of government flight information and cartographic services. Much of the work of this unit directly affects foreign airlines operating routes to the United States. An Airports Service has offices for planning and programming, and for standards.

The Aviation Standards Service has four offices: Flight Operations, Airworthiness, Aviation Safety, and Civil Aviation Security. The Office of Flight Operations is responsible for certifying aircrews and certifying and inspecting airlines, monitoring inflight performance of air navigation instrumentation, and maintaining and operating federally controlled civil airports. The Office of Airworthiness, a separate section of the Service only since 1979,[6] has three divisions: Aircraft Engineering, Aircraft Manufacturing, and Aircraft Maintenance. It is "responsible for the design, type, production, and original airworthiness certification of civil aeronautical products" and is also concerned with maintenance procedures.[7] Airworthiness officials monitor the planning and production of transport aircraft in the United States and the maintenance practices of American carriers.

The Office of Aviation Safety has separate divisions for Accident Investigation, Safety Analysis, and Special Programs. Among the responsibilities of the special programs division is the reporting of aviation safety data. The Office of Civil Aviation Security is concerned with security for domestic and international passenger and cargo air traffic. One of its four divisions, Intelligence and International Security, cooperates with appropriate agencies in other countries. The Office of Civil Aviation Security also directs FAA work on the carriage of hazardous materials.

Although each of the above-mentioned services has an impact on international civil aviation in that all American carriers flying abroad and all foreign airlines flying to the United States are subject to their regulation, a fifth FAA service focuses much more directly on international air transport. The Office of Policy and International Aviation Affairs has four divisions: Aviation Policy, System Plans, Environment and Energy, and International

Aviation Affairs (OIAA). The OIAA International Liaison and Policy division has three main functions: collection, evaluation, and dissemination of international air-transport information; development of international air-transport policies, plans, and programs; and provision of U.S. representation at ICAO. Its Technical Assistance Division annually offers training courses in the United States in all phases of commercial air transport to hundreds of foreigners. It also operates assistance programs in foreign countries. The OIAA International Analysis and Coordination Division develops policy, evaluates programs, and provides secretarial services for the Interagency Group on International Aviation, a government body established to enable different departments and agencies to discuss their views and make common recommendations on international aviation matters.

The FAA maintains a number of field offices abroad. Located in all regions of the world, these offices represent the FAA in relations with other U.S. agencies abroad and with foreign aviation agencies; exchange relevent information with appropriate foreign groups; promote American aviation interests; encourage common systems of air-traffic control; foster civil-aviation-assistance programs; monitor American carrier operations abroad with regard to efficiency, safety, and security; and perform other duties considered vital to the advancement of civil aviation.

The National Transportation Safety Board (NTSB) is an affiliated agency of DOT "independent of the Secretary [of Transportation] and the other offices and officers of the Department [of Transportation]."[8] The major responsibilities of the NTSB are: (1) investigation of aircraft accidents according to established procedures; (2) development of recommendations to the FAA that, once implemented, will prevent the future occurrence of similar accidents; and (3) publication of all reports of investigations and recommendations. The Board is empowered to hold hearings, compel testimony, supervise the removal of aircraft wreckage, and undertake other actions in pursuit of its investigative responsibilities.

The authority to impose NTSB recommendations as regulations lies not within the Board, but within the FAA which may adopt or reject NTSB recommendations as its Office of Aviation Safety sees fit. Adopted recommendations are issued as Airworthiness Directives (which have the force of federal laws) to airlines, aircraft manufacturers, and other appropriate bodies. Application of an Airworthiness Directive is enforced by the FAA; if not observed, the aircraft Certificate of Airworthiness may be revoked, and the aircraft prohibited from flying in U.S. airspace. Foreign airlines must comply with FAA Airworthiness Directives as these affect their aircraft entering American airspace; foreign-owned aircraft not flying in U.S. airspace cannot be subject to American regulation, but most foreign regulatory agencies adopt U.S. Airworthiness Directives as their own and enforce their application on home-registered aircraft.[9]

Although the FAA was subjected to severe criticism after the 1979 Chicago DC-10 crash,[10] it is recognized throughout the world as a major force in enhancing aviation safety. Particular respect is accorded the NTSB for its public reporting of accident investigations and recommendations. In many countries, aircraft accidents are considered so damaging to national prestige that investigations cannot be conducted under conditions conducive to fair, unbiased examinations of the facts. Findings perceived as reflecting badly on the national level of technology are not published, or, in some instances, even acknowledged. The NTSB has been exceptional in its adherence to a policy of openness and public accountability.

The Airport Authority

In some countries all civil airports are administratered, managed, and regulated by a single national authority. In other countries, administration and management of airports is a function of local authorities — county or municipal — and regulation a function of a national body, frequently a department of a larger aviation technical regulatory authority. The national agency establishes and enforces standards that are binding on all aircraft, domestic and foreign-registered, using home-country airports. Different standards concerning such conditions as runway length, lighting, firefighting capabilities, ground-based avionics, and ground support equipment are applied to airports permitting different levels of operations.

Although competent authorities may nominally control airports, their power to regulate all aspects of international airline activity at airports may be limited. Agreements allowing service at specific airports are negotiated by other government agencies — foreign ministries — that present airport authorities with a fait accompli, an agreement permitting particular international operations, often without regard to local conditions militating against service expansion, such as fuel shortages or airport congestion.[11]

Local nonaviation interest groups can also force airports to expand or, more often, limit operations to a degree undesired by the competent airport authorities. Noise abatement procedures, usually pressed by citizen lobby groups, may force takeoff and landing curfews and restrictions on flight patterns. Airport location and the nature of ground transportation may also be influenced by nonaviation interests, sometimes resulting in conditions adverse to international air transport development. Adjacent basing of military air force units at commercial airports can similarly limit civil aviation activity.

As is the case with aircraft, airport standards in one country may be affected, even regulated, by standards in another country. Just as the United States requires foreign aircraft using its airspace and American aircraft flying outside the U.S. to conform to its standards, so does the FAA require that foreign airports used by American-registered airlines conform to U.S. airport standards. On occasion, the FAA has prohibited American carriers from using certain foreign airports judged to be unsafe.[12]

Nontransportation Agencies and Institutions

The Foreign Affairs Ministry

The government agency charged with management of a country's foreign affairs ususaly has three primary responsibilities in regulation of that state's international air-transport industry. First, it establishes a general international civil-aviation policy to guide the government in its aviation relations with other countries. For example, a principle may be determined endorsing or prohibiting the operation of commercially nonviable routes for foreign policy reasons. If such a principle is endorsed, guidelines for reimbursing the carrier must be formulated. Second, the foreign affairs agency provides the political and economic background necessary to evaluate air transport relations with specific foreign countries. Working with foreign ministry area experts, it investigates the likely impact on general bilateral relations of various options available in air transport negotiations. It may extend the investigation to consider the impact of a particular agreement on regional relations, future negotiations, or some other area of concern. Third, the foreign affairs ministry usually conducts the actual negotiations, with input from other power bases, and formally concludes the agreement. Many governments establish an aviation office within their foreign ministries to execute the state international aviation program. Reflecting its functions, separate sections of the office may be concerned with policy, research, and negotiations.

In the United States, the Department of State provides background information on foreign policy implications of pending agreements to the President who must approve all international agreements. When these recommendations are in conflict with those presented by the CAB, the President has usually accepted the State Department position. In an effort to minimize such conflict, an Interagency Group on International Aviation (IGIA) brings together all concerned government agencies to prepare recommendations for State Department consideration, but experience suggests that State Department views have usually prevailed. Interagency conflict and IGIA will be examined below.

The Executive Branch

The Federal Aviation Act of 1958 empowers the President of the United States to approve certificates authorizing air carriers to operate international routes and permits allowing foreign airlines to serve U.S. destinations.[13] The act also allows the President to disapprove CAB orders rejecting or suspending international fares when "disapproval is required for reasons of the national defense or the foreign policy of the United States," and excludes Presidential decisions on foreign carriers serving the United States from judicial review by U.S. Courts of Appeals.[14]

In practice, Presidential ability to override Civil Aeronautics Board decisions (and those of other government agencies) has been interpreted rather broadly, and numerous actions taken by the President under this provision have led to charges of manipulation of international aviation for domestic partisan politics. For example, in 1977 President Carter overrode the CAB decision authorizing Pan Am to operate Dallas-London service, awarding the route to Braniff Airways. Most observers regarded the Presidential order as a favor to the congressional delegation from Texas, Braniff's base, in return for support in Congress by the Texas delegation of the Presidential energy program.[15] In consquence of this and other Presidential decisions, the Federal Aviation Act provision allowing such power has been periodically attacked in Congress, and the American Bar Association has recommended its repeal or amendment. Some critics, however, reject charges of presidential political interference, and support the view that presidential final authority in civil aviation is consistent with both Presidential prerogatives in foreign policy and the need for American capability to act quickly and decisively in international aviation matters. Lengthy court cases, such critics say, are the almost inevitable result of CAB attempts to resolve complex international issues.[16]

Statements defining U.S. international air transport policy are issued by the President periodically, some routinely and others in support of new principles or agreements.[17] International civil aviation policy has not been a factor in U.S. presidential campaigns, and interest in it has differed among individual chief executives.

The role in international civil aviation of chief executives of most other countries is less defined and much less public than in the United States. Policy issues are generally decided by the dominant political party and implemented through the foreign ministry. The chief executive may be a significant participant in this effort, if seldom a visible participant.

The Legislative Branch

The legislative branch of a democratic government can influence international aviation regulation in three ways. First, legislators supporting different political parties may view international civil aviation consistent with distinct and not always compatible political philosophies. One group may favor the nationalization of air carriers and the subsidization, for political reasons, of certain routes that cannot be operated profitably. Another group may back private ownership of airlines and operation of only pro-fitable routes. Some legislators may support the monopolization of all air service by a single airline, others may back the existence of multiple carriers. If more than one carrier does exist, opinions may differ regarding competi-tion between them. In some countries—for example, Australia and Canada (where one major airline is state-owned and another is privately owned)—aviation policy can be a major election issue.[18]

If election to the legislature is organized on a system of district representation, legislative influence on the regulatory system can be exercised by representatives supporting aviation programs perceived useful to or popular in their own districts. The instance of the Texas congressional delegation backing the efforts of Texas-based Braniff to obtain presidential authorization for Dallas-London service has already been cited. In 1978 and 1979, in an effort to avert loss of Pan American Boston transatlantic passenger service, the Massachusetts congressional delegation unsuccessful-ly tried to persuade the State Department to force amendment of the Ber-muda II agreement between the United States and Britain.[19]

Third, the U.S. Congress exercises an investigative and supervisory role in aviation through the functions of the Aviation Subcommittees in both chambers. The subcommittees hold hearings on matters of interest and are empowered to introduce legislation requiring changes in American aviation policy. In promoting such changes, Congress may well encounter opposi-tion from other government policy-making centers, such as the President, Department of State, and Civil Aeronautics Board.[20]

State corporations controlling several European airlines are responsible to national parliaments that may demand investigations and/or policy changes should the carriers incur financial losses or encounter other dif-ficulties. Airlines forced to operate economically nonviable political routes may turn to their parliaments for subsidy or for route cancellation. Parliamentary action on any of these issues may bring objection from other government policy-setting centers.

Special interest lobby groups concerned with issues related to aviation may generate sufficient support to force legislation backing their concerns. For example, neighborhood and environmental interest groups have forced legislation in several countries requiring stricter noise regulation. When such regulation has mandated airport curfews or retrofitting of engines, foreign airlines may attempt to claim exemption or may protest through diplomatic channels against regulations of which diplomats have little knowledge. Lines of communication between airlines of one country and legislatures of another are seldom direct, usually going through ministries of foreign affairs and frequently sacrificing clarity in the process. Some authoritarian governments with rubber-stamp parliaments profess disbelief that legislatures in other countries are empowered to enact regulations af-fecting foreign carriers as well as home-registered airlines.

The Department of Justice

Although the Federal Aviation Act of 1958 assigns to the Civil Aeronautics Board supervision over antitrust matters and certain other aspects of competitive practices, the Antitrust Division of the Transportation Section of the Department of Justice submits to the CAB its findings on pending relevant cases, including those concerning international routes.[21] The CAB considers such findings, but is not bound by them.

Because most other countries enforce a policy of monopoly operation by one airline of all scheduled international routes or of separate groups of international routes, antitrust questions generally do not arise outside of the United States. Competitive charter and inclusive tour carriers operating in several European countries with single airlines designated chosen instrument for scheduled international flights generally have not been subject to antitrust legislation. An exception exists in West Germany where a Federal Monopolies Commission has investigated mergers of competitive supplemental carriers.

Beyond antitrust questions, an airline is generally subject to judicial procedures in the same manner as are other institutions of similiar structure in a particular state. Liability in international air transport is governed by a uniform law adopted in 1929, the Warsaw Convention, and several protocols attached to it.[22]

Departments of Commerce, Trade, and Tourism

The specific functions of ministries of commerce and/or trade may differ from one country to another, but in all states these government agencies include among their objectives the strengthening of their national economy through exports. Sale to others of domestically grown, extracted, or manufactured products is pressed. Airline service is one of a number of "invisible exports"—among them other services, such as insurance and other modes of transportation—that, when purchased by a foreign consumer, may contribute positively to a country's balance of payments (exports verses imports) in the same manner as a more conventional material export.

In efforts to support their airlines in obtaining the greatest possible income, most governments have employed various procedures designed to direct traffic to the home airline. The most widely used means of increasing the earnings of a carrier is requiring that government employees use the home airline on all international travel, transferring to foreign flag carriers only when the home airline does not serve a desired destination. In those states in which all or most persons are employed by the government, the entire population may be a captive market for the home carrier. Taken to extremes, as it is in the Soviet Union, this policy extends to foreign businessmen who are told that proposals might be considered more sympathetically if they arrive and depart on the national airline. In the specific case of the USSR, a rather absurd situation had developed in which western hemisphere businessmen, not wishing to subject themselves to poor Aeroflot service on long transatlantic flights, fly the Atlantic on western carriers and transfer to Aeroflot in Europe. Although they do arrive in and depart from Moscow on Aeroflot, none can prove that use of the Soviet airline has any substantive effect on business negotiations. Other commonly used methods of traffic direction have been noted in chapter 2.

Tourism is another "invisible export" and a major source of foreign exchange for many countries, among them developing nations with few other products competitive in world markets. Most developing countries are located in warm climates and/or possess sites of great scenic interest which attract tourists from more affluent northern societies. Tourism also provides employment and may improve the visitors' image of the country. To exploit their tourist potential most governments maintain tourism offices, either as separate ministries or as divisions of another ministry, such as a ministry of commerce. Logic suggests that government tourism and air-transport agencies complement each other, that one industry enhances the other. Airlines transport tourists to and from the country and between sites within the country. Air service improves the accessibility of remote areas attractive to tourists. The airline gains from passenger traffic generated by tourism. Although such ties between the two industries are logical, some conflict between them is both inherent and a question of government policy. For example, tourism authorities want to attract more tourists and advocate almost any means of transporting them to their country that will facilitate their entry. Recognizing the ability of large, established airlines from affluent western states to promote travel, tourism authorities may press ministries of foreign affairs to allow western carriers whatever traffic rights they request. Aviation officials, however, are charged with protecting the interests of the national airline and may object to improved competitive conditions for foreign carriers. Government authorities, whether in a foreign ministry or in a ministry of commerce or trade which oversees one or both activities, may be required to develop a specific policy that favors one industry or attempts to achieve a balance between them. Advocates of each side will press their views and the result may hinge on the power of a particular personality.

Although the Department of Commerce in the United States is concerned with foreign trade and the American balance of payments, it has no statutory responsibility for civil aviation and no authority for enforcing any aviation-related policy it might adopt. Its lack of statutory influence in civil aviation notwithstanding, the U.S. Department of Commerce has issued reports and policy statements on the subject.[23]

The U.S. Travel Service, the government tourism agency, is under the aegis of the Department of Commerce, but its mandate is weak and its impact both upon overall government planning and upon the tourism industry is negligible. (The very minor role of the government tourism agency in the United States is an anomaly; in most countries, such offices enjoy relatively larger budgets and greater authority.)

The Postal Service

The requirements of postal authorities to improve mail service in the period immediately after World War I were among the leading factors in the rapid development of commercial aviation of that period. Airmail contracts issued by post offices in various countries provided the impetus for the formation of numerous airlines in both Europe and the United States. Many of these carriers, among them some airlines as prominent as Pan American, concentrated their early operations on airmail and were reluctant to carry passengers. Emphasis on airmail carriage continued into the early 1930s when the avialability of larger aircraft and a growing appreciation of political and economic benefits accruing from air transportation led to a gradually increasing role for passenger service. The World War II airlift experience proved the value of air transport of freight and stimulated advances in the postwar air-cargo industry. Although the provision of airmail service is important to both sender and receiver, postal traffic itself is only a small portion of total air traffic, accounting for less than 5 percent of the revenue of most airlines.

International air transport of mail is usually arranged by contract between the postal authorities and the appropriate carrier of the sending country which carries the mail as close to the destination as its route system permits. Although bilateral air-transport agreements between states may specify that airmail be carried by any airline without prejudice, airmail is almost always directed to the home-registered airline. In the United States, airmail rates are determined by the Civil Aeronautics Board and airlines are paid accordingly by the postmaster general. In fulfilling its rate-fixing function, the board has always attempted to ensure that contracts cover costs for the airlines; in some other countries, rates are fixed in such a way as to subsidize the home-registered airline—to not only cover costs, but provide a substantial profit as well. Airlines carrying mail of foreign countries are paid by postal authorities of the foreign country according to postal conventions between that country and the country of registry of the airline.

Department of Defense

Military control over airlines and the use of civil airlines for military purposes has been considered elsewhere in this volume. Should military forces control the carrier, as is the case in several Latin American and other countries, these forces will also exercise control over many aspects of regulation. A ministry of foreign affairs may negotiate bilateral air transport agreements, but armed services officers will limit its freedom to negotiate. The national air force is likely to supervise technical areas of regulation.

The use of civil aircraft for military airlift of men and materiel is common among countries of all political orientations. Employment of commercial equipment for large-scale peacetime troop rotations and materiel transfers can permit a reduction in the size of a permanent air force fleet and is usually justified for economic reasons. Military charter of civil aircraft, from both scheduled and supplemental carriers, is regulated in the United States by the Civil Aeronautics Board which fixes rates each year for the wet-lease of specific aircraft types. Documentation of such transactions is a matter of public record.

Impression of commercial aircraft into an airlift command for support of actual combat conditions generally occurs under an emergency situation and is organized differently than is a peacetime wet-lease for troop rotations. Many countries have well-defined plans in which all civil aircraft are included in an inventory listing their particular features; when necessary, specific aircraft are ordered into service as components in a military airlift command. In such circumstances, regulation of the equipment and their operations is transferred to military control.

Potential military use of civil aircraft has stimulated substantial interest by defense specialists in the commercial airline industry. Military adaptability of civil aircraft is closely studied in many countries and has led to some requests by the armed forces for modifications in aircraft design, instrumentation, or other features. In 1975, for example, the U.S. Air Force requested federal funding to subsidize installation of large cargo doors in all U.S.-registered widebody aircraft in order to facilitate loading of bulky, outsized materiel.[24]

Other National Agencies

In many countries a variety of additional nontransport government agencies may wield regulatory powers over international air transport. In the United States, for example, the Equal Opportunities Commission, Occupational Safety and Health Administration, and Environmental Protection Agency are among the federal agencies whose regulatory mandates in the social and health fields impinge upon civil aviation. Energy conservation and labor regulation also affect the operation of air service.

The influence in some states exercised by intelligence and espionage agencies may extend to exploitation or manipulation of an airline for purposes extraneous to air transport. As noted previously, Soviet employees of Aeroflot in foreign countries have been associated with espionage activity and several have been expelled by host governments.

Regional and Local Agencies

Depending upon the degree of national/regional/local decentralization in a state political system, regional and local agencies may have some regulatory impact upon international air transport. For example, environmental impact and noise restrictions may differ from one area to another, limiting takeoffs and landings at some airports and not at others.

Conflicts Between Government Regulatory Agencies

It is probably inevitable that conflicts between regulatory agencies within a single government erupt from time to time. Each agency represents a different constituency, each institution has its own priorities, and most groups perceive it necessary to compete with other groups for power and primacy.

Because the United States is both a pluralistic society and the home of a vigorous free press, interagency conflicts within the U.S. frequently become well known. In late 1977, as noted earlier in this chapter, President Carter overrode CAB recommendations in awarding carrier rights for the Dallas-London route. In 1978 the General Accounting Office and the Department of State differed on U.S. policy to be followed in response to high airport user charges and restrictive practices encountered by American carriers in foreign countries.[25] In 1978 and 1979 the administration and the Senate Aviation Subcommittee clashed over provisions of international aviation legislation introduced in the Senate by the latter.[26] In 1979 the following were among interagency conflicts affecting international civil aviation: the CAB and Department of Justice about IATA commissions; the CAB and Department of State about air service between New York and Saudi Arabia; the CAB and Congress about general U.S. aviation policy; the CAB and Department of State about the role of IATA; and the CAB and Departments of State and Transportation about cabotage.[27]

In practical terms, the Department of State "coordinates" U.S. international civil aviation policy, approving or disapproving recommendations of the CAB or other agencies, and leading the American delegation in international negotiations. Although the primacy of the Department of State is generally recognized, other agencies have tried to assert leadership authority. At such times disagreements have become public and some foreign officials have experienced "trouble fathoming just who was in charge in the U.S. [negotiating] group."[28]

In an attempt to resolve, or at least modify, the differences between the various government agencies, an Interagency Group on International Aviation (IGIA) was formed in 1960 pursuant to a request from the President. Represented on the IGIA since its inception have been policy-level officials of the following agencies: Department of State, Department of Defense, Department of Commerce, Civil Aeronautics Board, and Federal Aviation Administration (represented by the Department of Transportation since its establishment in 1966). Other agencies have been represented on the IGIA in later years. These are: Environmental Protection Agency, Federal Communications Commission, and National Transportation Safety Board. Additional agencies have participated in IGIA deliberations on an ad hoc basis, when appropriate, with the same status as regular member agencies. Among these have been: the Departments of Treasury and Agriculture, Department of Housing and Urban Development, Office of Management and Budget, and the U.S. Postal Service.

The specific purpose of IGIA is "to obtain the views of participating departments and agencies on international aviation matters requiring the establishment of Government policy or Government decision, which affect two or more agencies, other than the Department of State."[29] The Department of State reviews all positions before formulating specific policy. In some instances of agency conflict, compromise can be reached; in other disputes, the views of some are adopted and the positions of others are rejected. If a key foreign policy issue is not a factor, resolution of conflicts may be based on domestic politics or the forcefulness or a particular personality.

Although international civil aviation policy disputes probably occur in most countries, few outside the United States apppear to attract much press coverage. To this circumstance may be ascribed the greater decentralization of government authority in the United States which leads to a greater expression of opinions, a tradition of a free press, and a system of privately owned air carriers whose "protection" from controversy is not perceived as necessary as is that of some state-owned carriers by their owner-governments.

The Role of Nongovernmental Institutions in Regulating International Airlines

Although they possess no legal right to regulate the international air transport industry, several types of nongovernmental institutions exert influence upon regulatory systems in most pluralistic societies. Among the most active in countries with more than one international airline are airline trade associations — sometimes separate groups for scheduled, charter, and inclusive tour operators. These are lobbying organizations that monitor government legislation and other actions affecting their industries. Through persuasion of members of parliament, legislative aides, and other persons considered influential, trade associations try to obtain the best possible operating conditions for their member corporations. Their concerns range from bilateral agreements with other countries to safety regulations to tax laws. Some lobby groups, such as trade associations of scheduled and charter airlines, may be competitive with one another for the support of various power sources.

Another trade association competing for the interest of government authorities is that of the designers, developers, and manufacturers of aircraft, avionics, and other aviation products. For example, acting on behalf of manufacturers of avionics systems, a trade association may encourage regulatory bodies to require the installation of certain types of instrumentation in aircraft or at ground facilities. Individual manufacturers or trade associations representing them may be called to testify before government commissions investigating aircraft accidents. These manufacturers can and do influence the attitudes of legislators whose districts contain aerospace industries.

Professional associations and labor unions whose members are employed in the aircraft and airline industries also attempt to persuade government authorities to adopt regulatory policies perceived beneficial to their own members. The powers of unions to assert their influence through strikes or lobbying differs from one country to another. Employees of state-owned industries in some countries are severly restricted by law in the types of industrial action in which they are permitted to engage. Although such limitations may be consistent with other regulatory codes in authoritarian states, they also exist in nationalized industries in some democratic countries. In the United States, unions are free to strike if labor contracts cannot be negotiated successfully. A single union, the Air Line Pilots Association, represents most American pilots and maintains a strong lobbying presence in Washington, D.C. The power of unions representing other airline staff — flight engineers, flight attendants, flight dispatchers, mechanics, and clerical and agent personnel — is weaker; the lesser prestige of these positions and representation of each position by several different unions, according to airline affiliation, dilutes the authority of any one union to speak for a large number of personnel. Among the issues on which American airline unions have tried to force enactment of certain regulatory provisions is a requirement for three cockpit crew members in aircraft said by their manufacturers to be safe with only two cockpit personnel and new U.S. international air transportation policy allowing foreign airlines (and their foreign crews) greater opportunities to serve U.S. destinations. The American Institute of Aeronautics and Astronautics (AIAA), a professional association of engineers and scientists in aeronautics and astronautics, expends most of its organizational efforts in professional education and advancement, but does some lobbying to advocate certain regulatory measures.

Local chambers of commerce or similar booster groups frequently testify before legislative committees or government agencies for retention of air service to their municipalities if it is perceived threatened. An influential congressman, persuaded by residents of his district that the preservation or strengthening of specific air service is desirable, will use their testimony to support his case. Local chambers of commerce may press for allocation of national airport development funds or similar programs to improve the local air service infrastructure and thus enhance local air transport potential.

Reflecting trends toward activist politics in many spheres of life, aviation consumer groups have been organized in several western countries. These associations offer discounts at certain hotels, evaluate airlines in newsletters or magazines, and, in the United States, have appeared before government regulatory commissions as representatives of airline passengers. At least one such American association has generated some controversy because it encourages its members to purchase flight insurance, a product of an industry with which its founder and president has had extensive association.[30]

General and aviation media also exercise some influence on air transport regulation. News reports of specific procedures or of aircraft accidents and investigations can stimulate public interest in and legislative inquiries of various aviation practices. Editorials and other forms of advocacy journalism may promote regulatory changes.

Summary

The nature of air transport regulation in a specific country is determined by the general political system of the country, the powers of its state agencies, and the ability of private nonstate groups to influence state policies. These general attitudes are more important than the public or private status of airline ownership in a country; the style, intensity, and comprehensiveness of regulation differs among states in which each system is prevalent and, in some countries, both state-owned and privately owned airlines exist side by side.

Intervention by nonaviation government agencies in economic and political regulation of a country's international air transport is common throughout the world. Nonaviation political and economic considerations may force an airline to use aircraft inappropriate to its needs or to operate commercially nonviable routes to certain foreign points for foreign policy reasons. Domestic political conditions may also affect regulatory practice, influencing, for example, which home-registered airline in a multiairline state is authorized to operate specific foreign routes.

Less nonaviation intervention has occurred in regulation of technical aspects of national policies related to international air transport, doubtless because the safety issues so prominent in technical regulation inhibit such interference. The technical area most subject to political meddling appears to be accident investigation, a topic of extraordinary sensitivity affecting the national pride in many countries. Reports of accidents may be withheld or distorted to protect the national image.

Operation of an air-transport regulatory system in a single state requires that some means of resolving differences between various interest groups be found. Although policy coordination conferences may be held, a power elite may emerge and come to dominate regulatory issues, regardless of formal protocols about cooperation and equality of different agencies. Ministries of foreign affairs and executive branches of government dominate international air transport regulation in most countries.

In addition to aviation and nonaviation government agencies, a number of nongovernmental entities exert influence on the formation of state air transport regulation. Aviation-related trade associations, professional groups and labor unions, locality promotion groups, media, and other nongovernmental institutions may all attempt to influence air-transport regulation.

The degree of decentralization of government authority within a country and the extent of pluralism of expression is likely to determine the nature of the country's air-transport regulatory system. The status of the particular country — its political and economic importance and its location relative to key routes — may influence the role of its regulatory system in the international regulatory framework.

Notes

1. Almond and Powell, *Comparative Politics*, p. 196.

2. See Jacques Lauriac, *Air Transport Policies Regarding Public and Private Airlines* (Paris: Institute of Air Transport, 1979), p. 58.

3. See Robert M. Kane and Allan D. Vose, *Air Transportation* (Dubuque: Wm. C. Brown Book Co., 1969), pp. 84-85.

4. David Corbett, *Politics and the Airlines* (Toronto: University of Toronto Press, 1965), p. 325.

5. U.S. Civil Aeronautics Board, *Aeronautical Statutes and Related Materials*, revised ed. (June 1, 1970), "Department of Transportation Act," October 15, 1966, Section 2, p. 105.

6. "FAA Reorganizes Flight Standards Unit," *Aviation Week* 111:6 (August 6, 1979), p. 32. Although the reorganization was initiated beforehand, the crash of the American Airlines DC-10 in Chicago on May 25, 1979 provided additional thrust to the effort.

7. Ibid.

8. U.S. Civil Aeronautics Board, *Aeronautical Statutes and Related Materials*, Section 5, p. 111.

9. In 1979, following the DC-10 crash in Chicago, most foreign airlines suspended operations of their DC-10s in response to the FAA revocation of the aircraft's type certificate. Twelve European countries authorized recertification of their DC-10s after only twelve days, although the FAA withheld certification of U.S.-registered DC-10s for thirty-eight days. Although many foreign-owned DC-10s were flying outside the United States after twelve days, none was allowed to enter U.S. airspace for the full thirty-eight days.

10. Criticism centered on FAA inspection procedures at the aircraft manufacturing facility and of airline maintenance procedures as well as on FAA handling of the revocation of the DC-10 Certificate of Airworthiness. See Richard Witkin, "On Trial—DC-10 and F.A.A.," *New York Times*, June 3, 1979, sec. 4, p. 5; Eugene Kozicharow, "European Carriers Resent FAA Procedures Confusion," *Aviation Week* 110:23 (June 23, 1979), pp. 17–18; Editorial, *Washington Post*, June 6, 1979, p. A20; Editorial, *New York Times*, June 8, 1979, p. A30; Witkin, "Uncertainties in DC-10 Inquiry," *New York Times*, June 13, 1979, p. D25; Bradley Graham and Larry Kramer, "FAA's Credibility is Diminishing, both in U.S. and in Europe," *Washington Post*, June 24, 1979, p. A4; David North, "Criticism of FAA Maneuvers Mounts," *Aviation Week* 110:26 (June 25, 1979), p. 33; Witkin, "Panel Finds Major Flaws in Certification of Aircraft," *New York Times*, June 19, 1980, p. A1.

11. See "Unit Wants New Service Notification," *Aviation Week* 109:10 (September 4, 1978), p. 40; Richard G. O'Lone, "Deregulation Spawns Airport Burdens," *Aviation Week* 110:15 (April 9, 1979), pp. 25–30; and Jacques Plaignaud, "Air Transport Deregulation and Airports," *ITA Bulletin* 14 (April 9, 1979), pp. 317–320. Conversely, some governments have cited airport congestion and other problems as excuses to reject agreements not wanted for more sensitive economic or political reasons. For example, Japan has claimed airport congestion and fuel shortages in refusing to negotiate agreements with certain governments; such problems have not arisen in Japanese negotiations with Arab oil-exporting states. See, for example, Laurance Doty, "U.S. Holds Firm on Japanese Bilateral," *Aviation*

Week 107:4 (July 25, 1977), p. 38, and "Governments Pressure Japan on Air Service Issues," *Aviation Daily* 243:13 (May 17, 1979), p. 110.

12. See, for example, "FAA Suspends U.S. Flights into Bombay," *Aviation Week* 102:25 (June 23, 1975), p. 23.

13. U.S. Civil Aeronautics Board, *Aeronautical Statutes and Related Materials*, revised ed. (June, 1970), "Federal Aviation Act of 1958," August 23, 1958, 72 Stat. 782, Section 801, p. 68.

14. *Ibid*, 72 Stat. 795, Section 1006, p. 85.

15. See, for example: James T. Wooten, "Braniff Awarded Disputed Route Over C.A.B. Vote," *New York Times*, December 22, 1977, p. A1; "Pan Am's Outrage," Editorial, *Washington Post*, December 27, 1977, p. A18; "Move Over, Pan Am," *The Economist* (London) 7009 (December 31, 1977), p. 44; "Playing Politics with Airlines," *Time* 111:3 (January 3, 1978), p. 46; and "CAB Chairman Talks to Interavia," *Interavia Air Letter* 8950 (February 22, 1978), pp. D, E.

16. See John W. Barnum, "Presidents and International Aviation," *Regulation* 2:3 (May/June 1978), pp. 43–44.

17. See U.S., President, *United States Policy for the Conduct of International Air Transportation Negotiations; August 21, 1978* (Washington, D.C.: Government Printing Office, 1978), for a statement that both indicates general U.S. international aviation policy and supports a specific U.S. bilateral air transport agreement concluded within the same time period.

18. See Corbett, *Politics and Airlines* p. 301.

19. *Boston Globe,* May 20, 1978, p. 12, and February 22, 1979, p. 13.

20. See, for example "New International Air Bill Favorably Received," *Aviation Daily* 238:22 (August 3, 1979), pp. 169–170, and David R. Griffiths, "International Policy Draws Focus," *Aviation Week* 109:9 (August 28, 1979), pp. 23–24.

21. U.S. Civil Aeronautics Board, *Aeronautical Statutes and Related Materials*, 72 Stat. 767 − 72 Stat. 770, Sections 408-414, pp. 45–50.

22. Liability in international air transport is discussed in several aviation law texts. See especially Georgette Miller, *Liability in International Air Transport* (Deventer, The Netherlands: Kluwer, 1977).

23. See, for example, U.S., Department of Commerce, *National Interest Aspects of the Private International Air Carrier System of the United States* (Washington, D.C.: Department of Commerce, 1974).

24. See, for example, "USAF Mounts Drive to Increase Airlift," *Aviation Week* 102:2 (January 13, 1975), pp. 18–19. The requested appropriations were not granted.

25. Laurence Doty, "U.S. May Harden User-Charge Attitude," *Aviation Week* 108:7 (February 13, 1977), pp. 29–30.

26. See, for example, "Administration Opposes Key Elements of Inter-

national Aviation Bill," *Aviation Daily* 238:36 (August 23, 1978), pp. 281–282, and "Sen. Cannon to Pursue Removal of Presidential Review Powers," *Aviation Daily* 238:38 (August 28, 1979), p. 307.

27. "CAB Should Approve IATA Commissions on Foreign Sales — Justice," *Aviation Daily* 241:19 (January 26, 1979), p. 150; "News Digest," *Aviation Week* 110:6 (February 5, 1979), p. 21: "CAB, Congress Split Over U.S. Air Policy Approach," *Airline Executive* 3:3 (March 1979), pp. 24–26; "CAB to Stick to IATA Review Schedule Despite Pleas," *Aviation Daily* 244:40 (August 27, 1979), p. 314; "State Dept. Hits CAB on IATA," *Aviation Week* 111:9 (August 27, 1979), pp. 23–24; "State Department Opposes CAB Order," *Flight* 116:3676 (September 1, 1979), p. 634; "Administration is Split on Cabotage Issue," *Aviation Daily* 244:37 (August 22, 1979), pp. 289–290.

28. "Washington Roundup," *Aviation Week* 108:13 (March 27, 1978), p. 13. See also: "State, OMB to Oppose Transfer of International Aviation Policy Authority," *Aviation Daily* 236:15 (March 21, 1978), p. 113; Richard T. Witkin, "Other Agencies Opposing Adams on Bid for Top Role on Air Pacts," *New York Times*, March 24, 1978, p. D1; "Kahn Call for CAB to Conduct Aviation Policy," *Interavia Air Letter* 8975 (March 31, 1978), p. 2; Bron Rek, "IATA's Hope: Deregulation without Destruction," *Flight* 114:3637 (December 2, 1978), pp. 1999–2000; and "State Official Sees IATA Order as Possible Tactical Error," *Aviation Daily* 245:3 (September 6, 1979), pp. 17–18.

29. U.S. Department of Transportation, Federal Aviation Administration, Order 1230.12, "Interagency Group on International Aviation," June 7, 1977.

30. "Senate Aviation Subcommittee Will Review Passenger Association," *Aviation Daily* 243:39 (June 25, 1979), pp. 316–317.

6

The International Regulatory Framework: Bilateral Regulation of Air-Transport Relations between Two States

Commercial air-transport service between two sovereign states is governed by the provisions of a bilateral air-transport agreement concluded by competent agencies of the two countries. The agreement represents a compromise, reached during negotiations, between the positions of the two parties. Although no standard format exists, either for the negotiations or for the agreement itself, certain practices and procedures have become established over the years. These practices and procedures are the topics of this chapter.

Elements of an Air-Transport Policy

A consulting firm under contract to three agencies of the U.S. government identified ten major elements of a national air-transport policy in 1975.[1] Each can be developed in several alternative ways. (The first five elements, according to the firm, are primary policy elements in that they define the key factors of the international air-transport system—city pairs, route networks, number of carriers, degree of competition. The second five elements are secondary.)

1. **Nature of government-to-government negotiations regarding service type.** The issue concerns the type or types of service involved in negotiations—scheduled passenger, charter, all-cargo. Two or all three types may be covered in one set of negotiations, or each may be negotiated separately.

2. **Nature of exchange of rights.** Exchange of rights may be negotiated according to the pattern established in the 1946 Bermuda agreement (Bermuda I), the 1979 Bermuda agreement, or some other norm. Rights are most frequently exhanged on a bilateral basis, but multilateral exhanges have been made by several groups of countries, such as several British Commonwealth states.

3. **Degree of restriction in certifying an operator.** It has long been accepted that every country owns and controls the airspace directly above its territory and is therefore entitled to impose restrictions on aircraft flying

through it.[2] The restrictions are of two types, geographic and type of service. The most basic conditions are embodied in a series of principles originally termed the "five freedoms"; in recent years, several additional freedoms have evolved. The first two freedoms are technical in nature and are the subject of the International Air Services Transit Agreement (IASTA), an international covenant accepted by most member-states of the International Civil Aviation Organization (ICAO). These freedoms are:

First Freedom. A civil aircraft has the right to overfly the territory of another country enroute to a third country, without landing, providing the overflown country is notified in advance and approval is given. (The approval is usually pro forma.) This freedom is also called the "right of innocent passage." Example: flights between Canada and Mexico overfly the United States.

Second Freedom. A civil aircraft of one country has the right to land in another country for technical reasons, such as refueling or maintenance, without offering any commercial service to or from that point (discharging or picking up traffic). This is often called a "technical stop," as opposed to a "traffic stop." Example: before the availability of long-range aircraft, Shannon and the Azores were often used as technical stops on transatlantic routes.

Third Freedom. An airline has the right to discharge commercial traffic originating in its own country of registry in another country.

Fourth Freedom. An airline has the right to discharge in its own country of registry commercial traffic originating in another country.

Fifth Freedom. An airline has the right to carry traffic between two countries outside its own country of registry as long as the flight originates or terminates in its own country of registry. Example: the London-Frankfurt segment on a route New York-London-Frankfurt operated by an American carrier is a fifth-freedom segment. Fifth-freedom traffic rights are also called "beyond rights."

Sixth Freedom. An airline has the right to carry traffic that has neither its origin nor its ultimate destination as its own country of registry, but passes through, connects at, or stops for a limited period of time (stopover) at a point in the country of registry. Example: many European carriers have arranged their timetables so that their Europe-bound transatlantic flights connect with their flights to eastern Europe or the Middle East. They endeavor to route transit traffic through their own countries, establishing the involved airport as a "gateway" to various destinations. This type of traffic is often referred to as "gateway traffic."

Seventh Freedom. An airline has the right to operate entirely outside its own country of registry while carrying traffic between other states. Example: an American carrier flies a shuttle service between Tokyo and Seoul.

Eighth Freedom. An airline has the right to carry commercial traffic between two points in the same foreign state. In shipping, this type of traffic is called "cabotage." Example: a Japanese airline carries commercial traffic between Honolulu and San Francisco.

Whereas the first two freedoms concern transit rights and do not involve commercial rights, the remaining freedoms deal specifically with traffic or commercial privileges. Third- and fourth-freedom traffic rights cover commercial traffic between two states for the airlines of the two states. Sometimes a single aircraft will shuttle back and forth between the two countries, thus operating a "turnaround service." Third- and fourth-freedom traffic rights constitute the basis of bilateral air-transport agreements and are usually comparatively easy to arrange.

Fifth-freedom traffic rights, or beyond rights, are generally much more difficult to secure because they are perceived to encroach upon the "natural" rights of the countries of the intermediate and beyond points. Countries whose airlines operate long routes with several intermediate stops (for example, Paris-Athens-Teheran-New Delhi-Bangkok-Hong Kong-Tokyo) must negotiate fifth-freedom rights for every sector (for example, Athens-Teheran, Athens-New Delhi, Athens-Bangkok, Athens-Hong Kong, Athens-Tokyo; Teheran-New Delhi, Teheran-Bangkok, etc.). If one country declines to approve fifth-freedom rights on a particular sector, the airline cannot carry any commercial traffic between the two points. A sector without commercial traffic rights is called a "blind sector."

Sixth-freedom traffic is a combination of third- and fourth-freedom service from two different countries that results in a fifth-freedom situation for both of these countries. For example, the connection of a Sabena New York-Brussels flight with a Sabena Brussels-Tel Aviv flight is fourth freedom on the New York-Brussels service, third freedom on the Brussels-Tel Aviv service, and fifth freedom between New York and Tel Aviv. Such connecting or gateway traffic is of great importance to Sabena, KLM, Swissair, and several other airlines whose home airports are located advantageously in western and west-central Europe; with fairly small home markets unable to fully support their extensive networks, these airlines must attract substantial transit traffic to justify operation of various routes. Most advertise heavily for transit traffic, urging passengers in North America to use their airlines for one-stop service to, say, eastern Europe or the Middle East. Prominent in their advertising is the suggestion that Swissair, for example, offers far more comfortable and gracious service to Bulgaria than does Balkan, the Bulgarian carrier. The involved transit airlines deny that such traffic represents fifth-freedom rights and is thus subject to negotiations; it is, they say, simply a result of their ability to schedule their flights well, provide a needed service, and market their product. Airline and government authorities in the United States have charged some of the European airlines with operating as parasites off the "natural" American market, usurping traffic that should belong to U.S. carriers, at least on the transatlantic leg between the United States and an intermediate European point (where an American passenger could then board a European airline flight to Sofia because no American carrier finds it economically feasible to provide transatlantic service to Bulgaria). Some Americans claim that the European airlines have no right to advertise such transit service as a through service. The issue is one of controversy in the international air-transport community.[3]

Seventh-freedom traffic is so rarely allowed by sovereign states that it merits little discussion. In its earliest days of independence, a developing country lacking the capability to operate its own air service may allow a "merchant carrier" or the airline of the former colonial power to provide air-transport links between its own and foreign territory. More likely, the developing country would establish its own carrier and wet-lease aircraft for its operation.

Eighth freedom or cabotage traffic is generally allowed by sovereign states only when home-registered airlines are faced with a sudden, large-scale shortage of aircraft that serously damages the national economy or inconveniences a great number of passengers. In 1979 the Civil Aeronautics Board permitted several non-U.S. transpacific carriers (Korean Air Lines, Japan Air Lines, China Airlines, Air New Zealand, Qantas, Philippine Airlines, Singapore Airlines) to carry revenue traffic between Honolulu and California points when U.S. flag service usually provided on these routes was sharply reduced as a result of a strike against one major U.S. airline and the temporary grounding by the Federal Aviation Administration of all DC-10 aircraft.

Another aspect of geographic restriction is designation of terminals. The existence within a country of multiple attractive designations provides it with additional negotiating power. Should a foreign carrier already serving New York, for example, also want to implement service to Chicago or another U.S. city, its country of registry must negotiate the issue with the United States. The Americans would demand privileges in return. The United States leads all countries in the number of cities with international air-service links; ten to fifteen major urban terminals receive international flights. Canada, West Germany, Italy, India, and the People's Republic of China are among other countries with multiple international air terminals.

Great Britain derives great negotiating advantage from its control over Hong Kong.

The issue of multiple terminals also applies to single cities served by several airports. Use of a specific airport by foreign carriers may be restricted because of overcrowding, government policy to develop another airport, government intention to give the home airline an operating or marketing advantage, or some other reason. Usage of a particular terminal thus becomes a matter of national air transport policy and may be a subject of bilateral air transport negotiations.

Restrictions may also be imposed on the number of carriers permitted to serve a specific market. The United States usually strives to include in its bilateral agreements the right to designate multiple U.S. airlines to serve routes between the United States and a foreign country. Most other countries, however, have only one international airline or designate only one of several as "chosen instrument" for a specific route. Frequently, they demand reciprocity from the United States, refusing to allow multiple American carriers to serve a single route. They may be more liberal regarding different terminals, permitting different carriers to serve different airports.

Service restrictions concern limitations to specific types of service — scheduled passenger service, cargo service, and charter service. Governments have several options in developing a policy to guide negotiations of each: (1) a separate policy for each is developed and negotiated separately; (2) a unified policy encompasses all three and is negotiated as a single component; and (3) no differentiation between the three types is made, either in policy or in negotiations, thus allowing designated airlines to implement any service type at its own discretion.

4. **Capacity controls.** Capacity refers to the available payload — the number of commercial seats and/or tons of cargo — on a specific aircraft type multiplied by the flight frequency of that aircraft type during a specific time period (usually one week) over a specific route. The object of air transport capacity control is the maintenance of a general balance between capacity supply and traffic demand. "General balance" is not synonymous with precise equality. On an annual basis, scheduled service capacity should exceed traffic demand by a significant level; the surplus is available to absorb late bookings, traffic density variations on different sectors of a multistop route, seasonal variations (often managed by changing type of aircraft on the route, using lesser-capacity aircraft in off seasons), and directional traffic imbalance (especially important regarding cargo). The acceptable amount of surplus on most scheduled passenger routes is usually judged to be between 30 and 40 percent of capacity annually; a commercial

payload of 50 to 70 percent is generally considered the breakeven load factor, the commercial load an aircraft should carry on a given route to break even financially. (The breakeven load factor varies according to a number of criteria, including the efficiency of the aircraft used and revenue distortions caused by promotional fares.) When an airline consistently fails to achieve its breakeven load factor, capacity is in excess of actual need. Most governments and airlines prefer to institute some type of control mechanism to eliminate excess capacity and restore a capacity level responsive to traffic demand.

Capacity control policy differs among governments. The United States has generally favored fewer restrictions, preferring that airlines be allowed to institute capacity at their own discretion, according to the 1946 Bermuda agreement pattern. Should one carrier on a route consider that another has offered capacity in excess of reasonable traffic expectations, it can request that the respective governments initiate an ex post facto review. Few other governments support the American position. Almost all insist on negotiation of capacity control prior to implementation of service.

Capacity control can be negotiated by the carriers themselves, by governments as part of a standard bilateral air transport agreement, or by conferences of either governments or airlines operating commercial air service on major routes. In practice, either carriers or governments negotiate capacity on a bilateral basis, usually selecting frequency of service as the variable to be adjusted.

Adjustment of aircraft type may also be used to regulate capacity, each carrier agreeing to operate a specific or similar aircraft as a means of ensuring capacity equivalence. More often, however, insistence on aircraft equivalence is intended to restrict the entrance of a new type into the market in the service of one carrier. Airlines without the new type perceive a marketing disadvantage and seek to limit the use of the newer aircraft. The United States and Italy have clashed twice over such an issue, the first time in 1964 when TWA sought to introduce jet cargo service between the United States and Italy before Alitalia was able to offer comparable flights. Italy objected again several years later when Pan Am wanted to inaugurate Boeing 747s on its Rome service before Alitalia had widebody aircraft in its fleet. Soviet-bloc airlines, forced to delay acquisition of widebody aircraft until a Soviet model became available in the early 1980s, persuaded their owner-governments to prohibit foreign carriers from operating reciprocal routes with western-manufactured widebodies until that time. Few governments refusing to admit foreign widebody aircraft for reasons of pride are willing to acknowledge the pride factor. Most claim inadequate airport facilities or some other condition that could be overcome if the will to do so existed.[4]

Capacity control is often more stringently applied on fifth-freedom-right sectors than on third- and fourth-freedom operations. Some governments impose sales restrictions on fifth-freedom sectors originating in their territories, limiting foreign carriers to sales of, say, fifteen coach and five first-class tickets on specific fifth-freedom sectors. An airline operating a long, multistop route may have different capacity rights on each sector.

Although most governments and/or carriers choose to negotiate capacity restrictions and include them in bilateral air-transport agreements, some governments impose restrictions by fiat, implementing a policy with which other governments or foreign airlines do not agree but are powerless to affect. For example, the Soviet Union and most east European countries require that their own airlines be general sales agents in their own countries for foreign carriers. Foreign airlines are not permitted to sell tickets in Moscow for their own flights from Moscow; they must refer prospective passengers to Aeroflot, which routinely tries to persuade or deceive them into flying on the Soviet carrier. Capacity can also be manipulated by forcing a foreign airline into an unfavorable arrival/departure time, inconvenient airport-terminal location, limitations on advertising, or other measures not applied to the home carrier. In all such instances, foreign airline flights leaving the country carry far less payload than those entering the country, thus effecting a substantial directional traffic imbalance/excess capacity situation.

Joint Operation and Pooling. In addition to regulating capacity by frequency adjustments, aircraft type specifications, or manipulative/discriminatory measures, capacity can be controlled by reciprocal airlines entering into a joint operation (shared revenues and expenditures, sometimes joint use of a single aircraft) or a pooling agreement (shared revenues). Pooling, in its several versions, is the more common arrangement. The basic pooling agreement involves the pooling of all revenues earned by different carriers on a single route and allocation of the funds according to a specific formula. In some agreements, revenues are divided evenly, regardless of which carrier sells more tickets. In other arrangements, carriers pool revenues only up to a certain percentage of seats sold, for example, carriers pool revenues on seats sold until the aircraft is 70 percent full and any revenues earned after this figure is reached may be retained by the carrier that sells the additional tickets. Other pool agreements have more complex revenue allocation schemes. Most pooling systems provide for cooperative scheduling and some for joint marketing as well. Both cooperative scheduling and revenue sharing are factors in capacity control.

Proponents of pooling claim that it encourages more efficient use of equipment, reduces operating costs, lessens the need for heavy expenditures in marketing because competition is reduced, and offers protection against illegal discounting on ticket fares because a carrier would only diminish its revenue from the pool by putting less into it. Opponents of pooling charge that passengers are inconvenienced because the lack of competition on pooled routes reduces the incentive for good service.

Pooling agreements are common in Europe and on intercontinental routes connecting Europe with Canada, South America, and Australia and the Far East. Weak airlines from developing countries and communist states often favor pooling to ensure a greater traffic share than they could otherwise expect; pooling with a stronger western airline allows them to benefit from the latter's marketing expertise, superior reputation, and greater international traffic base. Some western carriers also favor pooling with communist state airlines, believing that such agreements provide protection against illegal discounting and marketing restrictions, both widely practiced by Aeroflot and the east European carriers. For most western carriers, pooling is a matter of some flexibility, depending upon the conditions prevalent on each specific route — most importantly, the traffic base, anticipated market share, anticipated extent of illegal discounting, and relative strength of the other carrier(s) on the route. If it perceives itself likely to capture a strong majority share of the market in competition with a weaker airline, a carrier is unlikely to favor a pooling agreement. Pooling is not practiced on any routes involving the United States, either by U.S. or foreign airlines. American aviation policy considers pooling incompatible with U.S. philosophy on competition. Until the CAB reinterpretation in 1978 of Sections 412(b) and 414 of the Federal Aviation Act of 1958, the Civil Aeronautics Board had been invested with the authority to approve pooling and relieve carriers from antitrust regulation, but implementation of such provisions was discussed only during the most servere excess capacity crises.

Capacity control can also be extended to cargo flights and charter/supplemental operations. Policy issues for governments regarding capacity control are the following: (1) the extent of control over each type of traffic; (2) whether each type will be negotiated separately or whether two or all three types will be negotiated in a comprehensive package; (3) the role of pooling; and (4) the functions of government and airlines in capacity negotiations.

5. **Pricing.** Pricing, or the setting of international tariffs, has traditionally been the major task of IATA Tariff Conferences. Organized on a regional basis, the conferences are open to IATA member airlines with international routes in the appropriate regions. Fares must be established unanimously by participating members. Even before the disruptions caused by the CAB show-cause order in 1978, however, a number of carriers with sizeable international route systems remained outside the IATA Conference system and reached independent fare agreements with reciprocal airlines. Some of these independently reached tariffs reflected existing fares and

rates on similar routes operated by IATA carriers, but others deviated by significant amounts from IATA standards. Additionally, many IATA airlines nominally accepting IATA fares routinely offered heavily discounted tickets to the general public. Thus, although the IATA Tariff Conferences dominated pricing procedures, several alternative mechanisms also existed. Following the 1978 CAB show-cause order and subsequent IATA reorganization, a number of airlines withdrew from IATA Tariff Conferences; these carriers and additional American airlines initiating international air service under CAB deregulation policies have implemented new fares on their own.

The principal aim of U.S. deregulation policy is protection and enhancement of consumer rights. In economic terms the policy calls for reduction of air fares to the lowest possible point. Some other governments, particularly those with inefficient state-owned carriers, support high tariffs to cover their higher costs. Many countries with unfavorable trade balances view international ticket sales as an important source of hard currency and thus also back high ticket costs. Governments/airlines holding different positions on the price issue may find it very difficult to reach agreement in bilateral negotiations. After determining the basic policy position on high or low tariffs, governments have the following policy options on methods of deciding tariffs: (1) adherence to IATA Tariff Conference procedures; (2) negotiation of pricing by carriers flying a specific route; (3) adoption of an open-rate system, allowing each airline to establish its own fares independently; (4) negotiation of pricing by governments; or (5) surveillance and approval by government(s) of fares established by conferences or airlines. Government pricing policy may also involve encouragement or discouragement of airline illegal discounting of established fares.

6. **Government support.** Government financial support for national airlines can be expressed in numerous ways, some of which have been noted earlier in this book. Government agencies may construct and maintain airports, air navigation facilities and services, training centers, and other institutions of substantial importance to commercial air transport. In most countries, the national government is the key source of support; in the United States, regional and municipal authorities support most major airports. National governments may subsidize flag carrier operations that cannot be sustained by airline revenues, especially for foreign policy or some other nonaviation government reason. Governments may also support airline acquisition of new aircraft through subsidy, provision of interest-free or low-interest loans, or some other assistance. Almost all governments require that government employees flying abroad on official business patronize the national flag carrier as far as possible. Some governments strongly urge private institutions and individuals to do so as well. Policy

issues for governments concern the types of support they wish to extend. In many countries, the support question is resolved less by rational discussion during routine evaluation of the airline than by application of emergency measures in response to a financial crises.

7. **Enforcement.** Enforcement of bilateral air transport agreements requires special mechanisms. A government might decide to support any of the following: (1) negotiations between designated agencies of the governments involved; (2) hearings by panel of representatives of designated agencies of governments involved; (3) referral to an appropriate judicial body; (4) hearings by a panel representing noninvolved airlines; or (5) third-party arbitration. Adoption of a specific policy does not guarantee its implementation; if other governments involved in the conflict find the policy objectionable they may force adjustments.

8. **User fees and charges.** The United States and many other governments base charges of airport user fees and other expenses on rules established by the International Civil Aviation Organization (ICAO). They may also be negotiated as part of a bilateral air transport agreement or as a separate agreement, or be determined by a single government according to its own standards and then imposed on all airlines using the airport. Some governments exempt their own state-held carriers from all or some of the fees and charges levied against foreign carriers.[5]

9. **Environment.** A number of governments impose their own environmental controls—principally noise suppression and air pollution reduction—on all airlines using specific airports. Curfews, designed to reduce noise during normal rest hours, are in wide use. Takeoff and landing patterns may be adjusted to avoid or limit excessive noise over residential areas. Alternatives to government-established controls are adoption of standards set by an international agency or imposition of no controls at all.

10. **Security.** Many governments impose their own security standards on all carriers serving their country, some even requiring that all flights originating in other states be subject to the same security procedures in the foreign country as in the standard-setting country. Alternatives to imposition of regulation by a single country are: (1) bilateral negotiation of security procedures; (2) adoption of standards established by an international organization; and (3) neither formally developing one's own standards nor adopting those of others, but relying on security practices widely in use in other countries to extend to one's own country sufficient protection. The need for a firm security policy differs from government to government in accordance with a particular airline's appeal as a terrorist target, presence of

terrorist groups, ability of citizens to leave the country by other means, and several other factors. The wide variety of government perceptions on the threat of terrorism has rendered the establishment of internationally accepted security standards very difficult.

Some western governments (and some opposition parties as well) publish policy positions on some or all ten aviation issues. They are far less likely to publish declarations on the influence of partisan domestic politics or foreign relations issues in the determination of international air transport policy. In numerous instances, nonaviation political factors have overwhelmed official air transport policies of governments, causing major inconsistencies in agreements and confusion among interested parties.

Domestic political interference in international air transport may be a function of executive-branch appeasement of influential local politicians who promise support on other issues in return for increased international air service from their areas. Alternatively, political support may be exchanged for governmental action beneficial to a locally based airline. An instance of presidential interference in a transatlantic route award case was cited in a previous chapter. Other countries with multiple international airlines — Canada, Britain, France, and Japan, among them — have also seen political pressure exerted on behalf of one carrier.

Political or political-economic interference in international air transport is far more varied than in domestic civil aviation, if only because of the diversity of political and economic systems in the modern world. In a previous chapter, the use of bilateral air-transport agreements as political instruments by the United States and Japan to gain favor with Arab countries (the United States in 1976 with Jordan and Syria, Japan in 1977 with Iraq) was discussed. A politically similar situation occurred in 1979 when the Department of State exerted substantial pressure on the Civil Aeronautics Board to approve a blocked-space agreement between Pan Am and Saudia, despite strong CAB feelings that the particular agreement was anticompetitive; according to the CAB, it threatened to bar other American carriers from service to Saudi Arabia. Delicate political relations between the United States and Saudi Arabia were more important than anticompetitive implications, argued the Department of State. The CAB approved the agreement "under duress."[6] Later in 1979 the CAB yielded to Department of State pressure in a conflict with the People's Republic of China, reversing an earlier decision not to expedite consideration of a proposed Pan AM/CAAC (the Chinese carrier) charter program. The initial CAB denial was based on the same concern that the board noted in the Pan AM/Saudia case, that is, that Pan Am participation in the program would give it an advantage over other American carriers that sought entry into the market and the resulting reduction in competition might adversely affect the

American public. Department of State officials said they encouraged expedition of the proposal so as (1) not to embarrass Vice President Walter Mondale, who was visiting China at the time, and (2) to motivate China to begin negotiations with the United States for scheduled service.[7]

A long-standing political/military trade-off explains American acquiescence to Icelandair low-fare service between the United States and certain European points (usually less prominent centers, such as Luxembourg and Glasgow). The route is permitted in exchange for Iceland's membership in the North Atlantic Treaty Organization (NATO) and location of a key U.S. Air Force base on its terrritory. From time to time, leftist political interests in Iceland have vigorously protested the presence of the American base, threatening to close the facilities upon attaining government power. On such occasions, the U.S. government has been quick to remind Reykjavik of the terms for continued Icelandair low-fare service between the United States and Europe. Similar warnings were extended in the early 1970s when the Soviet Union sought Aeroflot traffic rights into Iceland; concerned about the potential for electronic surveillance and other espionage activity provided by such flights, American authorities warned Iceland of the vulnerability of Icelandair-U.S. operating rights if the security of the military base was jeopardized. (The military base/low fares trade-off is seldom mentioned publicly; the American explanation for the low-fare service is usually that the Icelandair service operates at a substantial disadvantage with inferior aircraft and a compulsory stop in Iceland. However, in recent years, Icelandair has acquired competitive equipment and has secured permission from the United States for some nonstop service between the U.S. and certain European points. American authorities have approved the latter on the grounds of public interest, noting that no other service between the United States and Luxembourg existed.[8])

The Soviet Union has used civil aviation as a political instrument on numerous occasions, perhaps none more blatant than its efforts to force western recognition of East Germany by insisting that Aeroflot use East Berlin as an intermediate stop on its routes to West Germany and the United States. The Soviet carrier maintains commercially nonviable service to many developing countries; political presence and espionage activity are probably the most important factors in sustaining these routes.[9]

Exploitation of international summit meetings for the extraction of air transport rights is a common Soviet tactic, particularly when the summit partner is not eager to conclude the agreement sought by the USSR. Under pressure to give tangible form to the expressions of goodwill common at summit meetings, the parties involved may find new or expanded air-transport agreements a satisfactory instrument, especially if other issues are not adequately resolved. In 1973 the Soviets used the Brandt-Brezhnev summit in Bonn to extract from West Germany a one-sided supplement to the existing Soviet-West German bilateral agreement.[10] Also in 1973, the Nixon administration forced the CAB to delay publication of a complaint against more than one hundred Aeroflot violations of American air law, fearing an annoncement close to the visit of Brezhnev to the United States might embarrass the Soviets. The administration then forced the Department of State and the CAB into previously unscheduled air-transport negotiations with the USSR before and during the summit meeting; neither government body nor Pan Am favored the negotiations, but the Soviet Union threatened the success of the summit unless the negotiations were held. The USSR failed to achieve all of its aviation goals. However it did obtain several valuable concessions from the forced negotiations — the most important of these were access to the U.S. charter market and the addition of Washington, D.C., as a U.S. destination. Pan Am was awarded nominally equivalent, but effectively meaningless rights: access to the Soviet charter market and Leningrad as an additional Soviet destination. Given political controls in the USSR, Pan Am had no reasonable hope of generating charter traffic there, and Leningrad was (and is) not a viable transatlantic destination under conditions imposed by the Soviets. The Soviet Union was able to exercise its rights in the vastly more hospitable American political and economic environment. The agreement was assailed by many in Washington as extortion by the Soviets to assure a smooth summit meeting.[11] In 1975 a bilateral air-transport agreement that Luxembourg had not sought was concluded under pressure during a state visit to Moscow by the Luxembourg Grand Duke and Grand Duchess.

In 1977 the Executive branch of the U.S. government intervened in congressional hearings on the noise level of the Concorde supersonic jet. Both the British and French were eager to inaugurate transatlantic service with their jointly produced aircraft, but objections to the Concorde sonic boom and other noise problems forced a delay and eventual congressional hearings. National Security Adviser Zbigniew Brzezinski instructed two Department of Transportation officials not to testify, fearing that anti-Americanism aroused by U.S. objection to the Concorde might boost the fortunes of a Socialist-Communist coalition in forthcoming French elections.[12]

From 1968 until 1978, Pan Am maintained service between New York and Moscow one or twice weekly via a European intermediate point. Despite efforts to build traffic, obstacles to fair competition imposed by the Soviet Union precluded any possibility of economic viability for the American service. Periodic suggestions by Pan Am to the Department of State that the carrier might suspend its Moscow operation were answered by admonitions that such an action would not redound to Pan Am's favor in future dealings with the federal government. The New York-Moscow route was judged by the government to be valuable as a symbol of détente. In

1978, despite the previous government requests that it maintain service, Pam Am suspended its Moscow route. Early in 1979, William Seawall, chief executive of the airline, said that Pan Am had received "signals" from the U.S. government that there would be no more federal pressure on American carriers to serve foreign points for political reasons. American airlines were to plan their international networks on the basis of economics.[13]

If political intervention is inappropriate in specific instances, economic factors can be exploited to influence international air-transportation negotiations. For many years Ireland denied traffic rights in Dublin to American carriers, limiting that city to Aer Lingus on transatlantic routes while confining Pan Am and TWA to Shannon, a facility that had been built to serve as an intermediate refueling point between North America and Europe before the advent of long-range jet aircraft. The Irish claimed that American abandonment of Shannon would bring economic hardship upon southwestern Ireland, especially on the area's tourist industry. To dull the impact of such an occurrence, the United States is said to have offered to encourage American industries to establish operations in the region.[14] Under increasing American pressure, the Irish finally allowed U.S. carrier service to Dublin—but only with an intermediate stop in Shannon.

In 1976, seeking to acquire traffic rights in Toronto to supplement those already held in Montreal, Greece encountered firm opposition from the Canadian government which claimed that Toronto Airport was too crowded. Greece countered with offers of several multimillion-dollar concession deals, majority control in an oil prospecting consortium, an expensive property in Athens for Canadian diplomatic use, and permission for a Canadian archaeological group to dig in Athens.[15]

Dutch negotiators, always aggressive in negotiating international traffic rights for KLM, have little to offer in return. Amsterdam has limited attraction for foreign carriers. To compensate for lack of aviation reciprocity, the Dutch frequently resort to threats on nonaviation issues. For example, the Netherlands has threatened to withhold (1) contributions to NATO until the United States granted specific concessions to KLM, and (2) support for Israel in Common Market negotiations unless Israel granted KLM additonal frequencies on the Amsterdam-Tel Aviv route.[16]

Such a negotiating tool, whether political or economic, is known as a "nonaviation quid pro quo," that is, a nonaviation-related offer in exchange for air traffic rights. Nonaviation quid pro quos are seldom acknowledged publicly; they do not appear in conventional bilateral air transport agreements, but are formalized in "confidential memoranda of understanding" (variously abbreviated CMU or MoU) negotiated by governments. The major policy issue for countries is the extent to which they intent to exploit nonaviation quid pro quos in their negotiating practices. A centrally controlled government will find it easier to include nonaviation issues than will a more representative government; a centrally controlled state may also find inclusion of nonaviation issues administratively unavoidable. Small countries with few attractions to lure foreign airlines may find offers of nonaviation privileges to other countries indispensable for sercuring the international air traffic rights they covet.

In addition to nonaviation enticements extended for traffic privileges, aircraft sales are also used as ploys in negotiations. Airlines considering purchase of British- or French-manufactured aircraft have frequently been promised increased traffic rights into British or French territory as an incentive. In countries where both the aircraft industry and airlines are state-owned, such a policy is far easier to implement than in the United States.

Negotiations sought by one country can be exploited by another to acquire additional traffic privileges or to influence a third country, thus forcing the original applicant into situations it did not foresee. In 1978, for example, Malaysia refused to grant overflight rights to Britain for operation of Concorde flights between London and Singapore. The Malaysians claimed the Concorde would be environmentally harmful, but the British believed the refusal to be a ploy for extracting more extensive traffic rights for the Malaysian airline in Hong Kong and London.[17] In 1979 the United States and South Korea concluded a very liberal Memorandum of Understanding, awarding substantial traffic rights to new American carriers serving Korea. If implemented, the new flights could establish Seoul as a major Pacific gateway, a development that might persuade Japan to be more forthcoming in transpacific negotiations with the United States.[18]

The Process of Bilateral Negotiations

Two major approaches to initiation of bilateral air-transport negotiations are commonly used. A government wishing to start negotiations may approach the appropriate state agency of the second country, usually the foreign ministry or, less often, an aviation regulatory agency. In other instances, negotiations may be opened (or renewed) according to provisions of a previous agreement between the two states. General bilateral economic or cultural agreements may contain clauses calling for air-transport negotiations within a specific time period. Existing air-transport agreements may include provisions for review at specific intervals.

Negotiating delegations usually include representatives from at least three entities: the foreign ministry (possibly a negotiations specialist and an expert on the partner country), the relevant government aviation regulatory agencies, and the airline operating (or designated to operate) the route. Because several American carriers may operate a single route in competition with each other, the Air Transport Association of America (ATA), the national airline trade association, represents American airlines in bilateral negotiations. In some countries, a fourth party, the airline trade union, is also represented in the negotiating delegation. If service between the United States and a particular country is perceived to operate under unusual or difficult circumstances, a representative of the designated American carrier may be included in the U.S. delegation. Such a situation occurs infrequently.

A country initiating negotiations frequently presents its route proposals to the second country before the actual discussions begin. If that country objects to the proposals and is not obligated by existing agreements to conduct negotiations at specific times or within a specific interval after receiving a request for negotiations, it may refuse to commence discussions. The initiating government may then resubmit its proposals at a later date, or invoke nonaviation quid pro quos to enhance the appeal of negotiations. These may be punitive threats—such as the previously cited Dutch warnings that Holland would reduce its NATO commitment if the United States refused to grant additional traffic rights to KLM—or enticements, such as offering assurances of favorable future trade deals or support on issues to be brought before international organizations.

The key task of bilaterral air-transport negotiations is the determination of an equitable route exchange expressed in route rights of approximate equal market value awarded to each state. Market value is measured by (1) entry points or destinations, (2) traffic rights, (3) market opportunity and accessibility, (4) market potential, and (5) revenue potential.

An exchange of entry points or destinations based on reciprocal access to the most important commercial (or, alternatively, political, tourist, or other category) centers of the negotiating countries does not necessarily constitute a fair exchange. One such city may offer substantially greater marketing possibilities than the other due to population size, hinterland characteristics, standard of living, travel patterns of populace, or other factors. The value of New York as a destination is unmatched by any other city subject to transatlantic negotiations; foreign countries requesting access to it for their carriers may be asked by the United States for compensation in another aspect of route exchange.

The major issue in negotiation of traffic rights is usually the granting of fifth- and sixth-freedom or "beyond" rights. These rights may be more valuable than third- and fourth-freedom or "turnaround" rights, particularly on long routes. For example, the around-the-world service operated by Pan Am would be commercially nonviable without fifth-freedom rights from various Asian countries.

Market opportunity and accessibility to traffic may be limited for foreign carriers in certain countries due to coincidental or deliberate discriminatory factors extant in the local air-transport industry. For example, the home airline may possess such strong identity among potential customers that traffic rights—especially fifth-freedom rights—granted to foreign carriers offer little promise of traffic. Persons purchasing tickets for flights between London and Frankfurt will "naturally" consider British Airways or Lufthansa before even becoming aware that Pan Am, TWA, Air-India, and several other fifth-freedom airlines also offer service on the sector. The Soviet Union and several other party-states insist on appointing their own carriers as general sales agents for all airlines serving their countries, but their own airlines systematically deter potential passengers from patronizing the foreign carriers they purport to represent. Alternative transport modes may also restrict market opportunity and accessibility.

A study of various economic and political trends will suggest the market potential of an international route. For example, a liberalization of foreign-investment laws in a country might lead to an increase in business traffic between it and other states. Conversely, political unrest will reduce the traffic potential of a country. Airlines themselves may try to enhance the traffic potential of points on their networks by building hotels, operating automobile rental agencies, and otherwise improving the tourism infrastructure. Several large international carriers have invested heavily in such ventures; perhaps the best known relationships are those of Pan Am with Intercontinental Hotel Corporation and TWA with Hilton International.

Revenue potential depends on the system of tariffs applicable to the route. Important components of the system that affect the revenue yield of a given route are: the per-kilometer tariff, the prevalence of promotional fares, and the extent of illegal discounting. All of these conditions vary from region to region of the global air-transport network. For example, per-kilometer tariffs are lower on the North Atlantic route than on the North Pacific route. Promotional fares and illegal discounting tend to be more common on routes with excess capacity. Large-scale illegal discounting of ticket fares is routinely practiced by some airlines, infrequently employed by others.

Countries may choose to negotiate each one of these factors separately in relation to the particular route or routes under consideration, or may try to incorporate them in one of the five standard negotiating methods presently employed in bilateral air-transport relations. Most common among these methods is that of granting reciprocity in rights. In one variation of reciprocity, "visual reciprocity" or "double tracking," the two states agree to mutual air service on the same third- and fourth-freedom route, for example, carriers of the United States and the Netherlands each operate service between New York and Amsterdam under identical conditions. Another variation, "mirror image" or "equivalent exchange reciprocity," refers to an exchange that includes equivalent, but not identical, fifth-freedom rights. If an American carrier is granted a New York-Amsterdam-

Vienna-Rome route, the Dutch airline might be granted a Vienna-Amsterdam-New York-Atlanta route.

A second method of route exchange is known as the "most favored nation" approach. A country, considering itself equivalent to a second country, demands the same traffic rights that the other country enjoys with third countries. The key issue in this procedure is the determination of equivalence. Although two countries may be approximately equal in size and population, they may differ substantially in criteria of importance to air transportation, such as geographic situation (relation to other countries), tourism potential, or number of possible destinations.

The "lost opportunity" approach is a third method of route exhange. In this approach potential losses to airlines, if they do not acquire the routes under consideration, are evaluated. For example, if the United States and France fail to reach agreement on transatlantic routes, the United States loses less because its airlines could still carry passengers across the Atlantic to, say, Brussels where they could transfer to other airlines for flights to Paris. Air France could fly its passengers to Brussels where they could transfer to other carriers for flights to New York, but the Air France loss of transatlantic revenue is likely to be far greater than the American airline loss of Brussels-Paris revenue. Although Air France could presumably preserve North Atlantic revenues by flying American passengers to/from connecting flights in Montreal, it would lose direct access to the American market which is much larger than the French market. For this reason, the route is much more important to France than to the United States. The United States might feel justified in demanding compensation—in the form of extra capacity, additional traffic rights, or nonaviation quid pro quos—from France for the greater value the latter derives from the route.

A fourth method of route exchange may be called the "equivalent access" approach. This procedure emphasizes access to equivalent markets, although the relevant market for one airline may be a fifth freedom sector and for another airline a sixth freedom route.

Finally, a route exchange may be continent upon the granting of a nonaviation quid pro quo by one side as compensation for aviation rights granted by the other. A country without much aviation bargaining power may offer political, economic, military, or other concessions to obtain the aviation rights it desires. Air transport agreements are frequently negotiated in the context of broader trade agreements.

Format of Bilateral Air-Transport Agreements

No single internationally mandated format for bilateral air transport agreements exists. In general terms, commonality in format is prevalent within certain groups of governments, such as British Commonwealth countries and France and former French colonies. If the official languages of the two countries are different, the agreement is usually bilingual. If the two languages do not include one of the five UN languages (English, French, Spanish, Russian, Chinese), the agreement may be signed and executed in one of the these languages as well. The formal bilateral air transport agreement usually includes the following articles:

1. Preamble or statement of purpose
2. Choice of languages; if more than one language is used in the agreement, which is governing in case of dispute
3. Definitions — territory, airports, specified routes, all-cargo service, designated airline, revenue passengers, tariff, user charges, and other terms to be used in the agreement and annexes
4. Granting of rights — general statement of principles, referral to specifications in annexes
5. Designation and authorization of airlines
6. Application of laws including jurisdiction over foreign airlines
7. Designation of competent authorities including responsibilities of specific government aviation and other relevant agencies in both countries
8. Mutual recognition of each country's documentation, such as, certificates of airworthiness, crew licenses
9. Documents that must be kept onboard aircraft, including registration, Certificate of Airworthiness, crew licenses, log books, passenger lists, and freight manifests
10. Agreement to adhere to relevant ICAO standards such as navigation aids, registration of agreements and others
11. Procedures to be followed in emergency landings, accidents, or disasters on or over territory of signatory states; access to accident-involved aircraft, crew, passengers, freight; investigation procedures
12. Security procedures
13. Environmental protection and noise abatement procedures
14. Procedures for notification of schedule changes
15. Procedures for commercial operations, such as, maintenance of technical and commercial staff in foreign country (housing, location, and other necessities), issuance of long-term crew visas, advertising and sales regulations, and remittance of revenues
16. Tariffs and commissions
17. User charges
18. Customs duties, including exemptions for spare parts, fuel lubricants, and food onboard aircraft
19. Flight planning and air control procedures
20. Charter flights

21. Consultations
22. Procedures for amending the agreement
23. Procedures for terminating the agreement

Specific route schedules, capacity regulations, and tariff accords are usually included in separate annexes to the main agreement. The order of articles and annexes differs among various agreements. Some governments may prefer to combine, add, or delete certain provisions. According to custom of the signatory governments, air-transport agreements may be concluded as treaties, conventions, agreements, protocols, or exchanges of notes. In some countries, the head of state or an appointed representative thereof is empowered to make international agreements; in other countries, formal international agreements must be ratified by a legislature.[19]

Copies of bilateral air-transport agreements are usually printed by government publishing agencies and, in most western countries, are available in documentation libraries and in government bookstores. ICAO member-states are required to file copies of all of their agreements with that organization.

Particulars of nonaviation quid pro agreements, usually expressed in a "confidential memorandum of understanding," are not included in published bilateral air transport agreements. The memoranda of understanding are customarily filed in foreign ministries and are unavailable for public scrutiny.

Permits

If a government wishes to allow a foreign carrier to operate air service to its territory, but is unwilling or unable to conclude a formal air-transport agreement with that carrier's country of registration, it may issue an operating permit to the airline. Permits are usually issued by a ministry of transport, rather than by a ministry of foreign affairs, and contain most of the operational and commercial provisions of a standard bilateral agreement. Most permits are subject to annual renewal. A government usually elects to issue a permit, rather than conclude a bilateral air-transport agreement under one of three circumstances: (1) it is unable to determine the nature of the agreement it wants, a situation most common in developing countries inexperienced in international air transport and, perhaps, uncertain of the capabilities of their own fledgling airlines; (2) it is unable to reach agreement on all issues with a foreign country, but wishes to implement air service of some type; or (3) it is unwilling to extend the recognition to the other government implied in a formal bilateral agreement, but still desires some air links with that country. An example of the latter situation is charter service between Miami and Havana provided by Cubana de Aviación, the Cuban flag carrier, in 1979 under permits from the FAA and CAB. Similarly, before East Germany (German Democratic Republic) received international recognition from most countries in the late 1970s, flights by its airline, Interflug, between East Germany and western countries were operated under permits from the western governments. Permits also governed air-transport links between West Germany and east European countries. Repeated annual reissuance of permits is not regarded as a substitute for a bilateral air-transport agreement; formal agreements provide a much greater sense of permanence and are symbolic of good general relations between the countries involved.

Alternatives to Bilateral Air-Transport Agreements

In 1979 an official of the U.S. Department of State proposed that sovereign states around the world, particularly smaller states, consider a regional approach to negotiating air transport agreements. James Atwood, deputy assistant secretary for transportation affairs, suggested two types of regional agreements as models. The first would be a decision by neighboring states to form an integrated union for internal air transport. This, he said, would encourage more economically rational route structures, schedules, and tariff frameworks. The second type of regionalism advocated by Atwood was a pact between neighboring states to conduct negotiations as a single unit with other countries. Atwood pointed out that several important international air corridors — for example, the North Atlantic — are single markets, although several nations are involved at one or both ends. Each bilateral segment of the market is interrelated with each other and with the market as a whole. Other arguments for regionalism are that many long-haul markets can be operated more efficiently if carriers can serve several points at one or both ends of the long-haul sector and that a liberalization of air-transport policy might be facilitated by a multinational effort of nations working together.[20]

Although some multinational air transport efforts have proved successful over the years, others — East African Airways — have foundered on political and economic disputes among their constituent members. SAS thrives because its member-states share a common heritage and general culture, compatible political and economic orientations, and an absence of colonial ties requiring commercially nonviable air service.[21] Few other regional groupings can boast such commonality. In addition to practical barriers to cooperation, many nations would spurn regional negotiations for reasons of nationalism.

Summary

Fundamental to the process of bilateral air transport negotiations are the general air-transport policies of the negotiating states. Most countries adhere to certain positions on readiness to exchange various traffic rights, capacity control, pricing, user fees and charges, and other aspects of commercial transport. These positions are usually well known among international civil-aviation authorities and may even be published as formal policy statements. What is frequently less well known and even more rarely admitted is the intrusion in air-transport negotiations of partisan domestic politics or foreign relations issues irrelevant to the aviation questions at hand. Although the practice of using nonaviation quid pro quos to obtain air-traffic rights is fairly widespread, governments seem loath to admit it and rarely acknowledge public such trade-offs.

The object of the actual bilateral air-transport negotiations is an equitable route exchange, expressed in market value, and measured by destinations, traffic rights, market opportunity and accessibility, market potential, and revenue potential. If an equitable route exchange cannot be reached through exchange of these components, nonaviation quod pro quos are frequently used to effect an agreement.

Although no one particular format for bilateral air-transport agreement has been adopted by a large international aviation organization, the nature of articles within agreements is fairly constant throughout the world. Nonaviation quid pro quos are not included in air-transport agreements; they are recorded in confidential memoranda of understanding exchanged by foreign ministries.

It is likely that bilateral air-transport negotiations and agreements will continue to govern civil aviation relations between states for the foreseeable future. Political and economic incompatibilities, as well as local nationalism, would seem to preclude a significant role for regional participation in negotiations.

Notes

1. See *U.S. International Aviation Policy at the Crossroads: A Study of Alternative Policies and Their Consequences*, Vol. 1 (Boston: Harbridge House for the Department of State, Department of Transportation, and President's Council on International Economic Policy, 1975), pp. III-4 to III-12.

2. This concept is expressed in Article 1, Chapter I, of the Convention Relating to the Regulation of Aerial Navigation (informally known as the Paris Convention of 1919). The conference adopting the convention was organized by the victorious Allied powers after World War I for the purposes of developing an international civil aviation regulatory system and

determining a unified policy on aviation rights allowed to defeated Germany. See John C. Cooper, *The Right to Fly* (New York: Henry Holt and Co., 1947), chapter 2.

3. See Bin Cheng, *The Law of International Air Transport* (London: Stevens & Sons, 1962), pp. 13-16, 313, 323-324, 390-392, 406; and Andreas F. Lowenfeld, *Aviation Law* (New York: Matthew Bender, 1972), II-4.2.

4. See "LOT Denied Second US Gateway," *Interavia Air Letter*, 9497 (May 8, 1980), p. 2.

5. See "Brazilian Charges," *Aviation Week*, 110:14 (April 2, 1979), p. 21.

6. Pan Am/Saudia Blocked Space Agreement Approved Under State Pressure," *Aviation Daily* 241:20 (January 29, 1979), p. 156. The agreement provided that Pan Am lease Saudia a block of seats on four weekly 747SP flights between New York and Dhahran. Fearing that the pact might lead to its permanent exclusion from the Saudi market, TWA objected. TWA had been authorized to serve Saudi Arabia, but the Saudis refused to permit its entrance.

7. "China Wants Government Action on Charter Filing by Sept. 15," *Aviation Daily* 244:34 (August 17, 1979), p. 267; "CAB Weighs Bid for Charters to China," *Aviation Week* 111:10 (September 3, 1979), p. 29.

8. See the following: O'Connor, *Economic Regulation*, p. 108; *New York Times*, September 19, 1973; "Icelandic Nonstop Bid Sparks Protest," *Aviation Week* 110:23 (June 4, 1979), p. 27; "U.S. Makes Counter Offer on Icelandic Request," *Aviation Daily* 244:38 (August 23, 1979), p. 299; and "U.S. Airlines Criticize Icelandair Exemption Bid," *Aviation Daily* 246:15 (November 26, 1979), p. 117.

9. See the author's "Soviet International Aviation Policy," *Survey* (London) 24:2 (Spring, 1979), pp. 19-44.

10. See Article 5 in "Additional Protocol to the Agreement Between the Government of the Union of Soviet Socialist Republics and the Government of the Federal Republic of Germany on Air Communications of November 11, 1971," *New Times* (Moscow) 21 (May, 1973), p. 32.

11. "Soviets Seek More Routes in Talks with U.S.," *Aviation Daily* 207:35 (June 19, 1973), p. 274; Bernard Gwertzman, "U.S., Soviet Sign Pact to Step Up Airline Service," *New York Times*, June 24, 1973, p. 1; "Senator Assails Aviation Pact, Saying Soviet Discounts Fares," *New York Times*, June 29, 1973, p. 38; "Cannon Blasts Aeroflot, Criticizes White House," *Aviation Daily* 208:1 (July 2, 1973), p. 6; Laurence Doty, "Broad Charter Rights Won by Soviets in New Pact," *Aviation Week* 99:1 (July 2, 1973), pp. 22-23; and "Soviets to Press for U.S. Routes Despite Resistance by State Dept.," *Aviation Week*, 99:8 (August 20, 1973), p. 27.

12. Douglas B. Feaver, "Landing Rights for the Concorde: A Diplomatic Dilemma," *Washington Post*, September 8, 1977, p. C9.

13. "Pan Am to Seek New Domestic Route," *Aviation Daily* 241:13 (January 18, 1979), p. 98.

14. "Background to a Bilateral Row," *Flight* 100:3273 (December 2, 1971), p. 887.

15. "Greece Seeking Toronto Rights for Olympic, Offers High Price," *Exxon Aviation News* 43 (October 20, 1976), p. 2

16. O'Connor, *Economic Regulation*, p. 108; Thayer, *Air Transport Policy*, p. 78; "Pressure for Additional KLM Tel Aviv Rights," *Interavia Air Letter* 6078 (September 2, 1966), p. 4.

17. See "Concorde/Malaysian Talks Fail," *Interavia Air Letter,* 8993 (January 30, 1978), p. 5.

18. "US Airlines Granted Authority to Serve Korea," *Interavia Air Letter* 9286 (July 2, 1979), p. 4.

19. Bin Cheng, *The Law of International Air Transport*, especially part three, should be consulted for additional information on bilateral air transport agreements. Examples of clauses on various topics in agreements are included in several ICAO publications. See, for example, United Nations, International Civil Aviation Organization, *Standard Bilateral Tariff Clause* (ICAO Document 9228-C/1036), 1978.

20. James R. Atwood, "Regional Aviation Agreements: A Desirable Alternative to Bilateralism?" address at the International Aviation Symposium, Kingston, Jamaica, February 1, 1979.

21. Even SAS does not fully comply with the Atwood model. Although the jointly owned airline does operate service between the major cities of the three countries, each country has its own airlines to provide more comprehensive domestic and charter service. The owner countries of Air Afrique also have their own domestic airlines.

7 The International Civil Aviation Route System

The system of air routes connecting more than 140 different countries of the world is an agglomeration of thousands of individual transport linkages, some intended to provide commercial service and other designed to fulfill colonial, strategic, or other noncommercial purposes. Although the system provides a functional air-transport network, connecting virtually all inhabited areas of the globe, its operations are controlled by individual countries (through their airlines) or small groups of countries rather than by a supranational coordinating agency. It does not serve all areas equitably, but it does fulfill supply and demand conditions. An examination of this system requires consideration of route system structure, route types, and characteristics of major international routes.

The Structure of a Route System

Airline routes have no physical existence independent of actual transport operations. In this characteristic, air routes bear greater resemblance to sea routes than to rail or motor vehicle routes. Railroad and motor vehicle transport are defined by railway tracks and highways; aircraft are far less circumscribed in their movements, requiring only the facilities and services of airports now widely available and, in international air transport, agreement with other countries for use of airspace, airports, and commercial rights.

Actual structural elements subject to analysis in a route system are linkages (or route lines), nodes (also called junctions or intersections), networks, hinterlands, and hierarchies. The major types of linkages are trunk lines, feeder lines, and bridge lines. Trunk lines connect major centers in a system and are characterized by high traffic density. In a motor vehicle transport system, trunk lines are the multilane interstate highways. In an air-transport system, trunklines are often among the longer routes in a system and are frequently served by large-capacity widebody aircraft. Within the United States, trunk lines connect major cities in different areas of the country. Theoretically, certain heavily traveled international routes, such as London-New York, could also be termed trunk lines of the international air-transport system; traffic on this route is high, but dispersed among a large number of carriers. Feeder lines connect trunk lines with

159

points in a trunk line hinterland. Although direct flights connect many European, African, and Middle Eastern cities with New York, many flights between these eastern hemisphere points and London are feeder services for London-New York routes. A third types of linkage, a bridge line, connects two different air-transport systems. For example, numerous bridge routes over the United States — Canada border connect the United States and Canadian domestic airline networks.

Air-traffic nodes are airports that serve as junctions for various routes. Many important nodes are gateways — major exit or entry points for a region or transitional zones between regions. An archtypical example of an international air transport gateway is Vienna, capital and major city of a neutral country situated between two European political regions. Exploiting its neutrality, Austria has encouraged the development of Vienna as a center for international organizations and for headquarters or major offices of east-west trading firms and multinational corporations. Austrian Airlines advertising emphasizes the advantages of Vienna as a transit point between the two parts of Europe, and suggests that its service between East and West is much better than that available on eastern carriers. In the western hemisphere, Miami, a North American city with a large Spanish-speaking population, is a gateway between North and South America.

Linkages and nodes are components of a route network, a system of routes and intersections. Some networks are lineal, consisting in some cases of a single attenuated line that may appear to ramble through various intermediate points at irregular intervals as it stretches between its home base and a distant terminal. Air New Zealand international routes fit this pattern. Other lineal networks are characterized by a trunk line pattern — two or more roughly parallel routes that connect economic/industrial centers — but do not intersect with other trunk lines. Several American carriers operate coast-to-coast trunk lines in the United States. Perhaps the most common air-transport network system is a series of hub-and-spoke patterns, nodes with routes extending outward into a hinterland. Hub-and-spoke systems are typical of regional carriers, airlines that usually have one or a small number of major nodes dominating their networks. A hub-and-spoke system offers the advantages of centralized operations and economies of scale at the hub, and the disadvantages of congestion at the hub and disruption of the entire network if the hub is affected by bad weather or another problem. A gridline system is a network of routes whose junction pattern appears to form a number of approximate trapezoids and triangles. For example, routes connecting major west European cities produce both hub-and-spoke and grid patterns. A traffic flow diagram shows London, Amsterdam, Frankfurt, and Paris forming a discernible approximate trapezoid within which London-Paris-Amsterdam, London-Paris-Frankfurt, and Paris-Amsterdam-Frankfurt appear as prominent triangles. Each of the four cities is also a hub with its own spokes.

A hinterland is a tributary area of a specific airport. It is often defined by the pattern of linkages and nodes associated with the airport. For many years, the entire United States was a hinterland to New York for transatlantic flights; as additional American cities were awarded transatlantic service, other airports developed hinterlands. Some hinterlands overlap, and some airports are in competition for control over hinterland territory. Different airports and their hinterlands may function in a hierarchical relation to one another. For example, the airports of Milwaukee and Chicago may compete for hinterlands in certain domestic markets, but Milwaukee is dominated by Chicago for other domestic routes and for international service. Chicago, in turn, is dominated by New York for some international markets. Ultimately, the size of a hinterland depends on two factors: (1) ease of access to the airport, and (2) competition from other airports that serve the same markets.

The Traffic Base of Air Routes

Air routes can be classified according to their traffic characteristics. Some routes are associated with one particular type of traffic; others have a variegated traffic base, drawing traffic from several groups of passengers. Reliance on a single type of traffic is often very risky, especially when that type is discretionary traffic, a category very sensitive to economic and political changes and thus subject to disruption. A route with a broad traffic base is far more likely to be able to absorb upheavals in the surrounding non-aviation environment.

Ten categories of traffic markets can be defined. Each commercial air route in the world relies on at least one of the following markets for its traffic base.

1. **Business routes.** Business-based international routes usually involve industrial, commercial, or financial centers. A number of American and West German cities, London, Zurich, Bahrein, Singapore, Taipei, and Tokyo are among the cities generating large amounts of traffic of this type. Because many business passengers travel frequently (some on the same route repeatedly) and almost all purchase full-fare tickets, most airlines are especially eager to attract this market. Some carriers have developed a special "business class" with its own section of the aircraft and special cabin service.

2. **Personal traffic routes.** Personal traffic is discretionary and, unlike business traffic, often responsive to special fares, including charter flights. The attraction of personal travelers to reduced fare arrangements decreases the per passenger yield to the airlines. Three different types of personal traffic require some explanation.

Tourism-related traffic is a major market for many international airlines. Typically, international tourist routes originate in the affluent West. Their destinations vary; warm climates, historic and scenic locales, and special events have appeal to many vacationers. A major disadvantage to reliance on tourist traffic is its seasonality with attendant inconsistencies in capacity requirements. Some tourist routes may draw 60 percent or more of their annual traffic in a two- or three-month period.

Ethnic traffic (also called VFR — visiting friends and relatives traffic) is important to airlines of most countries with large immigrant and emigrant populations. Among the former are the United States, Canada, several South American countries, and Australia. Among the latter are Ireland, the Scandinavian countries, Poland, Greece, Italy, and Portugal. The population of Italy, for example, is approximately 60 million; another 55 million people of Italian descent live outside Italy. The route system of Alitalia, heavily influenced by the Italian dispersion, is designated to accommodate Italian VFR traffic. In 1974 Alitalia reported the ethnic share in a number of its markets: United States, 83 percent; Canada, 78 percent; Venezuela, 65 percent; Brazil, 70.5 percent; Argentina, 80 percent; and Australia, 70 percent.[1] The ethnic market share in traffic of both Olympic Airways and El Al is approximately 60 percent.

Ethnic composition of several large American cities is revealed by the particular foreign carriers serving their airports. That Aer Lingus, TAP-Air Portugal, and Alitalia each operate service to Boston is consistent with Boston-area demographic patterns. LOT, the Polish carrier, selected Chicago as its second U.S. destination after New York; Warsaw is the only city in the world to exceed Chicago in number of residents of Polish background.

Expatriate merchant-class populations in a number of developing countries constitute another type of ethnic market. Large groups of Indians and Pakistanis are shopkeepers and industrialists in other developing countries of the British Commonwealth; their presence in Kenya and Tanzania, for example, creates a demand for air links connecting east Africa with India and Pakistan. A comparable situation arises from the Syrian and Lebanese merchant-class population in many former French colonies.

Ethnic carriers frequently enjoy substantial appeal among expatriate groups and provide formidable competition to airlines of the expatriate country. Pan Am rarely did well on its routes to Scandinavian countries and yielded its certification for those destinations to Northwest without much complaint. TWA has similarly fared badly against El Al on routes between the United States and Israel. In each of these cases, however, the ethnic carrier has offered better service, including more nonstop flights, or otherwise proved more attractive than the nonethnic airline.

Unlike SAS, Alitalia, and most other European airlines, Aeroflot, the

Soviet carrier, is not supported by its diaspora. Most Soviet nationality groups living outside the Soviet Union—Russians, Ukrainians, Lithuanians, Latvians, among others—are political opponents of the Soviet Union and will not patronize Soviet products. In any case, relatively few such people visit the USSR. For some of the east European carriers, the situation is very different. Many diaspora Poles and Czechs, for example, support the national airlines of the ethnic homeland, and a large number of Polish-Americans visit Poland. Many members of east European diaspora groups, strongly anticommunist, justify use of state-owned airlines by claiming that their fares support "the people," not the system, and that the people are overwhelmingly anticommunist.[2]

Religious-pilgrimage travel constitutes a third type of personal traffic. Rome, sites of shrines, Israel, and Jedda (closest airport to Mecca) are among the most important destinations of religious or pilgrimage traffic. Travel to Jedda is probably the most interesting to commercial air transport specialists because it is one of the most seasonal markets in the world; it is an obligation of a Moslem to make a pilgrimage to Mecca at least once in his lifetime (if he possesses both the financial and physical possibilities) during the twelfth month of the lunar year. Each year in this period tens of charter aircraft are pressed into service to carry Haj (pilgrimage) traffic.

3. **Gateway traffic routes.** Gateway traffic is of two types, natural and contrived. A natural gateway is a commercial airport situated between two regions differing in political or economic system, ethnicity, or some other characteristic. Earlier in this chapter Vienna was cited as a gateway between Western and Eastern Europe. Although the Austrian government, the city of Vienna, and the Austrian flag carrier have implemented various measures to enhance the value of Vienna as a gateway, the chief factor in the gateway status of the city is beyond manipulation by Austrian officials—its site in a neutral country between two different blocs of governments. Many other gateways evolve naturally over a period of time, among them various U.S. coastal cities relative to the interior of the United States. Prior to the outbreak of violence in Lebanon and the rapid development of many other Arab airlines in the 1970s, Beirut was a gateway for much of the Arab world. Before the invasion of Cyprus by Turkish forces in 1974, Nicosia was a gateway for traffic between Arab countries and Israel. Larnaca, the airport serving Greek-held Cyprus, has absorbed some of that traffic, but Athens has developed its own gateway function in the Arab states-Israel market. Copenhagen is a gateway for other Scandinavian cities.

A contrived or artificial gateway is an airport whose location bears little relation to regional political, economic, or other differences, but whose function as gateway has been developed for commercial purposes. As examples, efforts by government, airport, and airline officials in Belgium, the Netherlands, Switzerland, and other suitably located European countries to establish home airports as gateways between North America and eastern Europe, Africa, or the Middle East may be cited. In each of these countries the flag carrier must attract substantial foreign traffic to support an international route network larger than that required by the indigenous population. Transport of large amounts of gateway/sixth freedom traffic helps to correct the passenger/capacity imbalance. For the national airlines of the three countries noted, this type of traffic accounts for more than one-third of all traffic carried. Such airlines are called "merchant carriers" by some observers, differentiating between them and airlines that rely more on the home market.

Whether natural or contrived, gateways consolidate and concentrate traffic at intermediate nodes, thus facilitating transport to relatively remote or less important destinations that could not support direct linkages with large numbers of points. The consolidation and concentration function may be performed by one carrier, as occurs in sixth-freedom traffic, or by several airlines in a coordinated or uncoordinated effort.

4. **Diplomatic traffic routes.** Diplomatic traffic refers to air travel connected with diplomatic relations between governments. For those capital cities with little industry other than government — among them Canberra, Brasilia, and Washington, D.C. — diplomatic traffic is a major component of all international air travel. Diplomatic traffic is also a significant factor in international air service to cities hosting large international organizations, such as New York and Geneva. (The corollary traffic on the domestic level is travel related to domestic government affairs.)

5. **Poor surface transport accessibility traffic.** Poor surface accessibility, whether considered on an international or domestic level, is an incentive to the development of strong air transport capability. On an international level, surface transport is competitive with commercial aviation in certain parts of western Europe; road and railway links are modern, convenient, and relatively inexpensive. However, in many other areas of the world surface transport is impractical or even irrelevant because of distance, topography, underdevelopment, or politics. The distance/time equation is a crucial factor in the displacement of ocean liners on the Atlantic crossing by air routes. Topographic and/or climatic barriers to surface transport linkages have stimulated the growth of air service in such countries as Canada, Norway, the Soviet Union, and Nepal. Underdeveloped road and railway systems have enhanced the value of air transport (which, under certain conditions, requires only a modest airport infrastructure) in Africa. The value of air-transport service to West Berlin, Israel, and Jordan has

been proved by the imposition of constant or sporadic political barriers to surface transport links with these entities.

6. **Strategic policy routes.** Enforcement of national strategic policy through exploitation of commercial air links can be attempted simply by transporting appropriate people and goods on existing commercial air routes of strategic significance. Certain routes of some carriers, however, appear to carry little commercial traffic and, in view of existing political/economic/military conditions along or beyond the route course, seem to be operated primarily, or even only, for strategic reasons. For example, the Soviet carrier Aeroflot operates several routes to developing countries that do not attract sufficient traffic to cover their costs. It is likely that some of these routes are maintained in an effort to establish presence in the context of superpower rivalry. Not only does the flag carrier appear at the capital airport once or twice each week, but an airline office is opened in town. The documented record of Aeroflot involvement with espionage in foreign countries suggests another possible motivation for commercially nonviable Aeroflot service. An additional Soviet motivation for some air routes is the establishment of intermediate bases and air corridors useful in support of friendly regimes or power groupings beyond the civil air route terminal. For example, Aeroflot routes to and stations in Algiers proved vital to Soviet supply of armaments to rebel forces in the former Belgian Congo (now Zaire) in 1964. In 1971 the Soviet Union used the Aeroflot infrastructure in Cairo in attempts to disguise military supply flights moving through the Egyptian capital en route to India during the 1971 India-Pakistan war. Flights through Soviet Central Asia were quicker, but had to overfly either Pakistan itself or Pakistan's ally and the Soviet Union's rival, China. The Egyptians also supported Pakistan, another Moslem country, but at that time were not in a position to complain to the Soviets about use of their territory as a transshipment point and exploitation of civil aviation links for noncommercial purposes.

Privately owned profit-making American carriers have occasionally operated strategic routes at the request of the U.S. government. The most recent example is Pan Am's ten-year long service to Moscow. When the U.S. airline first informed the Department of State that it wanted to suspend the route because of unacceptable financial losses, the department asked Pan Am to continue its operation in the interest of the country. Government officials mentioned the role of Pan Am's flights as a symbol of détente, an instrument of American visibility in the Soviet capital, and a means of facilitating communications between the U.S. embassy in Moscow and Washington. It was also suggested to Pan Am that its future dealings with the government might be less harmonious if it suspended its Moscow flights. Pan Am complied with Washington requests for several years, but finally withdrew its Moscow service in 1978. American policy on asking commercial airlines to maintain commercially nonviable service to sensitive destinations was changed shortly after the Moscow suspension, but could probably be altered again if a compelling need to do so was perceived by the President or the Department of State.

7. **Prestige routes.** Prestige routes usually are implemented and maintained by airlines at the request of foreign ministries perceiving it important to create an "image" (of political power, technological prowess, economic strength) in specific foreign destinations. The intentions of Kwame Nkrumah to establish a major airline with a farflung international network have already been noted. The heavily subsidized Concorde routes of British Airways and Air France can be considered contemporary prestige routes as can certain operations of Aeroflot. Operation of great numbers of prestige routes by Western and most developing country airlines is usually constrained by economic realities.

8. **Military-defense routes.** International military or defense routes are commercial routes operated to the perimeter of a battle area in support of a war effort. Characteristically, most traffic on military routes is directly related to the war. Pan Am routes to Saigon during American participation in Vietnam hostilities is a service of this type. Managed by civilians and commercially profitable, the flights carried passengers and freight vital to the U.S. military effort. Pan Am and other American carriers transported troops and materiel between the United States and Vietnam on special charter flights. Aeroflot flights to Hanoi during the same period, to Hanoi and Vientiane later, to Addis Ababa, and to other destinations in which the Soviets have supported military action have been of the same category. An important difference between the military routes of the superpower airlines is the civilian management of the American operations and the overall military role in Aeroflot administration and management.

9. **Colonial or vestigial-colonial routes.** Colonial or vestigial-colonial routes are those serving existing or former colonies of the colonial power registering the operating airline. Some colonial or vestigial-colonial routes are profitable, generating traffic from strong political, economic, military, tourist, or other ties between both countries. Other routes generate insufficient revenue to cover costs, but are maintained as a component in a government policy to facilitate and strengthen ties between the (former) colonial power and (former) colony. Airlines asked by their government to operate commercially nonviable service of this type may request government subsidy.

10. **Charter routes.** Although charter service can be operated on the same routes as scheduled service, providing that technical conditions are appropriate and the necessary bilateral arrangements have been made, some charter routes have been operated with such frequency that they have acquired their own character and features. European-Mediterranean charter traffic, the principal element of which is inclusive tours from northern Europe to warmer Mediterranean tourist areas, exceeds scheduled traffic volume on the same route. Examples of other special charter markets are North Atlantic ethnic/VFR traffic, and vacation tours from Japan to other Pacific islands. Although the charter market is dominated by discretionary personal traffic, other types of international traffic also utilize charter arrangments. For example, the U.S. armed forces frequently charter civilian aircraft to transport troops and materiel between the U.S. and its overseas bases.

Characteristics of Major International Routes

Commonly flown international civil aviation routes are usually considered as components in large regional route groupings, such as the North Atlantic or inter-African route systems. IATA has defined a number of such regions, some of which will be described below.

North Atlantic

The North Atlantic is the single most important route grouping in the world (see figure 7-1). It accounts for 25 to 30 percent of total international traffic in both scheduled and charter service. Its area encompasses all routes between Europe, Africa, and/or the Middle East on one side and North America, from Miami northward, on the other.[3] Over forty different airlines operate scheduled service on the North Atlantic, and additional carriers are active in North Atlantic charter or all-cargo service. Of the numerous city-pairs in the scheduled market, New York-London is by far the most important, accounting for 8 to 11 percent of total passenger traffic. New York-Frankfurt and New York-Paris each draw 4 to 6 percent of the total North Atlantic scheduled passenger traffic, followed by Toronto-London, 3 to 4 percent. Usually drawing less than 3 percent, but still important are routes connecting: (1) Los Angeles, Miami, Washington, Chicago, and Boston with London; (2) New York with Rome, Amsterdam, Madrid, Athens, Tel Aviv, and Zurich; and (3) Montreal with Paris.[4] Atlanta, Dallas, and Houston are new gateways for U.S.-involved North Atlantic flights. The leading three city-

Figure 7-1. Examples of Key Transatlantic Routes

———— New York - London is the most heavily traveled transatlantic route.

– – – – Miami - Frankfurt — Miami is increasingly important in international traffic.

—·—·— Rio de Janeiro is the South Atlantic gateway to South America.

Figure 7-1 (continued)

pairs in the North Atlantic charter market are also New York-London, New York-Frankfurt, and New York-Paris. A listing of other prominent North Atlantic charter city-pairs would differ somewhat from that of scheduled service city-pairs, reflecting tendencies of (1) Canadians to use charter flights more often than do U.S. citizens, and (2) U.S. residents of midwestern and western states to use charter service more often than do their eastern states compatriots.

TWA and Pan American are the leading U.S. airlines on the North Atlantic, each regularly carrying more than 15 percent of total scheduled passenger traffic. Both these airlines operate routes between several U.S. and various European points, in some instances in direct competition with each other. Reflecting the importance of the U.S.-London component of North Atlantic service, British Airways draws 10 to 15 percent of scheduled North Atlantic service involving the United States. Lufthansa and Air France each usually carry 5 to 6 percent of U.S.-involved scheduled North Atlantic traffic. Other leading carriers are SAS, Swissair, Alitalia, and El Al. American deregulation policies have allowed several additional U.S. carriers to enter North Atlantic scheduled service in recent years. Their impact has yet to be measured.

Air Canada carries about one-third of all scheduled passenger traffic between Canada and Europe. CP Air, the privately owned Vancouver-based airline which does not operate the same routes as Air Canada, flies 10 to 15 percent of Canadian transatlantic scheduled passenger traffic. British Airways draws approximately 20 percent, and three carriers attract 4 to 6 percent each—Alitalia, Iberia, and Lufthansa. Air France, KLM, and Swissair are also significant airlines in the Canadian North Atlantic market.

For many European airlines, scheduled routes on the North Atlantic are very important as feeder service to other routes in their system. Their home airports are used as gateways to collect sixth-freedom traffic for connections to points in eastern Europe, the Middle East, and Africa, as well as to secondary cities in western Europe.

In addition to third- and fourth-freedom traffic carriers on the North Atlantic, the route is also served by several fifth-freedom airlines that received transatlantic rights in return for beyond traffic rights through their countries accorded to North Atlantic airlines. The most important fifth-freedom carriers on the route are Air-India (New York-London) and El Al (New York-London, New York-Paris).

The North Atlantic route is one of the most problematic in the entire world. It suffers from serious overcapacity—stemming from the "prestige" perceived by some carriers or their governments in serving the United States, the value of transatlantic service as a feed-in to other routes in an airline network, the desire of many governments to use transatlantic service in support of their tourist industries, the expansion of North Atlantic service to additional gateways, and, according to opponents of American aviation policy, U.S. insistence on almost free access to U.S. markets. It is also affected by low per-kilometer tariffs relative to other route groupings. Lower tariffs result in decreased yields for the airlines, a situation exacerbated by the institution of promotional fares intended to attract passengers. Additionally, approximately 80 percent of total passengers represent discretionary traffic—vacationing and visiting friends and relatives—a volatile market characterized by dramatic seasonality and responsiveness to special fares.

The introduction of long-range jet aircraft on the North Atlantic in 1958 created vastly different travel conditions on the route. No longer were intermediate refueling stops necessary, thus increasing the comfort and convenience of passengers but adversely affecting the economies of refueling point areas no longer important to the airlines. Airports in Gander, Shannon, and the Azores had developed small industries centered on intermediate stops. Suddenly they were nearly irrelevant.

Mid Atlantic

The Mid-Atlantic route grouping is defined (by IATA) as including all transatlantic routes between Europe, Africa, and/or the Middle East on one side, and Mexico, Central America, the Caribbean, Bolivia, Colombia, Ecuador, French Guiana, Guyana, Peru, Surinam, or Venezuela on the other side. Mid-Atlantic scheduled international service accounts for approximately 4 percent of all international scheduled service; its share of total traffic in the international charter market is lower, less than 2 percent.

The leading Mid-Atlantic western hemisphere gateways are Mexico City, Caracas, Freeport/Nassau, and San Juan. European carrier service to Caracas (and sometimes to other gateways as well) frequently continues with an "Andean extension" to Bogota, Quito, Lima, or another city. Certain Mid-Atlantic western hemisphere gateways—among them Nassau, Mexico City, and Kingston—are tourism centers. Mexico City and Caracas, capitals of countries of rapid economic development, generate substantial business traffic. Colonial and vestigial-colonial traffic is important to a number of Caribbean nations. British Airways, Iberia, Air France, Lufthansa, and KLM are the most important European carriers in the Mid-Atlantic market.

Viasa of Venezuela and Avianca of Colombia, the leading western hemisphere Mid-Atlantic carriers, each serve approximately six European points. Mid-Atlantic service on Aeromexico, Air Jamaica, BWIA of Trinidad, and SLM of Surinam reflect their colonial pasts. Cubana also operates Mid-Atlantic routes, which reflect Cuban political orientation and transnational military involvements—destinations are Prague and East Berlin (via Madrid) in Europe, Tripoli and Baghdad (via Madrid) in the Middle East, and Conakry, Freetown, and Luanda in Africa.

Latin American countries are generally protectionist and many in the Mid-Atlantic area favor pooling agreements. These factors reduce the probability of excess capacity and contribute to favorable financial conditions for the airlines. The traffic growth rate in the Mid-Atlantic market has been strong.

South Atlantic

The South Atlantic route area includes traffic between Europe, Africa, and the Middle East on one side, and the western hemisphere south of the Mid-Atlantic on the other. Specific western hemisphere countries in the region are Argentina, Brazil, Chile, Paraguay, and Uruguay. South Atlantic routes account for approximately 3 percent of all international scheduled traffic and 2 percent of international charter traffic.

Rio de Janeiro is the principal western hemisphere gateway for the two routes in the South Atlantic group. The long range capabilities of the Boeing 747, Douglas DC-10, and Lockhead Tristar provide airlines with an option of nonstop or one-stop service between Rio and Europe, the more important of the two routes. Almost all airlines operating on the South Atlantic retain some one-stop flights, most using West African points for refueling. Air France, Swissair, Lufthansa, and Alitalia all stop in Dakar, and KLM refuels at the major Liberian airport, Robertsfield. Many European carriers extend their Rio service to Montevideo, Buenos Aires, and/or Santiago. Asuncion, capital of Paraguay, is not well served by transatlantic routes. Varig, the international Brazilian airline, operates nonstop service to three European points—Lisbon, Madrid, and Rome.

The second South Atlantic route connects South America with South Africa. Varig and South African Airways each fly between Rio de Janeiro and Johannesburg, and Aerolineas Argentinas and South African fly between Buenos Aires and Capetown.

As on the Mid-Atlantic route, carriers operating South Atlantic service generally favor regulation of capacity as a means of assuring financial stability. The very prominent position of Brazil in the Mid-Atlantic market makes the entire service dependent on political and economic conditions in that country.

The Americas

A number of separate international traffic flow patterns exist in the western hemisphere. They range in length from short/medium distance transborder flights to major intercontinental operations. Four route groupings are discussed below.

1. **United States-Canada.** U.S.-Canada service is extensive and diversified. Approximately thirty United States and fifteen Canadian cities are involved. The majority of traffic flows between mainland United States and Canada, but service also exists between Alaska and Canada and between Hawaii and Canada. Hawaii is a popular vacation destination for western Canadians as is Florida for eastern Canadians. State-owned Air Canada operates most Canadian service; U.S. routes of privately owned Vancouver-based CP Air connect western Canada with the western United States. American-operated service is shared by approximately ten carriers on a regional basis. For example, airlines whose route networks are concentrated in the eastern states (such as Delta, Eastern, and US Air) serve eastern Canada. Frontier and Western serve western Canada.

2. **South America/Caribbean-North America.** Miami and New York are the major U.S. gateways. With persons of Latin American heritage constituting approximately half of its population, Miami is officially bilingual and correspondingly attractive to visitors from South and Central America. It is a regional banking, trading, and shopping center for approximately 250 million Latin Americans. Nassau, Kingston, Caracas, and Bogota have especially strong air links with the Florida city. New York has especially significant traffic flows with Rio de Janeiro, Caracas, Port of Spain, and Aruba. (San Juan is also an important traffic point in relation to the U.S. mainland, but its status as chief city of a U.S. commonwealth defines its extensive connections with Miami and New York as domestic.)

Braniff and Pan Am are the dominant U.S. carriers in South America. In general terms, Braniff has exclusive U.S. franchise in western South America and is in competition with Pan Am in eastern South America. American and Eastern are the leading U.S. airlines in the Caribbean; Delta, Pan Am, and Republic also have some service in the region. Of the Canadian carriers, Air Canada flies to the Caribbean and eastern South America. CP Air serves western South America. Numerous Caribbean and South American airlines operate routes to the United States. Four carriers from Colombia alone have service to Miami. The largest Colombian airline, Avianca, serves several U.S. destinations and is among the major Latin carriers in the route grouping. Viasa, Varig, Aerolineas Argentinas, Lan-Chile, Aero Peru, and Ecuatoriana also serve more than one U.S. point. Of the Caribbean airlines, Air Jamaica and BWIA (Trinidad and Tobago) fly to Canada as well as to the United States. Dominicana operates service to several U.S. cities.

3. **Central America/Mexico-North America.** Air links between Mexico and the United States are very strong, reflecting heavy U.S. tourism to Mex-

ico, a large Mexican population resident in the U.S., and multifaceted commercial ties between the two countries. Mexico City is the dominant Mexican international traffic point, but important U.S. service also moves through a number of Mexican regional airports, among them Acapulco, Guadalajara, Mazatlan, Merida, Cancun, Monterrey, and Puerto Vallarta. Approximately thirty American cities have air service connections with Mexico; among the traffic leaders are Los Angeles, Dallas, Houston, Chicago, New York, and Miami. In all, fifty-four points in the two countries are covered in the Mexico-United States bilateral agreement.

Aeromexico and Mexicana each operate extensive U.S. service; with the exception of Mexico City-Los Angeles and Mexico City-Miami routes, the two carriers do not compete with each other. American, Eastern, Western, and Braniff are the leading American carriers in the Mexico-U.S. market. Several other U.S. airlines also operate Mexico-U.S. routes. Mexico-Canada service is provided by Aeromexico and CP Air.

Most air service between the small Central American countries and the United States uses Miami as the U.S. gateway. Service is provided by Aviateca of Guatemala, Belize Airways, TAN of Honduras, TACA of El Salvador, LANICA of Nicaragua, and LACSA of Costa Rica. Air Panama serves Miami, New York, and Los Angeles. Pan Am and Eastern provide American carrier service between some of these countries and Miami, and Pan Am and Braniff operate Panama City-New York service.

4. **Within South America.** International air traffic within South America is concentrated on two north-south axes — between the Caribbean and Buenos Aires through the Andean Pact countries and along the Pacific coast, and between Brazil and Argentina along the Atlantic coast. Buenos Aires is the southern terminus on both routes. Important city pairs on the Andean-Pacific route are: Caracas-Bogota, Bogota-Quito, Bogota-Lima, Lima-Santiago, and Santigao-Buenos Aires. Leading city-pairs on the Atlantic side are: Rio de Janeiro-Buenos Aires, Sao Paulo-Buenos Aires, Rio-Montevideo, and Montevideo-Buenos Aires. Landlocked Bolivia and Paraguay are less well served than are the coastal countries. Guyana, Surinam, and French Guinana are even more isolated from other South American states. In addition to the coastal routes daily nonstop service is available between Caracas and Buenos Aires.

Europe

Traffic in the European route grouping is second in volume to that of the North Atlantic. London exceeds all other European cities in traffic generation; its routes to Paris, Amsterdam, and Frankfurt are among the most heavily traveled in western Europe. Traffic is strong between almost all European commercial centers (except those so close to one another that surface transport is competitive) and between countries with strong ethnic or political ties, as with the Scandinavian states or England and Ireland. Due to their late entry into the western political mainstream and their relative economic underdevelopment, Spain and Portugal are less well integrated into the European air network than are most other Western countries.

With the exception of East Germany and Albania, east European countries and the Soviet Union have fairly strong civil aviation ties with many west European countries. Traffic flows are heaviest between Yugoslavia, the most liberal of the eastern states, and western countries, especially West Germany. On a city-pair basis, as opposed to country-pair ranking, Moscow-Paris, Moscow-Frankfurt, and Moscow-London are the most important routes. Unlike the Soviet Union where Moscow is an unrivalled primary city and magnet for international traffic, Yugoslavia is decentralized with several important regional power bases. Of routes between the Soviet Union and other eastern countries, Moscow-East Berlin has the heaviest traffic, drawing more than twice as many passengers as the Moscow-Paris service.

Charter service, usually as a component in inclusive tour packages, is an important factor in several country-pair route groupings. Typically, the greatest traffic flows involve vacations for relatively affluent north and central Europeans in southern Europe. The most important country-pairs, in approximate order, are United Kindom–Spain, West Germany–Spain, Scandinavia–Spain, Netherlands–Spain, United Kingdom–Italy, Scandinavia–Greece, Belgium–Spain, West Germany–United Kingdom, Scandinavia–United Kingdom, West Germany–Greece, West Germany–Yugoslavia, West Germany–Italy, and Scandinavia–Italy. In all, the United Kingdom and West Germany each generate 25 to 35 percent of originating traffic on European inclusive tours; Spain is the chief destination country, drawing over 60 percent of the European inclusive tour market. Italy, the next most important destination country, draws approximately 10 percent of the inclusive tour charter passengers. Most traffic on these routes is carried by private supplemental airlines, some of which have very close ties with particular travel agencies that specialize in inclusive tours.

Europe-Africa

Air traffic between Europe and sub-Saharan Africa ranks fifth in volume of major international scheduled traffic flows, greater than either the South or Mid-Atlantic. The most important city-pairs reflect colonial and political ties: London-Johannesburg, London-Lagos, Paris-Abidjan, Paris-Dakar, and London-Nairobi. Overall, Johannesburg is the leading sub-Saharan gateway, followed by Nairobi, Dakar, and Abidjan. Nairobi is the primary city in east Africa and an important tourism center. Dakar and Abidjan are key cities in francophone West Africa; among Dakar's attractions is its status as gateway for many flights between Europe and South America.

Africa

Regional, rather than continental, traffic patterns dominate international air service in Africa. Most numerous among the more heavily traveled routes are those connecting west African francophone countries, particularly if Abidjan (Ivory Coast) or Dakar (Senegal) is a destination. The route connecting these two capitals is the single most important francophone city-pair; other major routes in this grouping are Abidjan-Lome, Douala-Libreville, and Douala-Nouakchott. Lagos-Accra, a route connecting two former British west African colonies, is less well traveled than several francophone city-pairs. Only in the 1970s did African carriers mount significant west African air service crossing colonial lines. Despite transborder tribal continuities, adjacent former French and British west African colonies had much closer formal ties with Paris and London respectively than with each other. In the 1950s, a trip between Abidjan and Accra—two capital cities barely 300 miles (480 kilometers) apart—required three separate flights over several days: Abidjan-Paris, Paris-London, and London-Accra. An American airline, Pan Am, first connected cities in French and British West Africa. Pan Am opened a transatlantic U.S.-Africa service in the 1960s that extended down the western coast, linking several emerging states that had had limited formal contacts with each other. Pan Am continues its coastal route, but some African carriers now cross colonial lines as well; important city-pairs in this category are Abidjan-Lagos, Abidjan-Accra, and Abidjan-Monrovia.

International traffic between east African centers is less significant than that between comparable west African points. Political and economic instability in several east African states has limited the potential traffic base.

Service across Africa, between the two coasts, was also initiated by Pan Am which extended its transatlantic Africa service across the continent to the Indian Ocean. A combination of (1) distance/time factors, and (2) lack of historic ties between the two sides of Africa inhibit the development of contemporary contacts. The traffic base for air service even between prominent countries with the same colonial heritage, such as Nigeria and Kenya, is narrow. Limited transafrica service is offered by Pan Am, Ethiopian Airlines, Nigeria Airways, Cameroon Airlines, and Air Zaire.

Of some sensitivity to many Africans are the strong air links between

Johannesburg and several black African countries. These routes are of two types. First, many European carriers must make refueling stops at some point between Europe and South Africa. Although several black African countries do not accept such traffic, others welcome it—if only for the financial gain from fuel sales, landing fees, local traffic, and other commercial matters associated with the intermediate stop. Nairobi-Johannesburg is the single most heavily traveled route in sub-Saharan Africa, but all of the carriers on the service are non-African—Alitalia, British Airways, El Al, Iberia, KLM, Lufthansa, Olympic Airways, SAS, and Swissair. Kinshasa is another frequently used intermediate stop between Europe and South Africa. The second type of route is the service between Johannesburg and approximately twenty-five black-governed countries dependent upon South Africa to some degree for food, medical assistance, industrial and consumer goods, technical expertise, or financial support.[5] The South African cargo carrier Safair operates most of these flights. Airlines of several of the southernmost black states (among them Zambia, Malawi, Mozambique, and Zimbabwe) operate their own services to South Africa.

Europe/Far East—Middle East

More than many other regions of the world, the Middle East is subject to instability within individual governments and in relations between them. Political changes disrupt air transport route patterns and impede development of long-term networks. It is thus difficult to delineate specific city-pair routes of importance over long periods of time. The individual cities of Tel Aviv and Cairo have been consistent leaders in Middle East-involved intercontinental traffic; Baghdad, Kuwait, Bahrein, Damascus, and two Saudi Arabian ports—Jedda and Dhahran—also attract significant numbers of long-haul passengers. The importance of Beirut as a gateway diminished substantially during the 1970s due to political unrest in Lebanon and the increasing capability of airlines from other Arab countries to fulfill their own air-transport needs.

The leading European gateways to Arab countries are, in order, London, Paris, Frankfurt, Athens, Zurich, and Rome. Athens has assumed some of the gateway significance once held by Beirut.

Air traffic between the Middle East and Africa is limited, except for some pilgrimage traffic between Moslem African states and Saudi Arabia. Indians and Pakistanis working in the Gulf states are an important passenger group in Middle East–Asia air routes. The traffic flow between the Far East and the Middle East is limited in significance.

Several Middle East airlines operate air service to the United States drawing on (1) increasingly strong commercial ties between the Middle East and the United States, and (2) large diaspora populations in North America. Traffic between the Middle East and Latin America, though of limited volume, is growing for the same reasons.

The Israel-related component of Middle East transatlantic traffic far exceeds Arab-involved transatlantic traffic. Strong air links also exist between Israel and Europe. More moderate are traffic flows between Israel and Nairobi/Johannesburg. Connections between Israel and the Far East are impeded by the refusal of some Moslem states to grant first-freedom overflight rights for Israel-related service and the reluctance of some other Asian states to increase their ties with Israel for fear of offending Arab countries.

Intercontinental service to Iran, fairly well developed under the Shah, has been disrupted by the change of governments in the country. Iranair and foreign carriers have reduced international service involving Iran.

Middle East

The leading Middle East destinations for regional traffic are Cairo, Kuwait, and Jedda. In general, Middle East air traffic is diffuse; more than forty different regional international routes have significant traffic.

Until the institution of direct Israel-Egypt air routes in 1980 as a result of the 1979 Camp David agreement, air service between Israel and the Arab states was available only through connecting flights at non-Arab intermediate airports. Nicosia was a major transit point for this traffic before the Turkish invasion of Cyprus isolated the airport in 1974. The expanded Greek Cypriot airport at Larnaca now handles similar transit arrangements, but major marketing efforts by Greek authorities plus inferior transit service in Larnaca have given Athens (and Olympic Airways) increasing shares of Israel-Arab traffic.

South and Southeast Asia

Continuing tension, occasionally erupting into war, between India and Pakistan has impeded development of air-transport ties between these two most populous countries on the Indian subcontinent. The most consistent service between New Delhi and Karachi has been mounted by a nonregional airline, Pan Am, as a segment of its around-the-world route. Other nonregional carriers also offer fifth-freedom service between the two countries. Although demand for this service may not be high among Indians and Pakistanis, foreigners traveling in the area have always required transportation links between the two states. When relations between India and Pakistan are less tense, airlines of these two countries operate some transborder service as well. The most heavily traveled international air route in the region, Colombo-Madras, carries a substantial number of VFR passengers — Sri Lankans of southern Indian origin or their Indian relatives. New Delhi-Katmandu and Dacca-Calcutta are also important regional international routes.

Further east, in the southeast Asia–Pacific area, many more city-pairs show consistent and significant traffic (see figure 7–2). Bangkok–Hong Kong and Hong Kong–Tokyo are the two busiest routes, drawing passengers from the political/economic importance of the three cities involved and from the lack of alternate routes between southeast Asia and Tokyo. The agreement by the People's Republic of China in 1979 to open its airspace to overflights by foreign carriers may reduce some of the congestion on the Bangkok-Hong Kong-Tokyo route. Other heavily traveled routes in the area are Singapore-Djakarta, Tokyo-Taipei, Singapore–Kuala Lumpur, and Singapore–Hong Kong. Singapore's prominence in traffic statistics reflects the importance of the island-state as a banking, trading, and general commercial center in southeast Asia. The southeast Asia oveseas-Chinese population of some 15 million people, many of them important merchants and industrialists, is a key element in area traffic.

Europe-Japan

Routes between Europe and Japan are among the most heavily traveled in the world (see figure 7–3). Three route options exist: the southern route through south and southeast Asia, the polar route, and the transsiberian route. The southern route — also called the "silk route" because it approximates the historical course followed by silk merchants — is the longest of the three, usually requiring four to six intermediate stops between Europe and Japan. Two possible versions are: (1) West European point-Istanbul-Teheran-Karachi-Bangkok-Hong Kong-Toyko; and, (2) West European point-Beirut-Kuwait-New Delhi-Bangkok-Hong Kong-Tokyo. Many intermediate point substitutions can be made. Every major European carrier plus Pan Am and JAL operate at least one version of this route. Local carriers operate appropriate segments. Because few reasonable route options are available between Bangkok and Tokyo, the Bangkok–Hong Kong and Hong Kong–Tokyo sectors suffer from excess capacity and resultant illegal discounting and other problems as airlines compete for a market inadequate to fill their aircraft. The long distance and frequent stops on the southern route reduce its appeal to Europe-Japan travelers. Instead of attracting end-to-end traffic, its major function is the transport of one-stop or nonstop regional international traffic.

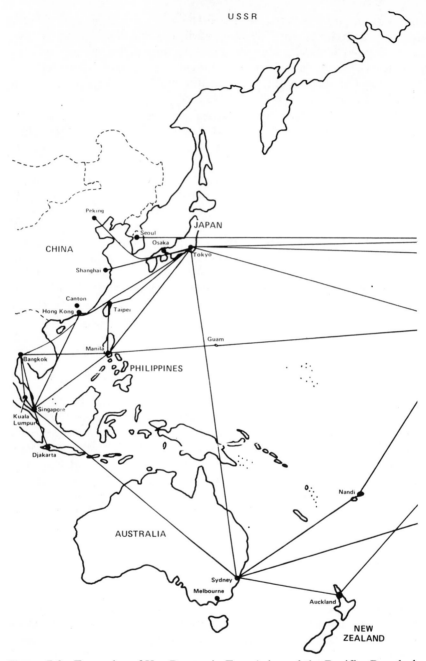

Figure 7-2. Examples of Key Routes in East Asia and the Pacific. Bangkok-
Hong Kong, Hong Kong-Tokyo, Singapore-Djakarta, Tokyo-
Taipei, Singapore-Kuala Lumpur, and Singapore-Hong Kong

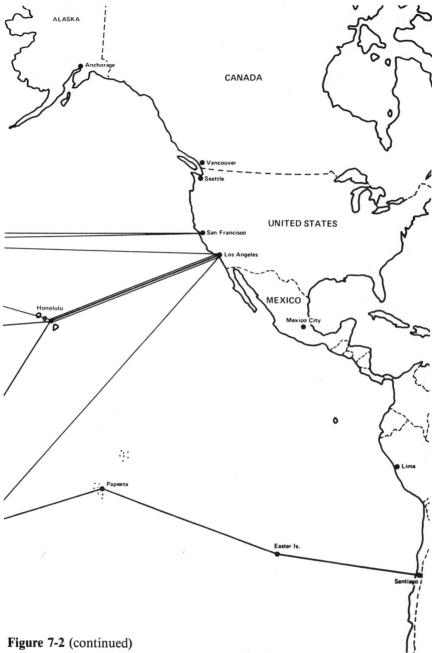

Figure 7-2 (continued)

are among the busiest routes in East Asia. The most heavily traveled transpacific routes are Tokyo-San Francisco, Tokyo-Los Angeles, and Seoul-Los Angeles

Figure 7-3. Three Air Routes between Europe and Japan

The polar route between Europe and Japan via an Alaskan intermediate stop was opened by SAS in 1957. Additional European airlines and JAL now operate the route as well, and American carriers fly between New York or Chicago and Tokyo via Alaska. The polar route permits rapid end-to-end one-stop service.

The transsiberian route between Europe and Japan most closely follows the great circle route around the globe and thus offers the most rapid Europe-Japan service. It averages three hours faster than the polar route, depending on the location of European city involved. Passenger appeal and fuel conservation make it very attractive to the airlines. Because the Soviet Union lies astride much of the route, the good will of the USSR is vital to its success. As early as 1938, a Swedish carrier proposed a joint transsiberian service in cooperation with Aeroflot. Increasing tensions in Europe and the outbreak of war in 1939 forced abandonment of the idea. In 1958, while negotiating for London-Moscow turnaround service, Great Britain requested transsiberian rights. Moscow rejected its proposal. More than ten years later, recognizing the potential hard-currency earning potential of the route and finally possessing civil aircraft (Ilyushin Il-62s) it considered competitive with western aircraft, the Soviet Union agreed to negotiations with Britain, France, and Japan. Protocols were signed and transsiberian service (London-Moscow-Tokyo, Paris-Moscow-Tokyo) inaugurated in 1970. Aeroflot and JAL operated service on both routes, and BOAC and Air France mounted service on routes involving their own countries. Several other European carriers have implemented transsiberian service since then. Because the long segments of the route permit longhaul aircraft to be operated at maximum efficiency; and because Japan has restricted market entry and capacity, transsiberian service has been very profitable for most carriers on the route.

JAL and several major European airlines operate all three Europe-Japan route options. Although the transsiberian service is shorter and profitable, the other routes are still viable. Carriers offering the polar service have been able to use widebody aircraft (in contrast to the transsiberian route where the Soviet Union, not having its own widebody aircraft until the 1980s, refused to allow other airlines to use western-manufactured widebody aircraft while crossing Soviet territory). These carriers can negotiate better pooling agreements when not dealing with the Soviet Union, and provide better service to tourists and families less able to cope with problems encountered in unscheduled weather or equipment-related landings on Soviet territory. Soviet society (including the political system, hotels, catering, and other aspects of the Soviet state) is ill-prepared to deal with unexpected groups of foreigners. At least one major transsiberian airline tries to direct casual tourists and family groups with children to the polar service where any difficulties are likely to receive more sympathetic and effective attention than is usual in the USSR.

A transsiberian service to Peking is a potential variation of transsiberian Tokyo service. A north European carrier proposed such a Peking route, but was refused by the Soviet Union, presumably because Moscow is not eager to facilitate contact between Europe and China.

The southern or silk route, as noted, attracts a different market than the Europe-Japan travelers desiring rapid end-to-end service. It is not competitive with the transsiberian route and therefore is unaffected by it.

North and Mid-Pacific

The North and Mid-Pacific route groupings, usually considered together, include routes between the western hemisphere and Asian countries north of Australasia. Primary Asian points are Manila, Hong Kong, Taipei, Tokyo, and Seoul. Peking may become significant in the future. Major western hemisphere airports are in Los Angeles, San Francisco, Seattle, and Vancouver. The polar route transpacific leg (via Anchorage or Fairbanks) is also part of this route grouping. Honolulu is an important intermediate stop for routes involving Guam, Manila, and Tokyo.

One of the major intercontinental route groupings of the world, the North/Mid-Pacific area is achieving high traffic growth rates. The principal factor generating this growth is the increasing discretionary income of the Japanese expressed in heavy tourist traffic to Hawaii and the U.S. mainland. The most heavily traveled routes in the region are Tokyo–San Franscisco, Tokyo–Los Angles, and Seoul–Los Angeles.

South Pacific

The South Pacific route grouping encompasses routes between the western hemisphere and Australasia. The most important Australasian point is Sydney; Auckland, Nandi, and Papeete are other regional points of some significance. In addition to routes between Australasia and North America, service involving Easter Island, Santiago, Lima, and Mexico City is also operated. Nandi and Honolulu are important intermediate points between Australia/New Zealand and North America, and Papeete serves the same function on routes to South America.

Unconventional International Routes

Although many international civil aviation routes are affected by political factors and some are mounted for political, rather than commercial, reasons, several are so entangled in politics that their operation differs markedly from most other routes. Three such international routes or route groupings bear special examination.

Berlin Air Corridors

The Berlin air corridor routes between West Germany (Federal Republic of Germany) and West Berlin are the most politicized air transport routes in international civil aviation (see figure 7–4). West Berlin is a West German enclave laying entirely with East Germany (German Democratic Republic), approximately 110 miles (176 kilometers) from the closest West German border. Though not a constitutional part of the Federal Republic, West Berlin enjoys close political, economic and cultural ties with it. In 1945 the Allied powers occupying Germany approved establishment of air corridors connecting three West German cities—Hamburg, Hanover, and Frankfurt—with West Berlin. Aircraft of the Allies were to be guaranteed safety if they remained within the 20-mile (32-kilometers) width of the corridors.

In June 1948 Soviet forces surrounding West Berlin blocked all surface transportation (autobahns, railways, waterways) connecting West Berlin with West Germany. Thus started the eleven-month Berlin blockade and the subsequent Western airlift to supply the city with all neccessities, including food and coal. The airlift succeeded despite adverse winter weather conditions and Soviet harassment. Soviet military aircraft buzzed the transports, occasionally firing a few shots nearby. Their crews trained searchlights on aircraft cockpits to blind Western pilots, Soviet forces raised barrage balloons alongside the corridors. In all, 733 incidents of harassment against Western aircraft were reported.[6]

After the Soviets ended the blockade in 1949, agreements were concluded with Soviet occupation forces to guarantee transport between West Germany and West Berlin over specified air, land, and water routes. East Germany (and the Soviet Union) still claim the entire city and harassment of transportation links is frequently increased during periods of East-West tension.

Airlines of the three Western allies operate nonstop flights between ten West German cities and West Berlin, usually on an exclusive franchise basis for particular cities corresponding approximately with the postwar occupation zones of the three powers. Frankfurt (Pan Am) has the most frequent connections, as many as fourteen daily flights; Dusseldorf (most flights by British Airways, some by Air France), Hamburg (Pan Am), and Hanover (British Airways) each generate eight to ten daily West Berlin flights: and Cologne-Bonn (British Airways), Munich (Pan Am), and Stuttgart (both

Figure 7-4. Berlin Air Corridors

Pan Am and British Airways) each generate more than five daily flights. Additionally, British Airways mounts two daily nonstop London–West Berlin flights and Air France mounts two daily Paris–West Berlin flights via Dusseldorf. Pan Am flies once daily between Zurich and West Berlin. Each of these flights must operate within one of the corridors when over East Germany.

Three purposes can be cited to support contined operation of the Berlin flights: (1) conventional commercial need; (2) manifestation of West Berlin independence from East Germany and ties with West Germany and the West in general; and (3) maintenance of a framework for reimplementation of the airlift should that become necessary. So vital does the West German government consider the Berlin service that each route receives a federal subsidy of 15 to 36 percent.

A long-standing problem of the corridor flights is the question of altitude restrictions. No specific limitations are included in the formal agreements, but according to customary procedures pilots maintain their aircraft at between 4,000 and 10,000 feet. At the time this practice was imposed, in the immediate postwar period, the Western Allies were using Douglas DC-3 transports that rarely climbed above 10,000 feet. However, the Boeing 727s and other aircraft used in recent years are inefficient at low levels and all aircraft are subject to weather difficulties at low altitudes. Whenever the Western Allies request permission from the Inter-Allied Air Safety Center in Berlin to fly above 10,000 feet, the Soviet representative at the Center claims that the safety of the flights cannot be guaranteed. The Soviets and East Germans reserve airspace above 10,000 feet for military flights. To make their point, Soviet military aircraft on occasion deliberately traverse the corridors in a north-south direction above and below western commercial transports flying in an east-west direction.

The Soviet Union and East Germany also object to flights entering West Berlin from foreign points and have protested nonstop service from London, Zurich, and other cities. The United States would like to open the corridors to carriers registered in countries other than the four wartime powers, but the USSR will not consider this possibility. On the contrary, East Germany does promote East Berlin Schönefeld airport as a major international terminal, trying to attract foreign airlines as much for the recognition and prestige their service might suggest as for the hard currency that might be gained from landing and other fees. Poor traffic potential and problems of access to East German territory from the West limit the appeal of Schönefeld for Western airlines. The East German carrier Interflug does do moderately well in generating its own transit traffic involving West Berlin, carrying passengers at large discounts between East Berlin and points in Asia or Africa, and providing connecting surface transport to/from West Berlin. Many non-Germans accept such arrangements.

In essence, air service involving West Berlin reflects the status of that city. Soviet restrictions reflect a policy to isolate and eventually absorb West Berlin into East Berlin and thus into East Germany. Western policy is to counteract Soviet efforts and keep West Berlin open, viable, vigorous, and firmly tied to the West.

Japan-Taiwan Service

In 1972 Japan extended full diplomatic recognition to the People's Republic of China and withdrew recognition from the Republic of China (Taiwan). Unofficial government relations between Japan and Taiwan were maintained and trade between the two countries, always strong, actually increased. Japan Air Lines (JAL) and China Airlines (CAL), the Taiwanese carrier, continued bilateral service, the former operating thirty-seven and the latter twenty-one weekly flights. For JAL, the Taiwan service accounted for 10 percent of its entire revenue. In addition to business links, the route between Japan and Taiwan is supported by a very large Japanese tourist flow.

Japan and the People's Republic of China signed a bilateral air transport agreement in 1974 that required Japan to impose upon China Airlines various restrictions that, if implemented, would drastically alter the nature of Japan-Taiwan air service. Among the Chinese demands were the following: (1) CAL would be banned from all Japanese airports that would be used by CAAC of the People's Republic; (2) CAL in Japan would call itself CAL-Taiwan; (3) CAL would close all offices in Japan and be represented there by independent agents; and (4) Japanese officials would announce that CAL did not represent a state and that the Taiwanese flag on CAL aircraft was only a trademark, not a flag. Upon hearing of the Peking conditions, Taiwan informed Japan that compliance with Chinese requests would result in Taiwanese exclusion of all Japanese aircraft from its airspace. Japan, which had earlier submitted to Arab pressures against El Al service to Tokyo, submitted to China as well, not believing that Taiwan would carry out its threats. Foreign Minister Masayoshi Ohira himself read the statement to newsmen that the flag on CAL aircraft did not represent a national flag and that the airline "CAL-Taiwan" did not represent a state.[7] Taiwan immediately canceled all Taiwan-Japan flights of both CAL and JAL, and withdrew permission for JAL to use Taiwanese airspace. The airspace restrictions forced JAL into a detour of 200-300 miles (320-485 kilometers) for its flights to Manila and other southeast Asian destinations. The extra distance added 40 to 50 minutes to each flight and substantial extra fuel expenditures.

Other airlines—Northwest Orient, CP Air of Hong Kong, Korean, and MAS of Malaysia—used fifth freedom rights to accomodate Taiwan-Japan traffic. JAL reported in 1975 that loss of the route in 1974-1975 had cost it $10 million. Its twice-weekly service to Peking was usually half full and could not compare with the Taiwan flights in revenue generation.[8] In July 1975, fourteen months after suspension of bilateral air services, Japan and Taiwan signed an "unofficial pact" to resume bilateral air service. Both countries were under pressure to find an acceptable compromise. Japan was driven by airline interests, pro-Taiwan interests within the ruling Liberal Democratic party, and Western allies who wanted to heal conflicts between anticommunist governments after the fall of Vietnam. Because the fifth freedom carriers flying between Japan and Taiwan were unable to attract large numbers of Japanese discretionary travelers (who, like other Japanese, are generally loyal to JAL), Taiwan had suffered a serious loss in tourist revenue.

Under terms of the unofficial agreement, a new Japanese foreign minister stated in Parliament that although Japan did not recognize Taiwan, Japan acknowledged that the Taiwanese flag was a national flag to those who did recognize Taiwan. However, it was impossible to revert to the pre-1974 situation in which JAL and CAL operated reciprocal turnaround service. Both Taipei and Peking rejected the proposal that JAL operate Taiwan and China service simultaneously. All Nippon Airways (ANA), the second largest Japanese carrier, was eager to replace JAL on the Taiwan route, but the Japanese government, which owns a significant minority holding in JAL, insisted that JAL retain a monopoly on international scheduled routes. In any case ANA was probably unacceptable to Taiwan because several of its board members have close ties to Peking. The Japanese government resolved the franchise issue by authorizing JAL to establish a wholly owned dummy subsidiary carrier that, for the sake of appearance, would be an entirely separate airline. In reality, its ties with JAL are strong and very evident. The new carrier, Japan Asia Airways, is directed by a board whose members are JAL officers. It is capitalized by JAL and operates cast-off JAL equipment, some purchased and some leased. Its aircraft livery is similar to that of JAL as are the uniforms of its crew. Its personnel (management and crews) were transferred from JAL. Japan Asia Airways mounts all Japan-based commercial service to and through Taiwan, including Tokyo-Taipei, Tokyo-Taipei-Hong Kong, Tokyo-Taipei-Manila, and Osaka-Taipei-Hong Kong routes.

In the late 1970s both Taiwan and People's Republic appeared to revise their positions on the issue of simultaneous service by third-country airlines. In 1979 the governments of the Philippines and China signed a bilateral air transport agreement permitting Philippine Airlines (PAL) to serve Chinese points while maintaining service to Taiwan. PAL operates a Manila-Canton-Peking route as well as a Taipei service. By then, both Taiwan and the People's Republic had eased their stands on person-to-person contacts between their citizens; China, in fact, had been urging the restoration of officially sanctioned communications, including transportation links, between the mainland and Taiwan as an initial step toward eventual reunification.

Cairo-Tel Aviv Service

Air service between Cairo and Tel Aviv was a provision of the 1979 Egypt-Israel peace agreement. Israeli government and El Al officials were eager that the national flag carrier operate the route on behalf of Israel. In Cairo, however, doubts were raised about the advisability of Egyptair mounting flights to Tel Aviv on behalf of Egypt. Although many Arab governments broke relations with Egypt after the peace treaty was signed, Egyptair and the airlines of most of these countries maintained reciprocal service between their major cities. Despite its official isolation, Cairo generated substantial Middle Eastern traffic because of (1) its gateway position at the "intersection" of North Africa, eastern Africa, and the Arabian peninsula, and (2) travel by thousands of Egyptians working in other Arab countries. Egyptian authorities and officials in various Arab states feared that should Egyptair also operate flights to Tel Aviv, boycotts against it in other Arab countries and even sabotage would occur.

Third-country airlines, among them TWA, KLM, and Olympic Airways, were proposed as potential Cairo — Tel Aviv operators. However, for various reasons, including threats of Arab boycotts and terrorist activity, such proposals were not implemented. Egypt adopted the Japanese solution, creating a new carrier to mount the Tel Aviv route. Thus, in March 1980, Nefertiti Aviation and El Al began reciprocal service as scheduled. Flight time is 50 minutes, compared with the day-long detour through Athens or Cyprus that had previously been necessary. Many passengers are third-country tourists on package tours combining Egypt and Isreal.

Summary

Some characteristics of the international civil aviation route network have remained constant for several decades. The North Atlantic route grouping has been and will continue to be the single most important route grouping in the world. In a postcolonial world, the ties between former colonial powers and their colonies endure as a major determinant in route structures of many airlines. Ethnic bonds between residents of different countries also remain a critical factor in route networks of many carriers. Despite expansion of service by airlines of developing countries and the Soviet bloc, the most heavily traveled international routes are those between Western industrialized countries and the most prized traffic rights are those in Western states.

The impact of rising fuel costs, increased use of charter airlines, and demand for greater influence of their carriers by developing countries is unlikely to be significant in the international system as a whole, although one or more of these factors may affect certain route groupings. Similarly, the emergence of "phantom" airlines to serve politically sensitive routes in the Middle East and Far East does not presage the appearance of large numbers of such carriers.

Notes

1. Michael Brown, "Alitalia—Good Management Isn't Enough," *Interavia* XXIX:7 (July, 1974), p. 643.

2. Several American travel agents specializing in east European ethnic travel have offered this explanation to the author.

3. Miami was included in IATA statistics for the Mid-Atlantic through 1978; since January 1979 it has been listed in the North Atlantic route grouping.

4. In this and other groupings of city-pairs, most routes are listed in a single directional pattern (that is, either north-south *or* south-north), regardless of any directional imbalance that may occur. Unless otherwise noted, the imbalance is not severe.

5. See John F. Burns, "Pretoria is Pressing Secret Trade with Its Black Africa Opponents," *New York Times*, April 8, 1979, p. 1.

6. Drew Middleton, "30 Years Ago, the West Won its First Round in Cold War," *New York Times*, June 26, 1978, p. A2.

7. Fox Butterfield, "Japan and China Sign Air Accord; Taiwan Cuts Link," *New York Times*, April 21, 1974, p. 1.

8. "Air Service May Resume Between Tokyo and Taipei," *Aviation Daily* 220:7 (July 10, 1975), p. 52.

8 The International Transport Aircraft Industry

The international transport aircraft industry includes manufacturers of airframes, engines, components, avionics, ground support equipment, aircraft furnishings, and other products vital to aircraft construction as well as related services, such as financing, leasing, and maintenance and overhaul. This chapter will concentrate on the international airframe and engine industries, aircraft selection and fleet planning, and financing new aircraft in the international market.

The combined fleet belonging to airlines of ICAO member states excluding the Soviet Union includes approximately 8,500 transport aircraft. Competition for supply of most of this market is keen; the manufacture and sale of aircraft abroad is perceived by governments to be beneficial to the national balance of payments, technological base, and potential for influence over other countries. Further, foreign purchase of home-manufactured aircraft enables larger production runs that reduce the cost of aircraft to home carriers (and to foreign carriers). Only in the Soviet Union and its most subservient satellite and client states is there no competition between aircraft manufacturers; the Soviet industry has a captive market. Elsewhere, the contest for sales is sharp.

The International Airframe and Engine Industries

American airframe and engine manufacturers dominate the international transport market. European and Soviet industries occupy secondary, yet important, positions, and several other regions have some significance in special markets.

The United States

Approximately 80 percent of all commercial aircraft in Western countries are produced in the United States. Before the European A300 Airbus penetrated the widebody market in the mid-1970s, the U.S. share of Western sales was as high as 96 percent. Three major airframe manufacturers (Boeing, McDonnell Douglas, and Lockheed) and two engine companies (Pratt & Whitney and General Electric) are the instruments of American domination.

Boeing. Of the products of the Boeing Company in Seattle, an American newsmagazine published in a 1980 cover story:

> They [Boeing aircraft] are the best, safest, most efficient aircraft anywhere. Boeing has earned the reputation of doing everything first class. The company's engineers are the most innovative and imaginative, its sales force the most dedicated, its service staff the most professional. What is more, everyone who has anything to do with buying, selling or flying commercial jets knows it. Says an executive of West Germany's national airline, Lufthansa, which has been flying largely Boeing aircraft since the start of the jet age: 'There is no secret at all about Boeing's success. The company just keeps coming up with the right plane, at the right time, at the right price.'[1]

Pacific Aero Products Company, the original name of Boeing, was founded in 1915. Its first aircraft, a fabric-covered wood-structured seaplane, made its initial flight in 1916. Given the extensive use of wood in early aircraft construction and the location of Seattle in a major lumber industry area, it is not surprising that another Boeing product in those early years was furniture. During the 1930s, the company began work on two military aircraft that were to see extensive service during World War II—the B-17 Flying Fortress and the B-29, both heavy bombers. In transport aircraft, Boeing lagged behind other manufacturers until 1958 when the first 707 was produced near Seattle. In late 1958 Pan Am inaugurated American jet service on the North Atlantic with 707s, thus bringing to an end the era of Douglas transport supremacy and beginning the current era of Boeing leadership.

Alone among contemporary aircraft manufacturers, Boeing is able to supply an airline with equipment suitable for almost all of its needs. The 737 meets the requirements of many carriers for a short-range jet. The 727, the best selling commercial aircraft in history, is a medium-range jet. The new 757, with two engines instead of the three on the 727, is also designed for narrowbody medium-range routes. Although no longer available for commercial purchase, the 707 is a long-range veteran and remains a key aircraft in many international airline fleets. The 747, Boeing's famous four-engine jumbo jet, is the original widebody and a familiar aircraft on long distance routes. A new widebody Boeing, the 767, is a two-engine jet for the medium-range market.

For airlines serving a variety of route lengths, such as United and Lufthansa, substantial cost savings can be derived from operating different models of aircraft manufactured by a single firm. Some commonality exists from one model to another in spare parts, maintenance and overhaul procedures, operating techniques, and other attributes. Certain economies of scale can be realized and, some claim, safety is enhanced by increased crew familiarity with aircraft characteristics. Not all airlines require four different models of aircraft, but even those carriers using two types can gain by purchasing both from the same manufacturer. Only Boeing offers airlines a wide choice.

McDonnell Douglas. More so than Boeing, McDonnell Douglas Corporation is identified by the general public as a major defense contractor. It is, in fact, among the largest defense contractors in the United States. Its Douglas Aircraft Company in Long Beach produces only two civilian transports, the short-range twin-engine DC-9, and the three-engine long-range widebody DC-10. The latter has suffered from some passenger backlash against it following a 1979 crash of the type in Chicago that killed 273 people. Significant segments of the traveling public avoid flying on the DC-10, advertising campaigns of other manufacturers and of airlines flying other types feature ill-disguised campaigns against it, some carriers with DC-10s have sold them, and sales of new DC-10s have slipped sharply.

Douglas is probably the best known manufacturer of propeller-driven transports in the world. Its DC-3, which first flew in 1935, was produced in great numbers prior to and during World War II (nearly 11,000 in the United States, 2,000 in the Soviet Union under license, and others elsewhere) and saw postwar commercial service well into the 1970s with several developing-country airlines.[2] The DC-6B (first flight in 1951) and DC-7B/C (first flights in 1955) were four-engine propeller-driven workhorses on transatlantic and other intercontinental passenger runs until rendered obsolete by the advent of jet transports. Many operators converted the displaced DC-6s and DC-7s into freighters which then saw lengthy service on cargo routes.

The DC-8 long-range 4-engine jet aircraft was never as successful as its Boeing 707 counterpart. Less efficient to operate, the DC-8 was manufactured in lesser numbers and taken out of production earlier than the 707. It was, however, an important aircraft on intercontinental routes of some large carriers (among them Air Canada, KLM, SAS, Swissair, UTA, and JAL), and the DC-8 63 "stretch" version has remained popular in its cargo version into the 1980s. The DC-9 twin-engine short-range aircraft is competitive with its Boeing 737 counterpart and has been developed in several range and capacity variations.

Lockheed. Another very prominent defense contractor, the Lockheed Corporation produced several noteworthy propeller-driven transport aircraft in the 1940s and 1950s. The four-engine Constellation was a rival to the DC-6B and DC-7B on transatlantic service prior to the jet era. The four-engine Electra turboprop, designed for short- and medium-range routes, was first flown in 1957 and saw service in the fleets of several U.S. carriers. However, several serious accidents marred the image of the aircraft, reducing its acceptability to the American market and thus diminishing its sales potential. Nonetheless, the Electra was a mainstay of the Eastern Airlines east coast shuttle for many years, surviving well into the jet age.

Production of the L-1011 Tristar widebody jet in the 1970s and 1980s marked the return of Lockheed into the commercial aircraft field. Similar in performance and appearance to the DC-10, the Tristar has not sold as well. The Tristar uses Rolls Royce engines and thus receives some British government support in marketing, an important factor in its purchase by several Commonwealth airlines.

Pratt & Whitney. A subsidiary of United Technologies Corporation, Pratt & Whitney is the largest manufacturer of aircraft engines in the world. It is one of three companies in the world to produce the high bypass ratio fan jet engines that power Western widebody aircraft.[3] Its primary widebody market is the Boeing 747 and 767, but Pratt & Whitney large fan engines can be used on other widebodies as well. Smaller Pratt & Whitney engines are standard on all Boeing and Douglas narrowbody aircraft and on many military types.

General Electric. General Electric CF-6 high bypass ratio fan jet engines are standard on most DC-10s and A300/A310s, but can also be used on some Boeing widebodies. For example, Lufthansa decided to order GE engines for its new 747s, instead of the more common Pratt & Whitney powerplants, in part to standardize on the GE engine for its entire widebody fleet. The German carrier also operates GE-engined DC-10s and Airbuses.[4]

GE has developed a new high bypass ratio fan jet engine for narrowbody aircraft, specifically for DC-8s and 707s. Airframes of these aircraft are expected to remain structurally sound for many years, but their original low bypass ratio engines are unable to conform to U.S. noise control regulations effective from 1984. The new engine, designated CFM56, not only meets noise requirements, but also is more efficient in fuel consumption and enhances aircraft performance in takeoff thrust, range, and other characteristics. The CFM56 was developed jointly with the French engine firm, SNECMA, and is produced in both countries.

Other companies. Additional firms in the United States produce airframes, but these generally are for military use, general aviation, or another purpose not relevant to international commercial air transport. Among the companies are Beechcraft, Cessna, General Dynamics, Grumman, and Fairchild. Similarly, several firms manufacture engines of various types not frequently used on aircraft flying international transport routes. Bell Helicopter, Boeing Vertol, and Sikorsky Aircraft (a division of United Technologies Corporation) are the leading U.S. builders of helicopters.

Europe

Britain. In 1978 the ruling Labor party nationalized most British aerospace manufacturers, bringing approximately 80 percent of the industry (in terms of sales volume and number of employees) under the management of the state-owned British Aerospace Corporation, known as BAe. In 1979 a subsequent Conservative government declared its intention to "denationalize" the newly formed state corporation. The issue of ownership may continue to be a source of dispute between British political parties. (Even before nationalization, the independence of some nominally privately owned British aerospace firms was subject to compromise as a result of heavy government subsidy.)

BAe is organized in two "groups," a Dynamics Group (consisting of the former British Aircraft Corporation Guided Weapons Division and Hawker Siddeley Dynamics), and an Aircraft Group (formerly British Aircraft Corporation, Hawker Siddeley Aviation, and Scottish Aviation). The former is concerned with missiles, space systems, and related products. The latter has manufactured both military and civilian aircraft, including the supersonic Concorde. In 1978 BAe joined Airbus Industrie as a 20 percent partner; its particular responsibility is construction of A300/A310 wings.

Jet transports built by Britain alone have been unable to compete with American counterparts; they have been sold mainly to British carriers, other Commonwealth airlines whose governments are subject to British pressure, and carriers not known for their operating efficiency, such as Tarom of Romania and CAAC of China. The BAC (Vickers) VC-10, a long-range aircraft with four rear-mounted jet engines, entered service in 1974 with BOAC. Only 54 copies were manufactured, far too few to recover costs. Although comfortable for passengers, the VC-10 lacked the range capabilities and operating efficiencies of American aircraft in the long-haul market. Production of the Hawker-Siddeley Trident, a three-engine medium-range jet, was terminated in 1978 after 117 copies.

The BAC One-Eleven, a short-range jet with rear-mounted twin engines, has been more successful, but it is not competitive with the Boeing 737 or DC-9 in free market conditions. A production run of approximately 250 copies is projected in Britain and license production is planned in Romania. The Hawker Siddeley 748, a short-range twin-engine turboprop, enjoys a better record. It is widely used for both commercial and military service in industrialized as well as developing countries.

The third firm in the world (in addition to Pratt & Whitney and General Electric) to manufacture high bypass ratio, fan jet engines for widebody aircraft is Rolls Royce. A component of BAe, Rolls Royce produces the RB 211 engine standard on the Lockheed L-1011 Tristar. Variations of the RB 211 can also be used on the 747 and Airbus. Many British narrowbody aircraft — including the VC-10, Trident, and BAC-111 — are also powered by Roll Royce engines.

France. Two French firms manufacture commercial aircraft airframes. Aérospatiale, fully nationalized, was the major French partner in production of the Concorde, and is the primary French contractor and the overall manager of the Airbus program. It also manufactured the short/medium range twin-engine Caravelle, which received more attention than its small production run of 280 aircraft would suggest. The Caravelle was never developed to its maximum advantage and its production resulted in a financial loss to the manufacturer. Another Aérospatiale project, the Corvette business jet, was cancelled in 1977 after construction of 40 aircraft of a planned run of 300. Aérospatiale also produces several different models of helicopters.

The French government acquired 21 percent of the capital of Dassault-Breguet in 1979. The shares carry double voting weight, according to French legislation, thus giving the government a 42 percent voice in company decisions, substantially above the 33 percent legally required in France to form a blocking minority. Better known for its military aircraft, Dassault also produces the successful Falcon business jet. Another attempt at civil aircraft manufacture ended in financial disaster in the 1970s when construction of the Mercure twin-engine jet designed to replace the Caravelle was terminated after only 10 were built. Sales of approximately 320 were needed to recover a large government subsidy. The aircraft had two major shortcomings: entry into the market after American counterparts were well established and inadequate range in comparison with American models.

Two French companies manufacture aircraft engines. The major portion of SNECMA (Société Nationale d'Etude et de Construction de Moteurs d'Aviation) output is in the military field, but the company is developing and producing high bypass ratio fan jet engines for both narrowbody and widebody aircraft in cooperation with General Electric of the United States. The CF6 series engine is standard on the Airbus and some DC-10s and can be used on certain other widebody aircraft as well. The new CFM 56 is designed to replace the relatively noisy and inefficient engines on DC-8s and Boeing 707s. Turbomeca, a privately owned firm, produces a variety of turbojet, turboprop, and turboshaft (helicopter) engines that power military and civil aircraft.

Netherlands. Though not prominent in international service, aircraft of the Fokker company of Amsterdam are in wide use around the world. The F.27 short-range twin-engine turboprop has sold well in several versions for twenty-five years. Several hundred F.27s were built under license in the United States by Fairchild. The F.28 short-range twin-engine jet fulfills requirements for a jet aircraft with smaller capacity and lesser range capabilities than Boeing or Douglas short-haul equipment. Fokker is a participant in the Airbus program and is active in other collaborative projects.

From 1969 to 1980, Fokker operated as a partner in the VFW-Fokker consortium. Dissolution of the German-Dutch organization was sought by West Germany to facilitate reconstruction of its own aerospace industry.

Other West European countries. West German industry produces no civil aircraft on its own, but is a major participant in the Airbus program and is active in other aspects of aerospace technology. VFW (Vereinigte Flugtechnische Werke), MBB (Messerschmitt-Bolkow-Blohm), and Dornier are among the largest firms. CASA (Construcciones Aeronauticas, S.A.) of Spain manufactures a small STOL (short takeoff and landing) transport that has sold well in developing countries. Italian industry includes production of helicopters and military aircraft under license, components and airframe sections for large transport aircraft built in other countries, and support equipment. Swedish industry is strongly military-oriented.

Multinational European firms. Eager to acquire a major share of the international transport aircraft market, west European aerospace firms are pooling their capabilities — technological, industrial, and financial — in an effort to compete with major American manufacturers. Because many participating industries are state-owned or state-supported, cooperating governments are often heavily involved. They in turn encourage state-owned airlines to purchase the multinationally produced aircraft, thus creating a situation approaching the "captive market" condition of Aeroflot and most east European airlines relative to Soviet aircraft production. Given the influence several west European countries still maintain in numerous former colonies, the potential market advantage extends well beyond the European region.

The most successful cooperative European aircraft to date is the A300 Airbus and its several variations. A twin-engine medium to moderately long-range widebody, the Airbus is produced by the consortium "Airbus Industrie" in Toulouse. Aérospatiale and Deutsche Airbus (VFW and MBB) each hold shares of approximately 38 percent, followed by British Aerospace, 20 percent, and CASA of Spain, 4 percent. Fokker and Belgian Belairbus are Airbus Industrie associates. Some components — including the wings and portions of the fuselage — are produced in participating countries outside France and shipped to Toulouse for assembly. Development of several Airbus variations is planned in an effort to create a "family" of aircraft suitable for the diverse needs of an airline with routes of different lengths and traffic densities. A widebody replication of the Boeing family of narrowbodies — 707, 727, and 737 — with substantial commonality of spare parts, operating techniques, and other attributes is the goal of the producers. The major competitor of the basic Airbus is the Boeing 767. Neither the 767 nor the Airbus is directly competitive with the 747, the L-1011, or DC-10, all of which have longer range and higher capacity capabilities. Additionally, although fuel efficiency should be enhanced by the fact that the Airbus and 767 each have only two engines, most carriers prefer three- or four-engine aircraft for overwater flights.

Aircraft industries in Europe continue to seek opportunities for collaboration in developement of new aircraft. Some confine their efforts to other companies in Europe, others pursue the possibility of joint projects with American or Japanese firms. In all instances, multinational production is perceived important in raising development capital, broadening the technological base, and enhancing access to wider markets.

The Soviet Union

The Ministry of Aircraft Production organizes, administers, and conducts the production of all aircraft in the Soviet Union. Aeroflot and the airlines of most party-states constitute a captive market for its output. Although they have tried to export their civil aircraft to the international market since the 1960s, the Soviets have been able to achieve significant sales only to countries dependent on the USSR — to other countries in Comecon (Council for Mutual Economic Assistance, a USSR-imposed version of the Common Market for the Soviet bloc) and client states among developing coutries.

Design work in the ministry is done by bureaus specializing in transport aircraft, fighters, bombers, helicopters, or engines. Five transport design bureaus exist, each named after its founder — Antonov, Beriev, Ilyushin, Tupolev, and Yakovlev. Upon announcement by Aeroflot of specifications for a desired new aircraft, several of the bureaus develop and submit designs to the airline which then selects the version to be produced. Production may be undertaken at several plants concurrently, none of them attached to the relevant design bureau.

Aircraft designed by the Tupolev and Ilyushin bureaus dominate Aeroflot international routes in the 1980s. The twin-engine Tu-134 and Tu-154 trijets are used on short- and medium-range routes respectively as well as on some longer multistage largely overland routes. The rear-engined Il-62 jet is widely used on long-range routes. The four-engine medium-range Il-86 widebody airbus entered scheduled service in the 1980s, more than ten years after Western widebody aircraft began scheduled service. Although not prominent in international service, several other Soviet aircraft should be noted. The Yakovlev Yak-40 and Yak-42 trijets, intended for shorter routes than those on which the Tu-134 is used, have been intensively promoted for export, but have not sold well. Completing its first flight in 1971, the Il-76 high-wing four-engine jet freighter is used extensively on medium- to long-range cargo flights within the Soviet Union. It is also used on Aeroflot's limited international cargo service and, in a military version, by the Soviet armed forces. The long-range Tupolev Tu-114, replaced by the Il-62, is noteworthy for its four counter-rotating turbo-prop engines. Another turboprop, the four-engine medium-range Ilysuhin Il-18, was widely used on Aeroflot service to developing countries and is still operated on Soviet domestic routes. It resembles the Lockheed Electra in structure and function — and even exceeds its American counterpart in accident occurence. The twin-engine Antonov An-24 turboprop has been constructed in several variations and is widely used in the Soviet Union and client states for several tasks, including freight carriage and troop transport. An aircraft of limited range, it was also used on Aeroflot multistage routes to developing countries until replaced by jet aircraft.

Eleven different design bureaus develop engines for Soviet aircraft. Most prominent among them in providing powerplants for Soviet jet transports are the Soloviev and Kuznetsov bureaus. Soviet engine technology does not meet Western standards. Their engines are considered inefficient, consuming vast amounts of fuel, and mechanically unreliable. Soviet industry has been unable to produce large high bypass ratio fan jet engines. From time to time, the Soviets have implicitly acknowledged their inadequacies by attempting to purchase small numbers of Rolls Royce RB 211 and General Electric CF6 powerplants, but the British and U.S. governments have forced suspension of relevant negotiations. On several occasions, with a variety of equipment, the Soviets have purchased small quantities, sometimes a single unit, of advanced Western products which they subsequently reproduce illegally for their own needs.

The Soviet Union is widely believed to have copied a number of transport aircraft designs from Western sources, either because of their own technological inability to create wholly new aircraft or a perceived need to build aircraft similar to "stylish" Western equipment. The noted designer Sergei V. Ilyushin admitted in a Soviet newspaper article that he designed the Il-62 with rear-mounted engines because rear-engined jets were then stylish in the West. He would have preferred an aircraft with wing-mounted engines.[5] The Il-62 is viewed in the West as a poorly engineered copy of the VC-10; the Il-18 as drawing heavily on the Lockheed Electra and Bristol Britannia; the An-24 as derived from the Fokker F.27 and Handley Page Herald; the An-72 STOL freighter as a copy of the Boeing STOL YC-14 military freighter; and the Tu-144 SST as a copy of the Concorde. The Soviet SST is known among many Western aviation professionals as the "Concordchik" or "Concordski." In each case, the lag-time between design work on the Western and Soviet models is appropriate to Soviet duplication of Western efforts. In several instances, Soviet aircraft engineers had visited Western aircraft plants where the relevant aircraft had been produced or Soviet agents had attempted to obtain detailed plans of Western aircraft through espionage.[6]

Attempts to copy Western aircraft have not resulted in Soviet-built duplicates because inadequate Soviet technology yields inferior products. Specific problems in the Soviet industry prevent the construction of aircraft equivalent in quality to Western counterparts. Among these problems are:

1. separation of design bureaus from production facilities, resulting in inconsistencies between designs and capabilities of the aircraft construction industry;
2. lack of coordination between airframe and engine design bureaus, resulting in inappropriate matching of engines to airframes;
3. uncertain delivery date of aircraft from factory and testing centers to carriers, thus complicating airline planniing;[7]
4. relatively unsophisticated metallurgical and other technology leading to excessively heavy aircraft by Western standards;
5. inefficient engines with exceedingly high specific fuel consumption;
6. low mechanical reliability of engines;
7. poor spare part support, leading to frequent cannibalization of some aircraft to keep others flying; and
8. design/performance characteristics that directly or indirectly lead to safety problem.[8]

East European Countries

Three east European countries manufacture civil aircraft. The Polish industry, subordinate to the Polish Ministry of Mechnical Construction, has three major airframe production facilities. It is the second largest builder of agricultural aircraft in the world, exceeded in output only by the United States. It also produces a Soviet light helicopter and the An-28 propeller-driven twin-engine feederliner under Soviet license; a jet trainer; the Piper Seneca twin-engine light aircraft under U.S. license; and major components of the Soviet Il-86 Airbus. Included in the output of the Polish engine industry are light aircraft powerplants and engine parts for Pratt & Whitney of Canada.

In pacts concluded in 1978 and 1979, British Aerospace agreed to transfer One-Eleven construction technology to Romania. Implementation of the agreement occurs in stages over a period of years, beginning with Romanian assembly of British-supplied components and culminating in Romanian manufacture of the entire aircraft. A similar arrangement provides for Romanian assembly of the Rolls Royce engines used on the One-Eleven.[9] Forerunner of the One-Eleven agreement was a 1968 agreement with the Britten-Norman Company, also of England, for the assembly of the ten-seat Islander aircraft. Additional agreements were concluded in 1970 and 1978 with Aérospatiale for license production of Alouette and Puma helicopters. The Romanians, apparently, are as eager to assert their independence from the Soviet Union in aircraft manufacture as in other fields.

Czechoslovakia produces aerobatic aircraft, gliders, military jet trainers, and a very short range fifteen passenger twin turboprop. Known as the Turbolet or L-410, the latter is used by Aeroflot for feeder service routes.

People's Republic of China

Lacking a strong technological base, the People's Republic of China is unable to sustain a modern aircraft industry. Some Soviet aircraft — propeller-driven transports, military types, and helicopters — have been built under license, but Sino-Soviet acrimony and Chinese dissatisfaction with the Soviet product (due to operating characteristics and safety-related shortcomings) have combined against the likelihood of further significant license arrangements between the two countries. The Chinese manufacture some unsophisticated aircraft on their own and have attempted to copy several Western types without license. These copies are not known to be successful; even replication of foreign aircraft (based on information freely available in the West) requires research/development and manufacturing capabilities unavailable in China. Discussions about production of Western aircraft under legal license in the People's Republic have been held with several Western firms, but the level of industralization in China suggests delayed implementation of such projects. Specific aerospace inadequacies are only one aspect of Chinese difficulties; the general economic infrastructure — including communications, surface transportation, and computer technology — is too primitive to support a modern aircraft production capability.[10] The 1980 contract for Chinese manufacture of landing-gear doors for the DC-9 Super 80 does not require great sophistication.

Other Countries

Many governments encourage or actually support the development of a home aircraft industry, perceiving it valuable in strengthening the national technical base, providing a domestic source for military and military-related equipment, and conserving/earning foreign exchange. Both developing and industrialized countries are among the states supporting local aircraft construction. Though none approaches the volume of the American or even major European industries, several other countries have industries of commercial or political importance.

Two state-owned firms produce commercial aircraft in Canada. Montreal-based Canadair, formerly a subsidiary of General Dynamics, was acquired by the govenment in 1975. Its output includes the business/commuter Challenger jet (originally developed as a Learjet) and various special-purpose small aircraft for cargo transport, firefighting, amphibious and other uses. Toronto-based de Havilland, purchased by the government from Hawker Siddeley in 1974, manufacturers the Dash-7 short-range fifty-passenger turboprop, the very successful Twin Otter eighteen-passenger feederliner, and the twin turboprop Buffalo military transport. Boeing, Douglas, Pratt & Whitney, and Rolls Royce each have subsidiary firms in Canada.

Embraer (Empresa Brasileira de Aeronautica S.A.) was established by the government of Brazil in 1969 for the specific purpose of producing and marketing a light twin turboprop transport aircraft suitable for both civilian and military use in Brazil and abroad. Since then, government ownership has been reduced to a small minority holding, and the aircraft construction program itself has been quite successful. The twin-engine Bandeirante has sold well in both Brazil and foreign countries, other small aircraft have been developed, and Embraer is producing several foreign-designed small aircraft under license.

Israel Aircraft Industries produces two aircraft with civilian application, the Arava STOL twin-engine utility aircraft and the Westwind executive jet.[11] Both can be used for several military purposes, for example, the Arava in paratroop configuration and the Westwind with radar systems for patrol and surveillance work. IAI also manufactures military fighters, jet trainers, missiles, and other military products. Its Bedek maintenance division overhauls Boeing 707s for resale and does major maintenance work for a number of foreign airlines, some registered in states whose governments are hostile to Israel.

Several firms in Japan manufacture helicopters and small fixed-wing aircraft, but the Japanese aerospace industry has not developed any successful transports. The YS-11 short-range twin turboprop did sell fairly well in domestic and foreign markets, but the program was poorly managed and failed to show a profit. Approximately 80 percent of Japanese aerospace orders are placed by the Japanese government; in contrast with many other sectors of Japanese industry, the aerospace balance of trade is negative, with imports almost ten times greater than exports.[12] A consortium of three Japanese manufacturers—Fuji, Kawasaki, and Mitsubishi— is a risk-sharing participant in construction of the Boeing 767. Approximately 15 percent of the airframe is built in Japan and more than 100 Japanese engineers work in the 767 program in Seattle.

The Supersonic Transport

In 1979 the British and French governments announced termination of Concorde supersonic transport aircraft production after only sixteen had been built. Launched by a treaty between the two governments in 1962, construction of the Concorde began in 1965. Commercial operation of the aircraft began in 1976, Air France offering Paris-Dakar-Rio de Janeiro flights and British Airways offering London-Bahrein service. Air France inaugurated daily Paris-New York flights in 1977. Additional transatlantic service followed.

The Concorde has been plagued by problems since its inception. Construction costs soared far beyond initial projections, resulting in at least six cost estimate revisions after 1962. The program drained resources away from subsonic aircraft development that might have been more profitable. The purchase price of the Concorde rose along with the revised cost estimates, eroding the pool of potential buyers. Sales prospects were further dimmed by production delays of at least five years, placing the SST on the market in the mid-1970s when the most likely airline purchasers were already committed to large buys of widebody jets. Certain operating characteristics of the Concorde raised further doubts about the commercial viability of the aircraft: profligate fuel consumption, exceeding the requirements of a 747 by four times on the North Atlantic route; severely restricted capacity (100 passengers and limited baggage); limited range; and adverse environmental consequences (sonic booms and take-off/landing noise). To recover some of the exorbitant costs of operating the aircraft, fares were set at 20 percent above first class service, thus limiting passenger market size on all but a few routes. Both Air France and British Airways sustained severe annual losses on Concorde operations, between $4.5 and $10 million. No airline would voluntarily purchase an aircraft with so many glaring weaknesses;[13] state-owned Air France and British Airways were captive markets for the French and British aircraft industries and the two governments were forced to subsidize their losses. By 1979 France and Britain determined that further financial support of the Concorde construction program could not be sustained, but that operation of existing SSTs by the two airlines should continue with subsidy.[14]

The Soviet supersonic transport, the Tupolev Tu-144, is widely believed to have been copied from the Concorde,[15] although inferior Soviet technology precluded an exact replication of the French-British aircraft. Its problems are legion and well-documented, the Soviets having taken the unusual step in 1977 and 1978 of asking Concorde officials for technical assistance on various problems. Among their many specific concerns were fuel-system pipes, emergency power supply, fireproof paints, navigation-piloting equipment, speed stability control unit, fire-fighting system, interior furnishings, and methods of improving the strength of the fuselage and undercarriage units.[16]

Knowledge of Soviet problems with the Tu-144 was widespread, well before the 1977/1978 official Soviet requests for assistance. Most attention was focused on the low bypass ratio Kuznetsov NK-144 engines which consumed so much fuel that the range of the Tu-144 was only about half that of the Concorde. Other engine difficulties contributed to excessive cabin noise and vibrations, particularly during high speed operations. In common with other Soviet aircraft, excessive structural weight is also a problem for the Tu-144 and is a factor in its high fuel consumption. Structural problems are believed to have caused the very public fatal crash of a Tu-144 at the Paris air show. Another Tu-144 was destroyed in a 1978 Moscow-area crash.

Throughout the Soviet SST's checkered history, USSR officials have repeatedly issued optimistic forecasts about its imminent entrance into international scheduled service. In 1969 Aeroflot announced a 1971 target date for transatlantic routes. In early 1971 Tu-144 flights to Calcutta were announced for later that year. The international inauguration of Soviet SST service was soon declared to be planned for 1973, then 1974. By mid-1973 passenger flights were scheduled for 1975-76. In 1978 the Ministry of Civil Aviation and Aeroflot confirmed that the aircraft had been withdrawn from a domestic route (Moscow-Alma Ata) implemented less than a year earlier and that the SST had been grounded indefinitely.

In February 1979 the Soviet Union cited "ecological reasons" for refusing permission for Air France to operate transsiberian Concorde service between Paris and Tokyo. Although they had previously belittled Western concern about potential SST-caused damage to the environment, Soviet officials suddenly decided that Siberian wildlife would be endangered by overhead Concorde flights. Western observers were quick to note that the professed Soviet concern over its ecology was more likely a screen to cover their determination that a Soviet SST precede foreign SSTs in overflying Soviet territory enroute to other countries.[17]

In mid-1979 the Tu-144 was reported by the Soviets to have been re-equipped with new Kolesov engines that were 50 percent more fuel efficient than the Kuznetsov models used earlier. The aircraft was said to be in regular service between Moscow and Khabarovsk, a distance of some 6,200 kilometers. No claims were made about impending international service.[18]

From the vantage point of the 1980s, it seems clear that the technological base for developing commercially viable and ecologically acceptable supersonic transport aircraft did not exist in the 1960s and 1970s. Unforeseen fuel price rises also played a major role in curtailing the longevity of the Concorde. Any new SST must have more efficient engines and better capacity and range capabilities. The Office of Technology Assessment in the U.S. Congress issued a report in 1980 stating that long-term prospects for development of an advanced U.S. SST were "significant," although fuel prices and availability could not be predicted. It declared that substantial progress has been made in a number of key technologies relevant to the SST and suggested that Congress support a major research program to define and reduce development problems.[19] (An earlier proposal for major

U.S funding of SST development was rejected by Congress in 1971. Funding of a minor research program continues.)

Aircraft Selection and Fleet Planning for International Service

Airline operating efficiency requires a high degree of fleet standardization, yet many airlines must operate a variety of routes best served by aircraft of different range and capacity characteristics under varying conditions of competition, seasonal fluctuation, and other factors. Carriers select aircraft with these criteria in mind, realizing that no fleet of reasonable size can possibly fulfill the precise demands of each route. Compromise in fleet planning is inevitable, and some routes are thus less efficiently operated than others. In some instances, achieving a balance between all the relevant aviation measures is complicated by the intrusion of political or other external considerations irrelevant to airline operations.

One or a combination of three factors is usually cited by airlines as a reason for purchasing new aircraft. These include: (1) anticipated traffic growth, (2) network expansion, and/or (3) need to replace existing aircraft (because of low efficiency, age, environmental problems, or competition).

Evaluation of particular aircraft is based on technical performance relative to needs, financial costs of acquisition and operation, and availability. The technical performance characteristics of aircraft should be appropriate for the routes on which it is operated. Range and payload are two key variables; each aircraft type is most economically operated over a specific distance, usually the maximum distance it can fly nonstop with a full payload. If it is operated beyond this distance, payload must be reduced in order to accommodate extra fuel; if it is operated at shorter distances, its cruising speed is usually reduced below maximum efficiency levels and its (nonrevenue earning) ground time increased. Because a given aircraft must operate over several routes within a general range grouping, it cannot be expected to always operate at maximum payload/range efficiency. Parallel to the trade-off between payload and range is a trade-off between capacity and frequency—whether a route should be operated on a high capacity-low frequency basis, for example, one daily 747 flight, or a low capacity-high frequency basis, for example, two daily 707 flights. Other technical performance elements are runway/airport requirements and environmental performance. Some runways have weight restrictions (either in absolute terms or in distribution of weight over the aircraft "footprint" when it lands). Some airports are poorly equipped to load/unload widebody aircraft. Environmental performance is concerned chiefly with ground, takeoff/ landing, and flight noise, and with fuel emissions.

If the aircraft in question are to be operated on international routes, each of these issues must be considered relative to conditions in each country to be served. For example, some countries whose airlines do not have widebody aircraft in their own fleets will not permit foreign carrier widebodies in their airspace or airports. This particular issue is significant for an increasing number of airlines eliminating or greatly reducing their long-range narrowbody fleets in favor of the generally more efficient long-range widebody aircraft. Discrepancies also exist between countries in application of environmental protection standards.

Acquisition costs of aircraft include the cost of the aircraft, spare parts, ground and support equipment, training, and financing. Operating costs vary with range and payload. Fuel consumption, fuel efficiency, maintenance costs, and maintenance efficiency are other key factors in determining operating expenses. Fleet standardization and commonality also have an impact on aircraft costs. Crew training and aircraft maintenance expenses are significantly reduced when new equipment is of the same model as aircraft already in the fleet or, if another model, at least from the same manufacturer. Selection of aircraft intended for use in international service might also take into account the number of additional airlines using the same equipment at mutually-served foreign destinations. Similarly-equipped airlines often form spare parts pools at foreign points, particularly at airports not served with great frequency and thus not able to justify the maintenance of comprehensive spare parts stores by each foreign carrier.

Contemporary fleet planning is often done through use of a computer simulation model of the airline system designed to determine the proper fleet size and composition for projected needs. Individual carriers, aircraft manufacturers, and various consultants have produced model frameworks to establish aircraft requirements, fleet-assignment patterns, financial requirements, and other conditions vital to the planning process. Airline resources (aircraft, route authority, etc.), market demands, financial policies and cost structure, corporate strategy, and constraints are all considerations.[20]

Financing Aircraft Purchases in the International Market

Between 1980 and 1989, according to one estimate, IATA-member airlines will require $100-125 billion to cover the cost of new flight equipment.[21] Because the transport aircraft industry is concentrated in the United States and a few other countries, many aircraft sales and purchases are international transactions. Financing this trade may be complex, involving several methods of raising capital. These options differ from country to country and are discussed below.

Internal Financing

Privately owned airlines and many state-owned carriers are expected to finance a significant proportion of their capital requirements from internal sources. A state-owned airline that consistently loses money and is heavily subsidized simply to survive is unlikely to be among the carriers in this category.[22]

External Financing

Aircraft manufacturers. Most foreign manufacturers operating under free market conditions offer financing assistance to attract customers, particularly if the purchasing airline is a new client. Flexible payment terms, free crew training, and other incentives are frequently offered potential customers.

Own government. Many carriers, particularly those that are entirely state-owned, are able to secure financial grants, loans (at favorable rates), and/or loan guarantees for new equipment from their governments of registry. Government financial support for equipment purchase frequently brings with it government participation (and pressure) in the process of aircraft selection.

Government of aircraft manufacturer. Most Western governments have established state financial institutions similar to the American Export-Import Bank (Eximbank) to support export of home manufactured goods. Because it is a key component in U.S. domination of the international transport aircraft market, the role of the Eximbank deserves attention. It is a self-sustaining, profit-making, and wholly owned U.S. government corportion that provides loans and loan guarantees, and assists in mobilizing private capital financing in support of U.S. exports. One-fifth to one-third of Eximbank total credit authorizations support export of commercial jet transports and related equipment.

Eximbank guidelines generally require that the buyer pay at least 15 percent of the purchase price in cash. A direct loan of up to 65 percent of the financial sum at a minimum of 8.75 percent interest over a ten-year period is offered along with guarantees for supplemental loans raised privately. Eximbank itself may coordinate private loans through PEFCO (Private Export Funding Corporation), an organization of banks, savings and loan associations, insurance companies, and other institutions active in lending. The most favorable terms are offered to developing countries and in support of aircraft sales faced with heavy foreign competition. For example, a foreign airline could expect to receive far better terms for purchase of a Boeing 767, which is competitive with the European Airbus, than for a long-range 747, which has no foreign competition. Especially large sales may also receive favorable terms.

The low Eximbank rates provide a government subsidy of sorts to the U.S. aircraft industry, facilitating aircraft sales and eliminating some of the finance burden the industry itself might have to carry. U.S.-registered airlines are not eligible for Eximbank subsidy; however, they do have access to long-term financing through U.S. money markets unavailable to foreign firms.

Other governments, particularly that of France, have been much more generous in supporting exports of their aircraft industry. In successful efforts to sell twenty-three Airbuses to Eastern Airlines in 1978, Airbus Industries provided Eastern with a no-cost four month lease of four of the aircraft. It also paid Eastern legal fees, FAA certification charges and certain other expenses associated with integrating the A300 into the Eastern fleet. Both France and Britain have included traffic rights in their respective territories in aircraft sales packages. Barter of material goods as a means of financing equipment purchases, to be covered below, is encouraged by some producer and some customer countries.

Countries with aircraft industries involved in multinationally manufactured equipment must agree on a formula for joint financing of sales. The governments of Japan and Italy, whose industries are participating in construction of the Boeing 767, have agreed with the United States that each country, through its export credit institution, will provide financing for the aircraft in direct proportion to their involvement in production.

Private sources. The private capital market is the primary external funding source for purchase of U.S.-manufactured aircraft by U.S. airlines. Banks, savings and loan associations, and insurance companies are the most commonly involved institutions.

Barter. Developing countries and other states with balance of trade problems often prefer that barter arrangements with the selling company or country cover a major portion of aircraft costs. The 1968 sale of BAC One-Elevens to Tarom, the Romanian airline, was facilitated by the British firm's agreement to establish a Swiss trading agency to sell Romanian products that the Romanians had been unable to sell in the West with Romanian labels. The Yugoslav carrier JAT has financed a portion of its DC-9 and DC-10 purchases by bartering Yugoslav hams, mopeds, and several other items to McDonnell Douglas. The American company has used some of the hams in its own cafeterias and has sold other Yugoslav products on the U.S.

market. Douglas has also accepted African spears and New Zealand lamb bicycle seat covers as partial payment for aircraft.[23]

The Soviet Union, unable to sell Soviet aircraft on the open market in competition with Western equipment, has long attempted to attract customers in developing countries by accepting goods in barter for aircraft. Aviogenex, a supplemental carrier, is the only one of four Yugoslav airlines to use Soviet aircraft. It is owned by a federal import-export agency, most of whose trade is with the Soviet Union, and has obtained its fleet of Tu-134A short-range jets in exchange for animal hides and similar products bartered to the USSR. In 1970 the Soviets offered Tu-134s to Turkish Airlines for surplus Turkish tobacco or for "virtually any commodity Turkey wanted to get rid of." The Soviet aircraft "were almost free," said one Turkish official.[24]

India, heavily dependent on the Soviet Union for arms, has been a frequent target of Soviet civil aircraft barter arrangements. In the mid- and late-1970s the USSR not only made intensive efforts to persuade Indian Airlines to acquire Yak-40, Tu-134, and Tu-154 aircraft, but also offered to include aviation fuel in the deal to compensate for extraordinarily high fuel consumption of the Soviet engines. The USSR would have accepted payment in rupees or in barter goods.[25]

Barter sales are most easily arranged by state-owned aircraft industries whose positions as units in larger entities facilitate distribution of the barter goods in the economy. Private American firms, other than McDonnell-Douglas, have not been eager to participate in such exchanges.

Leasing. Certain changes in U.S. tax laws in the 1960s and in 1970 combined to make aircraft leasing attractive to American carriers and the American finance industry alike. Some leasing is commonly done on a lease-purchase basis, other leasing with no commitment (but perhaps with an option) to buy. Seven reasons may be cited in support of leasing:

1. leasing eliminates the need to borrow large sums of money;
2. leasing eliminates progress payments to manufacturers;
3. leasing offers protection against inflation because payments remain fixed throughout the contract period;
4. leasing may provide tax benefits, depending on the carrier's profit/loss situation;
5. leasing simplifies accounting for tax purposes;
6. leasing reduces the risk of being saddled with technologically or otherwise obsolescent aircraft; and
7. short-term leasing permits seasonal routes to be served without purchase of aircraft that would be inefficiently used for much of the year.[26]

The specific tax advantages that may obtain in the United States might not exist in other countries, but leasing has many adherents in other nations as well because of its additional advantages. Some lessor institutions are companies established specifically for that purpose. A number of American and European scheduled and supplemental airlines also lease aircraft as a major component of their corporate activity.

Social and Political Problems in the International Transport Aircraft Industry

Although its significant manufacturing capacity is concentrated in a small number of countries, the international transport aircraft industry touches almost every nation in the world. Its product is highly valued, not only for its transport function but also for the economic and technological power it is perceived to represent. A single aircraft may cost more than $60 million—and no airline owns only one aircraft. Aircraft are inherently mobile, their manufacturers almost inherently conspicuous. It is an industry susceptible to pressure from several quarters. Two types of pressure are particularly noteworthy.

Protectionism

It has been noted earlier in this text that states with aircraft industries are usually very protective of these industries, imposing various political, financial, and bureaucratic barriers to purchase of foreign-manufactured equipment by home airlines. Home airlines are perceived by some governments as economic instruments; one of their functions as such is the protection of the home aircraft industry. If both the airline and the aircraft industry are owned by the state, pressure on the airline to purchase locally made equipment is easily exercised. Most east European carriers and Aeroflot are a captive market for Soviet aircraft production; although state-owned carriers in both Britain and France have been allowed to purchase some American equipment, they too have been compelled to operate less efficient home-manufactured aircraft.

Recognizing the forces of protectionism, the American civil aircraft industry has entered into several multinational production ventures in the hope that involvement by foreign companies in the construction process will spur the airlines of the same states toward purchase of the equipment. The use of Rolls Royce engines on the Lockheed L-1011 Tristar has boosted its sales in countries in which Britain enjoys influence. Similarly, Boeing agreement to participation by Japanese and Italian firms in production of its 767 is aimed at securing Japanese and Italian purchase of the aircraft (although Alitalia operates the Airbus, a direct competitor of the 767). The multinational construction base of the Airbus assures it consideration in equipment decisions taken by the airlines of Airbus consortium member-states. Protectionism can also be generated by carriers; in 1978 SAS decided to consider the possibilities for industrial off-set orders for Scandinavian firms when the airline evaluated new equipment.[27]

In an attempt to ease protectionism and facilitate free trade, participating countries in the "Tokyo Round" of discussions of the General Agreement on Tariffs and Trade (GATT) decided in the 1979 Aircraft Agreement to eliminate by 1980 all tariffs on civil aircraft, engines, related spare parts, and ground flight simulators. The countries involved are the United States, Canada, the Common Market countries, Sweden, Norway, Switzerland and Japan. Sponsored by the United States, the Aircraft Agreement also requires governments to avoid "unreasonable" pressure on airlines or manufacturers to purchase equipment from particular sources; to avoid attaching inducements or economic sanctions to the sale of equipment; and to observe certain additional measures intended to insure that decisions to purchase civil aircraft and related equipment are made on commercial and technological grounds alone.[28]

Certain clauses in the agreement are imprecise and may be subject to varying interpretations. Further, although other countries may join the agreement, no incentive exists for them to do so. Some countries with relatively small aircraft industries are strongly opposed to it, viewing protection of their own domestic markets fully justifiable and not a concern for foreign states. The fact that other countries have signed the agreement allows nonadherent states to benefit from tariff absence in signatory countries while maintaining protectionist tariffs for their own domestic markets. These flaws notwithstanding, the agreement has the potential to reduce sales tensions between the major Western manufacturing countries.

Bribery

The aviation world was rocked during the 1970s by a series of revelations concerning wide-scale bribery of potential purchasers by aircraft manufacturers. Press reports indicated that all major U.S. airframe producers and numerous non-U.S. airlines and air forces were involved. The American manufacturers admitted their guilt, implicitly and explicitly, and scandals erupted around the world. Prince Bernhard of the Netherlands was determined by a Dutch government commission to have an "unacceptable relationship" with Lockheed and was forced to resign from a variety of military and business positions. A Japanese executive implicated in a scandal concerning sales of Grumman reconnaissance aircraft to the Japanese government committed suicide, and Prime Minister Kakuei Tanaka had been forced to resign in an earlier Lockheed case. McDonnell Douglas was also involved in Japanese payoffs. Although the single most publicized relationship was probably that between Lockheed and the Saudi Arabian agent Adnan Khashoggi, investigations disclosed similar (if smaller scale) activity in numerous other Middle Eastern countries, in Asia and the Far East, in Canada and Latin America, Europe, and Africa.

Bribery—expressed as excess commissions, consulting fees, kickbacks, or whatever—is an accepted (if unpublicized) component of trade and commerce in many areas of the world. It is not accepted in mainstream American business, but American companies perceived it important to accommodate foreign custom. American firms are caught in a conflict: such activity is clearly illegal in the United States, but quite normal and even necessary for the conduct of business in many international markets. The extensive and unflattering publicity accorded the various participants in the bribery cases may do more to limit its further occurrence than application of U.S. laws. If foreign officials fear press exposure, the pressure on U.S. firms to engage in such practice may be substantially eased.

Summary

Manufacturing capability in the international transport aircraft industry is concentrated in a very few countries and has been dominated in the post-World War II era by the United States. Equipment of Boeing and Douglas, in particular, is known around the world. Narrowbody jet aircraft produced by British and French firms have not sold well under free market conditions, and no Soviet-manufactured aircraft of any type has been successful in a competitive environment. Because maintenance of a strong aircraft industry is widely perceived as contributing to a national technological base, improving defense capabilities, conserving and earning valued foreign exchange, and projecting an image of power and scientific competence, most aircraft industries are strongly supported and protected by governments. Outside the United States, government ownership of aircraft industries is common.

Realizing that none of their industries can compete with American manufacturing capability on an individual basis, Western countries (including Japan) have entered into numerous cooperative aerospace construction projects. Not only do they pool their technological and financial resources, but they also combine their own protected markets into a larger, transnational purchasing unit. Colonial and ex-colonial ties extend the joint market beyond regional boundaries. Even U.S. firms able to undertake projects on their own are seeking foreign partners as a means of broadening potential markets.

Financing aircraft purchases is complex and varies in nature among different countries, that is, some state-owned airlines receive substantial government grants, government loans, or government loan guarantees to cover aircraft costs. In all free market situations, government export credit institutions offer financing assistance to foreign carriers as inducements to buy particular home-manufactured aircraft. Barter transactions, granting of traffic rights, and other incentives may also be offered. So competitive is the international sales environment that bribing of purchasing agents has also been widely practiced.

Factors of pride and anticipated commercial gain will doubtless continue to spur competition between aircraft manufacturers. Some new producers, such as Romania, cannot be expected to capture a significant share of the market, but Romania and other countries may seek collaborative projects with established manufacturers. Some Westen producers could be subject to pressure from their own governments to invite cooperation from certain other countries for foreign policy reasons. The very fact that the international aircraft industry is perceived to be important assures government interest in it.

Notes

1. "Masters of the Air," *Time* 115:14 (April 7, 1980), p. 55. Reprinted by permission from *TIME*, The Weekly Newsmagazine. Copyright Time Inc. 1980.

2. The DC-3 is one of the most remarkable aircraft of all time. During World War II, it was the standard medium-range U.S. military transport (known then as the C-47, C-53, and C-117). In civilian use, it accommodated as many as thirty-six passengers and was also known as the Dakota.

3. The Pratt & Whitney designation for large fan jets produced in the late 1960s, 1970s, and through the early 1980s is JT9D, followed by a short series of numbers/letters indicating specific model variations or different appellations for the same model for different aircraft. For example, the JT9D-59A and JT9D-70A are almost identical, but the former is intended for DC-10-40 and A300 aircraft, and the latter for the 747. The JT9D-7R4 engine series is offered for A310 and Boeing 767 widebodies.

4. See David A. Brown, "Lufthansa Reequipping Its Fleet," *Aviation Week* 107:13 (September 26, 1977), pp. 27-29. The General Electric designation for large fan jets is CF6, followed by a number/letter series for specific models.

5. *Izvestiya*, March 16, 1966. The "stylish" Western aircraft that determined the design of the Il-62 were probably the Caravelle and the VC-10.

6. For example, the Paris manager of Aeroflot was expelled from France in 1965 on charges of employing illegal means to obtain plans of the Concorde.

7. The elapsed time between the first prototype flight and introduction of a new U.S. aircraft type into airline scheduled service during the 1970s was usually 300 days. In Western Europe, the time period was 600 days, in the Soviet Union 1,200 days. The Soviets face major delays in testing new aircraft (demonstrating airworthiness) due to inadequate wind tunnel facilities and computer technology during the design process. Many problems discovered and corrected during preproduction computer testing in the West must be worked out during postproduction environmental testing in the Soviet Union.

8. A near-collision of a LOT Il-62 and Braniff 747 on the ground at Kennedy Airport in New York in the late 1970s was caused by operational deficiencies in the Soviet-manufactured Il-62. Inadequacies in the Il-62 design prevented the LOT pilot from executing a move ordered by the air traffic controller. See Henry Lefer, "LOT Aims to Stretch International Wings," *Air Transport World* 16:12 (December, 1979), p. 52.

9. A good account of the initial stages of the project is given in "Romania's One-Elevens," *Flight International* 117:3764 (March 15, 1980), pp. 852-854.

10. See the following: "Chinese Aircraft Industry—Status Report," *Interavia Air Letter* 8623 (November 3, 1976), pp. A-B; Jay Mathews, "China Said to Clone a '708' from Boeing Jet It Bought," *Washington Post*, May 9, 1980, p. A1; and "Y-10 Called Development Effort, Not Boeing Copy," *Aviation Week* 112:20 (May 19, 1980), p. 32.

11. License for production of the Westwind was purchased by IAI from North American Rockwell, the original developer of the aircraft, when the U.S. firm was forced to divest it in an antitrust case.

12. Mark Lambert, "Japan's Aerospace Industry," *Flight* 110:3526 (October 9, 1976), p. 1143.

13. The British "second carrier," privately owned British Caledonian, refused to accept a Concorde "allocated" to it by the British government.

14. See Joseph M. Grieco, "The Concorde SST and Change in the British Policy," *World Politics* XXXI:4 (July, 1979), pp. 518-538.

15. Expulsion of the Paris Aeroflot manager from France in 1965 for espionage related to Concorde production has already been noted. See also: "KGB Paid $12,500 for Concorde Secrets," *Aviation Daily* 197:23 (October 4, 1971), p. 187; "How Russia Spies: A New Game," *Newsweek*

LXXVIII:15 (October 11, 1971), p. 32; and "Tu-144—1965-78," *Flight* 114:3628 (September 30, 1978), p. 1229.

16. See "Technical Aid Sought for Tu-144," *Aviation Week* 109:23 (December 4, 1978), pp. 26-27.

17. See "Concorde Banned from Soviet Airspace," *Flight* 115:3648 (February 17, 1979), p. 443.

18. "Supersonic Tu-144D Has New, Fuel Efficient Engines," *Aviation Daily* 244:6 (July 10, 1979), p. 46.

19. Douglas B. Feaver, "Hill Office Backs Development of Supersonic Airliner," *Washington Post*, March 31, 1980, p. A5, and "Prospects for U.S. SST are 'Significant'—Congressional Report," *Aviation Daily* 248:22 (April 1, 1980), p. 174.

20. See Nawal K. Taneja, *The Commercial Airline Industry* (Lexington, Mass., Lexington Books, 1976), pp. 97-101.

21. Roy Allen, *Capital Financing and Re-equipment of the World's Commercial Airline Fleets in the 1980s* (London: The Economist Intelligence Unit Ltd., 1979), p. 43.

22. Taneja, *The Commercial Airline Industry*, pp. 77-91, explains in some detail how internal and certain other types of financing for equipment is managed.

23. See "Airline Observer," *Aviation Week* 110:14 (April 2, 1979), p. 31.

24. Comments made to the author in Turkey in 1972. Although the purchase terms were undeniably attractive, Turkey rejected the offer because of Tu-134 high operating costs, uncertain spare parts supply, undesired fleet diversification, and other factors.

25. See "Additional B.737s for Indian Airlines," *Interavia Air Letter* 8645 (December 3, 1976), p. 1, and "Soviet Inducement," *Aviation Week* 106:7 (February 14, 1977), p. 41.

26. See Taneja, *The Commercial Airline Industry*, pp. 85-86.

27. "Scandinavian Offsets Required in Future," *Interavia Air Letter* 9008 (May 2, 1978), p. 7.

28. See Chris Bulloch, "The 'Tokyo Round' Aircraft Agreement," *Interavia* XXXIV:7 (July, 1979), pp. 655-656, and Ernesto Preidi, "The GATT Agreement on Trade in Civil Aircraft," *ITA Bulletin* 21 (June 2, 1980), pp. 477-483.

9

Unlawful Interference with Aircraft

The expression "unlawful interference with aircraft" is the technical term used to describe all illegal acts committed against civil aircraft, including armed seizure (hijacking) and sabotage. Unlawful interference with aircraft, when executed for political reasons, is considered an act of terrorism. No single definition of terrorism is widely accepted, but it can be defined for its use in this book as "the systematic use of murder and destruction, and the threat of murder and destruction, to terrorize individuals, groups, communities, or governments" into conceding to political, social, or economic demands. Terrorist violence is characterized by "indiscriminateness, inhumanity, arbitrariness, and barbarity."[1]

The first known hijacking of an aircraft occurred in 1930 when Peruvian revolutionaries seized control of a Peruvian transport in efforts to flee the country. This incident appears to have been an aberration in the development of civil aviation during the interwar period. As airline service was restored in eastern Europe during the postwar years, persons eager to escape the closely guarded frontiers of countries perceived to be oppressive resorted to aircraft hijacking. Between 1947 and 1961, twenty-five successful and seven unsuccessful hijackings from eastern Europe were attempted. The pattern was repeated in Cuba after Fidel Castro came to power: twenty-five aircraft were hijacked to the United States during the first two years of the new government. Since then, incidents of unlawful interference with aircraft have multiplied in numbers, apparent purpose, and geographic region of occurrence.

Scope of the Problem

Those who commit acts of unlawful inteference with aircraft can be classified in three categories according to their major motivations: the emotionally disturbed, the criminal, and the politically militant.[2] These categories cannot always be neatly separated. Some criminals are emotionally disturbed. Some political militants are also emotionally disturbed or have criminal backgrounds. Some emotionally disturbed are drawn to extreme politics or to crime. Within limits, however, the classification of terrorists into three types is proper and useful in

219

determining their principal motivation and in intelligently choosing methods for handling terrorist activity. The primary concern of this chapter is with the politically motivated performer of unlawful interference with aircraft.

Participants

Participation in acts of unlawful interference with aircraft is not common to all terrorist groups. Among the better known terrorist organizations that are not associated with this type of activity are the Irish Republican Army, ETA (Euzkadi Ta Askatasuna, Basque Homeland and Liberty) separatist group, and FALN (Fuerzas Armadas de Liberación) of Puerto Rico. The groups most closely associated with seizure and sabotage of civil aircraft are several Palestinian organizations, Rengo Sekigun (United Red Army) of Japan, and Ustashi (Insurgents), the Croatian separatist group.

Palestinians. A 1980 report of the U.S. Central Intelligence Agency identified forty-seven different Palestinian terrorist groups.[3] Of these, fewer than a dozen are of substantial size and only four of these have committed acts of unlawful interference with aircraft.

Al Fatah. Al Fatah was founded in 1957 in Egypt. Led by Yasir Arafat, it is nondoctrinaire leftist in ideology. In 1971 Fatah established a "special operations" group, Black September (so named in commemoration of September 1970 when King Hussein destroyed the terrorist power base in Jordan), to carry out terrorist attacks "independently," and thus enable Arafat to adopt an image of a responsible statesman. By 1974 the pretense of Black September independence was so transparent that its separate name was no longer used. Among its numerous actions during its three-year existance were three incidents involving aircraft: (1) attempted assassination of the Jordanian Queen Mother by a bomb which exploded in her aircraft after landing in Madrid; (2) hijacking of Sabena aircraft to Israel in which all terrorists were killed or captured when Israeli forces stormed the aircraft; and (3) hijack of Lufthansa 727 which was later released in exchange for the three surviving perpetrators of the Munich Olympics massacre. Black September is probably most widely known for its 1972 massacre of eleven Israeli athletes and coaches at the Munich Olympics and the 1973 murder of three diplomats (two American, one Belgian) at the Saudi embassy in Khartoum. Since the demise of Black September, Fatah itself has claimed responsibility for various cross-border raids into Israel from Lebanon and time-bomb explosions in Israel.

Fatah has strong connections with European terror groups. It receives arms, training, and military support from the Soviet Union, Czechoslovakia, and East Germany, and financial subventions from several oil-rich Arab states. Many Palestinians working in the Gulf states and elsewhere also contribute funds.

Popular Front for the Liberation of Palestine [PFLP]. The PFLP was established in 1967 after the Six-Day War by Dr. George Habash. An amalgamation of several smaller terrorist groups, the PFLP is doctrinaire Marxist in ideology with nationalist Palestinian, regional Arab, and worldwide revolutionary aims. The PFLP is ruthless in its operations. Its most widely known aviation-related attacks are:

1. multiple hijacking in 1970 of three aircraft to Dawson Field in Jordan, one to Cairo, and destruction of all four on the ground;
2. hijacking of Lufthansa 747 to Aden in 1972 and extortion of $5 million from Lufthansa for its release;
3. Lod Airport massacre of twenty-seven people in 1972 by Japanese Red Army on behalf of PFLP;
4,5. attempts by groups of German and Arab terrorists to destroy El Al aircraft at Orly airport in France in 1975 with rocket-propelled grenades;
6. attempt of three Arabs and two Germans in 1975, foiled by Kenyan police, to fire SAM-7 missiles at an approaching El Al 707 in Nairobi;
7. 1976 hijacking of Air France Airbus to Entebbe, ended by Israeli rescue; and
8. 1977 hijacking of Lufthansa 737 to Mogadishu, terminated by West German rescue operation.

The PFLP also perpetrated the 1975 attack on OPEC offices in Vienna and numerous other nonaviation and aviation-related actions.

The PFLP has strong ties with radical Arab states and with terrorist groups in Europe, Japan and Latin America. It receives various types of support from the Soviet Union, East Germany, North Korea, and Cuba. Financing is raised from aforementioned sources as well as from protection and blackmail schemes, counterfeiting, bank robbing in Lebanon, narcotics, and smuggling.

Popular Front for the Liberation of Palestine-General Command. The nucleus of the PFLP-GC was a small group, the Palestine Liberation Front, founded in 1959 by Ahmed Jabril, a former Syrian Army officer. It became a branch of the PFLP in 1967, breaking away a year later over policy disputes. The PFLP-GC has conducted cross-border raids into Israel and other types of terrorist activity; its most widely known aviation-related operations have involved sending altitude-sensitive explosives onboard

Israel-bound aircraft, either in postal parcels or concealed in luggage carried by unwitting young women. Actions of this type include:

1.   1970 parcel explosions onboard Swissair and Austrian aircraft, causing the former to crash with death of all onboard and the latter to make a safe emergency landing;
2,3,4. three 1971 unsuccessful attempts to place concealed explosives on El Al aircraft in luggage carried by naive young women discovered by El Al. security procedures; and
5.   1972 airborne explosion of tape recorder checked by young women aboard El Al aircraft which managed to land safely.

Syrian intelligence officers are the dominant "outside" force in the PFLP-GC.

National Arab Youth for the Liberation of Palestine [also called Arab National Youth of Revenge, Revenge Squad of the Martyr Ghafour, and other titles]. The NAYLP was founded in 1972 by Libyan President Muammer Qadaffi. It has specialized in aviation-related operations, including:

1. machine-gun and grenade attack at Athens airport in 1973, killing five and wounding fifty-four;
2. a plan to attack El Al aircraft near Rome with SAM-7 missiles in 1973 foiled by Italian police;
3. 1973 firebombing of Pan Am aircraft at Rome airport, killing thirty-three;
4. altitude-sensitive bomb onboard TWA aircraft failed to detonate properly after takeoff from Athens in 1974; and
5. altitude-sensitive bomb concealed on same TWA 707 flight two weeks later exploded at 28,000 feet, causing crash of aircraft and death of all eighty-eight onboard.

This group appears to have split up following the execution of its leader by Fatah in 1974. Two final terror attacks were committed after his death.

    The number of Palestinian attacks on aircraft diminished substantially in the late 1970s, apparently in recognition of (1) the international ill will generated by such actions, and (2) the failure of the attacks to cause a significant decrease in travel to Israel or in use of El Al Israel Airlines. Nonetheless, Palestinian involvement in unlawful interference with aircraft continues, albeit at a reduced rate. In 1980 Israeli security agents discovered an altitude-sensitive bomb in the luggage of a West German citizen preparing to board an El Al aircraft in Zurich. The would-be passenger had been paid by another German known to have contacts with Palestinian terrorists to take the suitcase to Israel and had not known of the luggage contents.

Rengo Sekigun [United Red Army]. Established in 1969 as a splinter group of a left-wing student association, the URA is radical and nihilistic in ideology. It has committed numerous robberies and murders in Japan, and in 1970 nine URA members hijacked a JAL domestic flight to North Korea. In the same year, it began a lasting relationship with the PFLP, receiving arms and training from the Palestinians in return for cooperation in staging attacks where an Arab presence might attract unwelcome attention in preparatory work. In 1972 three URA members massacred twenty-seven people in Lod airport, Israel. In 1977 five URA members hijacked a JAL DC-8 to Algiers, exchanging the aircraft and 151 hostages for $6 million in ransom from the Japanese government and the release of six URA members from Japanese prisons. The URA is quite small and is dependent on the PFLP for any actions outside Japan. Fusako Shigenobu, its woman leader, has been in the Middle East and in Europe since 1971. Many of its other members have also left Japan.

Ustashi. The Croatian Revolutionary Brotherhood is an organization of long standing, based on Croatian hostility to Serbian dominance in contemporary Yugoslavia and predecessor governments. Right-wing nationalist with fascist tendencies, the Ustashi collaborated with German occupation forces during World War II. In pursuit of Croatian separatism, Ustashi forces have committed at least sixty "significant" terrorist acts since 1962.[4] Most such incidents involve bombings of Yugoslav property and assassinations of Yugoslav diplomats abroad, but Croatians have also engaged in acts of unlawful interference with aircraft. In 1972 a Croatian-planted bomb destroyed a JAT DC-9 over Czechoslovakia, killing twenty-nine people. Nine Croatians hijacked a SAS DC-9 later in 1972 from Goteborg to Malmo and then to Spain, releasing the aircraft after Sweden released seven Croatians imprisoned for earlier terrorist acts. In 1976 Croatians hijacked a TWA aircraft to Paris. A New York City policeman was killed when trying to disarm a bomb planted by Croatians in connection with the hijacking incident.

The fewer than fifty Croatians thought to be actively involved in the commission of terrorist acts enjoy considerable sympathy and some tangible support from Croatian diaspora communities in Australia, the United States, Canada, Spain, West Germany, Sweden, and other countries. Its right-wing ideology has discouraged international links with other terrorist groups, most of which are strongly leftist in philosophy. From time to time, prominent Croatians and Serbs in exile have been murdered in counterattacks widely believed to be perpetrated by agents of the Yugoslav government.[5]

Other groups. In 1978 and 1979 black nationalists of the Zimbabwe African People's Union (ZAPU) shot down two Viscount aircraft of Air Rhodesia with SAM-7 missiles. Of the fifty-six persons on the first aircraft, thirty-eight were killed on impact and ten of the eighteen survivors were murdered by nationalists on the ground. All were civilians. In the 1979 incident, all fifty-nine persons onboard, most of them tourists, were killed in the crash. A third aircraft was hit by bullets shortly after the second missile attack, but landed safely. ZAPU was led by Joshua Nkomo and received strong support from the Soviet bloc, particularly from East Germany which is reported to have supplied ZAPU forces with the missiles and other armaments.[6] Nkomo's group admitted commission of all three attacks. A rival group, the Zimbabwe African National Union (ZANU), won a landslide victory in independent Zimbabwe's first free elections in 1980. ZANU, led by Robert Mugabe, received some support from China, and conspicuously snubbed the Soviet Union and most East European states upon accession to power.

Terrorism against civil aviation has also been practiced by the Eritrean Liberation Front, one of two groups seeking Eritrean independence from Ethiopia. Receiving substantial aid from the Soviet Union at the time, the ELF attacked several Ethiopian Airlines aircraft on the ground and hijacked others during the late 1960s and early 1970s. Subsequently, armed Ethiopian security guards were carried on all flights and, on several occasions, gun battles between hijackers and agents broke out in midair.

International Support

The transnational nature of terrorism is a phenomenon dating from the Japanese Red Army execution of the Lod airport massacre on behalf of the PFLP in 1972. Since this action, collaboration between various sovereign states and terrorist groups in the execution of terrorist campaigns has been widely recognized.[7] Not all groups or states actually commit acts of unlawful interference with aircraft, but each extends support to groups that do hijack or sabotage civilian aircraft.

Groups. Groups involved in general terrorism represent almost all populated continents. In Europe, the major organizations are: the Red Brigade (Italy), Red Help (Netherlands), Red Army Faction (West Germany), IRA (Northern Ireland), Basque ETA (Spain), and South Moluccans (Netherlands). In the Middle East, in addition to the groups already mentioned, active groups include: Saiqa (a component of the Syrian army), the Palestine Liberation Army (military force of the PLO), the Fedayeen of Iran, and Turkish People's Liberation group. The major western hemisphere groups are: Tupamaros (Uruguay), Montoneros (Argentina), Sandinistas (Nicaragua), ELN (Bolivia), MIR (Chile), and FALN (Puerto Rico). In Asia, as well as the United Red Army of Japan, Moslem separatists in the Philippines have connections with terrorist groups in other countries.

States. Both Soviet-bloc and Arab states extend major support to terrorist groups. In the Soviet bloc, the Soviet Union is the most actively involved, supplying various terrorist groups with arms, training, intelligence, and logistic and diplomatic assistance. East Germany provides arms, training, intelligence, personnel and funding. Czechoslovakia has achieved some notoriety for its supply of arms; it also contributes training and money. Cuba offers personnel, extensive training, and diplomatic support. Bulgaria, Poland, Hungary, and Yugoslavia have been less involved, but each has provided training, and Yugoslavia granted conspicuous haven to Illyich Ramirez-Sanchez, better known as Carlos, in 1976. North Korea also offers training. China has trained some Palestinian terrorists, but its relations with many terror groups have been strained by Sino-Soviet tensions.[8]

South Yemen, Iraq, Syria, Algeria, and Libya provide the most diverse support among Arab states. Each supplies arms, training, funding, havens, false passports, and diplomatic services. Lebanon provides extensive training facilities, haven, and some diplomatic support—all probably unwillingly. Saudi Arabia grants generous financial subsidies, bribe money to dissuade radicals from initiating action within Saudi Arabia itself.

Chaotic conditions in Lebanon motivated several Palestinian organizations to transfer some operations to Cyprus in the mid-1970s. The Mediterranean island has subsequently become a major base for terrorist activity, particularly for logistics, finance, and intelligence services. Soviet arms are delivered to Palestinians in Cypriot ports, and Arab subsidies are transmitted through Cypriot banks. "Summit meetings" of international terrorist leaders have been held on the island.

Air-Transport Industry Response to the Problem

The most evident industry response to the problem of unlawful interference with aircraft is the imposition, spurred in some countries by government regulation, of security procedures designed to prevent hijackings and sabotage. A multimillion dollar weapons and explosives electronic detection industry has developed to facilitate surveillance of passengers and baggage, and security requirements are now a key factor in design of new airports. Security standards, however, are not internationally regulated, and implementation of procedures varies widely from country to country.[9]

The impact of air terrorism on airlines has been most severe on carriers in countries affected by terrorism in general. In late 1977, after three West German terrorists committed suicide in a Stuttgart prison, other members of the Red Army Faction charged the German government with assassination of the inmates and threatened to blow up three Lufthansa aircraft in revenge. Because two Red Army Faction members were among the terrorists arrested in Nairobi the previous year for complicity in an attempt to fire SAM-7 missiles at an El Al aircraft, speculation was strong that missiles would be fired at Lufthansa aircraft. Landing and takeoff patterns were altered for Lufthansa in Germany and other countries, and general security procedures intensified. Traffic fell precipitously as nervous Germans transferred to other airlines or, when practical, used surface transportation. No terrorist act was perpetrated against the airline, but Lufthansa earnings dropped sharply for a period as a result of reduced traffic.[10]

Events generated by the terrorist presence in Lebanon have seriously weakened Middle East Airlines, once the leading Arab carrier. In mid-1968 a PFLP unit left Beirut airport on a mission to board an El Al aircraft at an intermediate airport and hijack it to Algiers, thus inaugurating the Arab air terror campaign. In response, Israeli forces raided Beirut airport later that year, destroying eight of MEA's eleven aircraft. Although the Israelis were careful to avoid injuring anyone and MEA was able to recover most of its direct financial loss through insurance, its indirect financial losses—from leasing of aircraft, revenue loss, need to dispose of spare parts no longer usable, and greatly increased war risk insurance—were substantial.

Fighting between Palestinian/leftist factions and other forces in Lebanon escalated into war in 1975 and 1976. Beirut airport was subject to frequent attack, from looters as well as military units, causing severe damage to MEA property and some loss of life. As fighting raged, traffic demand fell and maintenance of operations became impossible. MEA was compelled to transfer its management and fleet to Paris, a move facilitated by Air France's 28 percent ownership of the Lebanese carrier. Until conditions permitted resumption of service from Beirut, MEA wet-leased many of its aircraft to other airlines. However, long after the end of the "official" civil war and MEA's return to Beirut, continuing instability in Lebanon reduces the MEA traffic base and prevents full exploitation of the carrier's ample managerial experience and expertise.[11]

The impact of air terrorism on El Al has been more constant and more costly in strict financial terms, but far less damaging in traffic growth. El Al security procedures are the most stringent in the industry, annoying and antagonizing some passengers. Other travelers, however, are attracted to the Israeli carrier by the very implementation of such measures, believing that El Al is the most "hijack-proof" airline in the world. Hijacking is only one aspect of its unlawful interference problem; El Al has also undertaken action to prevent damage to its fleet caused by concealed explosives or by missiles. To limit the impact of the former, El Al has reinforced the structure of its cargo holds, a move that proved its worth in 1972 when a PFLP booby-trapped tape recorder that had not been detected in predeparture inspection detonated in flight. The strengthened hold absorbed the force of the blast, allowing the aircraft to land without injury to passengers. Few would gainsay the safety benefits of structural reinforcement; this measure, however, has exacted a weight penalty and may reduce the aircraft payload potential. To decoy or divert missiles guided by infrared sensors (such as the shoulder-launched SAM-7 Strela), El Al has installed infrared jamming devices on the trailing edges of its engine pylons. Again, the action has been costly.[12]

The Political Response to the Problem

A variety of institutions—governmental and nongovernmental, national and international—have debated possible solutions to the problems of international terrorism in general and unlawful interference with aircraft in particular. That no solution has been found is apparent in the continuation of terrorist attacks and assaults against international civil aviation. An examination of involved institutions readily explains some of the differences.

International Institutions

The United Nations, the principal international air transport organizations (ICAO, IATA, IFALPA), and several other international institutions have all addressed the problem of unlawful interference with aircraft. Resolutions have been adopted and conventions passed, but no action of any of these groups has had a significant impact on politically motivated interference with civil aircraft.

The United Nations. Between 1969 and 1979 the General Assembly adopted eight resolutions concerning international terrorism. Three specifically addressed unlawful interference with aircraft (#2551 of December 12, 1969, #2645 of November 25, 1970, and 32/8 of November 3, 1977), two dealt with the taking of hostages (31/103 of December 15, 1976 and 32/148 of December 16, 1977), and three attempted to justify international terrorism by calling for study of its causes (3034 of December 18, 1972, 31/102 of December 15, 1976, and 32/147 of December 16,1977).[13] Resolution 32/8 of 1977 was proposed and adopted in response to two related incidents: the PFLP hijacking one month earlier of a Lufthansa aircraft to Mogadishu, during which the pilot was murdered, and the subsequent pressure for action exerted against the United Nations by IFALPA. Initiated by Austria, Australia, and the Nordic countries, the original text of the resolution was modified to meet objections from Arab and certain other states. For example, a clause was added stipulating that any action taken against hijacking should be "without prejudice to the sovereignty or territorial integrity of any state," an illusion to the Israeli rescue of Air France passengers at Entebbe in 1976—an action that did not have the approval of the government of Uganda. The modified resolution failed to note that the government of Uganda was an active participant in the Entebbe hijacking and its leader, Idi Amin, when approached by a retired Israeli army officer and former friend, refused to do anything on behalf of the hostages. In contrast, the Somali government, eager that the Mogadishu incident end, conferred with West German leaders and gave permission for the rescue assault on the Lufthansa 737.[14]

As previously noted, some member-states of the United Nations are actively engaged in the commission of acts of international terrorism. Others provide support services to terrorists. Still others are anxious to ingratiate themselves with foreign governments backing terrorism. The sum of all of these states is sufficient to prevent the General Assembly from adopting any measures unreservedly critical of terrorism. Even if the General Assembly, Security Council, or other United Nations body did condemn international terrorism, resolutions merely express a consensus of opinion. Few call for specific action.

International Civil Aviation Organization. ICAO is a specialized agency of the United Nations with a broad mandate to deal with air transport issues. It has adopted three conventions on unlawful interference with aircraft: the Convention on Offences and Certain Other Acts Committed on Board Aircraft (known as the Tokyo Convention) of 1963, entered into force in 1969; the Convention on the Suppression of Unlawful Seizure of Aircraft (known as the Hague Convention) of 1970; and the Convention on the Suppression of Unlawful Acts against Civil Aviation (known as the Montreal Convention) of 1971. The major points of the Tokyo Convention are that the country in which a hijacked aircraft lands is obligated to (1) restore the aircraft to those legally entitled to its possession, and (2) permit passengers and crew of the aircraft to continue their journey as soon as practical.

The Hague Convention was written in response to the 1968 PFLP hijacking of an El Al aircraft to Algiers in which twenty-one Israeli passengers and eleven Israeli crew members, as well as the aircraft, were held for five weeks by the Algerian government before their release. The Hague Convention specifies that contracting states must: (1) either prosecute or extradite hijackers; (2) facilitate passengers and crews of hijacked aircraft in continuing their journey as soon as possible; and (3) return hijacked aircraft and cargo without delay.

The Montreal Convention reflects the increasing number of sabotage incidents involving civil aircraft. It obligates signatory governments to impose severe penalties for: (1) attacks on lives of persons onboard aircraft in flight; (2) acts such as sabotage and bombing that seriously damage aircraft or endanger safety in flight; (3) acts that destroy, damage, or interfere with the operation of air navigation facilities; and (4) communication of false information that endangers the safety of aircraft in flight. Each of the above three conventions is undercut by two realities: (1) not all ICAO member-states have adopted them, and (2) no measures exist for enforcing them.

The admission of the Palestine Liberation Organization to ICAO as an observer in 1974 further compromises the agency in dealing seriously with the unlawful interference with aircraft issue. Although its observer status does not entitle the PLO to vote on matters before ICAO, it does allow the PLO to attend ICAO sessions on air terrorism.[15] The incongruity of representatives of an organization responsible for numerous acts of unlawful interference against aircraft observing committees trying to curb such activity appears not to have impressed the majority of ICAO member-states.

Arab states and organizations are not alone in obstructing ICAO progress in dealing with air terrorism. A study of ICAO resolutions on unlawful interference issues shows a consistent pattern of non-Arab Moslem-dominated, third world radical, and communist-led countries failing to support (by voting against or abstaining from) measures unreservedly critical of air terrorism or introducing and backing politicized resolutions on the problem. For example, in a 1975 ICAO Council vote to adopt an annex on security to the (Chicago) Convention on International Civil Aviation, six predominantly Moslem states (Arab, African, and Asian) and Idi Amin's Uganda abstained. In a 1973 meeting of the ICAO Legal Committee, France joined the Soviet Union and a group of Arab and African member-states in voting down a United States-Canadian resolution that would have invoked mandatory sanctions against countries failing to punish hijackers.

The politicization of ICAO is little different from the politicization of nonaviation UN agencies, such as the World Health Organization or the International Labour Organization. It does, however, effectively preclude the undertaking by ICAO of any significant action to deal with the problem of unlawful interference with aircraft. Certain technical regulations have been adopted—such as recommending screening of passengers and their baggage, and recommending frequent patrolling of airport grounds—but even these recommendations cannot be enforced, and they do not begin to consider the more basic issue of the unacceptability of interference with aircraft as a means of achieving political goals.

International Air Transport Association. Although many of its member airlines are owned by governments, IATA has been less subject than ICAO to political manipulation. The domination of the association by Western carriers and the intense identification of airline executives with the potential tragedy inherent in every instance of unlawful interference with aircraft combine to minimize the opportunity for politicizing the aviation terrorism issue. However, unity of attitude toward the problem does not invest the association with the authority necessary to effect internationally binding regulation concerning unlawful interference against aircraft. For example, imposition of sanctions against countries failing to punish or extradite persons found guilty of air terrorism is the province of organizations of states, not airlines. The inability of ICAO to initiate any practical action to control unlawful interference with aircraft suggests that IATA member airlines could not persuade their governments of registry to undertake measures deemed appropriate by the carriers. Although it may issue resolutions condemning air terrorism (and has done so), the mandate of IATA to exert any significant influence on solving the problem is severely limited.

IFALPA. Hijackers and pilots of hijacked aircraft almost always encounter each other in situations of direct confrontation; several pilots have been murdered by hijackers, and others have been killed in incidents of sabotage against aircraft. Acutely sensitive to the dangers faced by its membership, the International Federation of Pilots Associations has tried to exert pressure on ICAO to adopt measures controlling air terrorism. IFALPA organized a worldwide strike of airline crews in 1972; although only partially effective because of political and legal barriers to work stoppages in some countries, the action did focus international attention on the air terrorism problem. In 1977, following the murder of a Lufthansa pilot in the Mogadishu hijacking, IFALPA threatened another international strike if the United Nations did not adopt formal measures to curb air terrorism. The ensuing UN action, a resolution on the safety of international civil aviation, had had no practical effect.

The potential impact of IFALPA on the issue of unlawful interference with aircraft is constrained by two conditions. First, pilots of airlines registered in states whose governments condone interference with aircraft for selected political reasons are unable to support IFALPA conduct, however strongly they might wish to do so on a personal basis. Pilots in some other states may be prevented from striking or participating in other IFALPA action by legal procedures unrelated to politics. The absence of both groups from an IFALPA consensus reduces the impact of any IFALPA initiatives. Second, in common with IATA, IFALPA has only limited power to effect controls over unlawful interference with aircraft. Governments alone have final authority.

Western Countries

The Western countries—NATO members, Austria, Switzerland, Sweden, Japan, Australia, and New Zealand—have failed to achieve a common position in responding to the air terrorism issue. Their different approaches generally reflect the policies of their respective governments on the Israeli-Arab conflict. Groups of these countries have adopted resolutions or conventions deploring terrorism and advocating procedural controls at airports to discourage unlawful interference with aircraft, but none of the legal texts prescribes regulation of such controls or means of assuring their implementation.[16]

A partial exception to this lack of common Western resolve is the "Bonn Economic Summit Declaration" on international terrorism concluded on July 17, 1978 by the governments of Canada, the United States, United Kingdom, France, West Germany, Italy, and Japan. The signatory states pledge to undertake the following actions: (1) to cease all flights of their own airlines to a country refusing to extradite or punish hijackers and/or return a hijacked aircraft; and (2) to halt all incoming flights from that country by any airline or from any country by airlines of the country concerned. However admirable the intent of the declaration, several uncertainties are inherent in its formulation. No guidelines are given regarding: the length of time considered acceptable for extradition/punishment of hijackers or return of the aircraft before imposition of sanctions; standards for determining satisfactory prosecution of hijackers; the length of time sanctions should remain in effect; and whether genuine political refugees who commandeer aircraft for escape to another country should be treated in a different manner. In addition to these weaknesses, the declaration has attracted no additional signatories beyond the original seven countries.[17]

The United States. The United States has been more consistent than most Western countries in its opposition to unlawful interference with aircraft. Cynics may attribute U.S. concern to its lesser dependence on Middle East oil, the smaller incidence of Arab terrorist attacks in the United States, the greater distance of the United States from the Middle East, or the ability of the so-called "Jewish lobby" in the United States to focus American policy on issues of its own specific interest. More likely, most Americans appear to share a feeling of genuine revulsion toward terror attacks, a feeling reflected in American news media and in U.S. government decision making. The American experience with numerous hijackings to Cuba, in an era that generally preceded Palestinian attacks on aircraft, may have caused many to view air terrorism as totally unjustifiable.

In support of its statements condemning terrorism, the Department of State has refused to license the export of both military and civil aircraft to Libya, claiming that similar aircraft have been misused by the Libyan government in recent years for transport of troops and materiel used in terrorist activity. Libya has already paid for some of the equipment. Should Libya transfer its purchases to European firms, it is less likely that their governments would block deliveries.[18]

Although adopting a firm course against Libya, the Department of State and the Executive Branch have shown less willingness to commit the United States to a hard line against all countries associated with air terrorism. In hearings before a congressional committee considering an antiterrorism bill requiring mandatory application of sanctions against countries sheltering hijackers and saboteurs, representatives of the Department of State and the President have urged Presidential discretionary authority to invoke sanctions instead. Almost all other witnesses have supported mandatory sanctions.[19]

European countries. The European countries—particularly France, West Germany, and Italy— have been markedly inconsistent in their approach to combatting air terrorism. On one level, having determined a substantial degree of both cooperation between European terror groups and transborder mobility of individual terrorists, law-enforcement officials in most west European countries are coordinating their fight against terrorism. In addition to cooperative efforts, several European countries maintain highly skilled antiterrorist commando units trained to rescue hijacking hostages. On another level, however, many of the Common Market countries have implemented a policy of appeasement toward Arab terror groups by releasing captured terrorists from prison long before their terms are completed or by attempting to accommodate radical Arabs with sympathetic political statements.[20] Presumably the rationale for this policy includes perceptions of continued access to Middle East oil, favorable markets for exports, and immunity from future Palestinian terror attacks. It is nonetheless inconsistent with their simultaneous war against non-Arab terror groups known to cooperate with Palestinian units.

France. Of all the west European countries, France has been the most obstructionist in implementing a common Western policy against air terrorism. As noted earlier in this chapter, France joined the Soviet Union and a group of Arab and African states in voting down a United States-Canadian proposal before the ICAO Legal Committee in 1973 that would have required ICAO member-states to invoke sanctions against countries failing to punish hijackers. In 1976 France vetoed a Common Market draft treaty dealing with mandatory extradition of terrorists, and in 1977 it released from custody a Palestinian terrorist leader wanted in both West Germany and Israel.[21] France has been in the forefront of Western countries seeking political accommodation with Arab extremist groups. It does, however, participate in joint efforts of European states to combat European extremist groups.

West Germany. Although West Germany acted decisively to end the hijacking of a Lufthansa aircraft to Mogadishu and has vigorously pursued members of the German Red Army Faction, it too has released Palestinian air terrorists from prison before serving their full terms. It is, however, far less obstructionist in seeking a common Western antiterror policy than is France.

Italy. Arab terrorists convicted in Italy are routinely deported before serving prison sentences. Several have been involved in attacks on aircraft, and others have been arrested for possession of surface-to-air missiles intended for use against El Al aircraft. In 1980 the former chief of the Italian secret service reported in an Italian weekly magazine that in 1972 Italy concluded a verbal "nonaggression pact" with Palestinian terror groups, agreeing to provide "benevolent assistance" to the Palestinian cause in return for a Palestinian commitment to refrain from attacking targets in Italy or belonging to Italy.[22]

Nonaligned Countries

Few non-Arab truly nonaligned countries have had extensive direct experience with air terrorism. Several have had aircraft hijacked by native dissidents and others have had airports used as intermediate stops by foreign hijackers, but the air terrorism problem generally is not of great moment to most nonaligned states. In the diplomatic arena, most nonaligned counries have supported the radical Palestinian position, agreeing to the formulation that terrorist attacks are acceptable means of fighting "misery, frustrations, grievance, and despair."[23]

Arab Countries

It has been noted previously in this chapter that many Arab states offer support to terrorist groups through supply of arms, training, funding, havens, false passports, and/or diplomatic services. Among the diplomatic services is obstruction of international legislation aimed at curbing air terrorism, a task joined by all Arab countries, not only those considered radical. For example, Morocco and Oman, both strongly oriented toward the West, have supported radical Palestinian positions in voting on relevant resolutions in the UN, ICAO, and other international forums, and some moderate Arab countries have praised particular Arab terror attacks.[24]

Soviet-Bloc Countries

Supply of arms, training, intelligence, and logistic and diplomatic assistance by Soviet-bloc countries to Arab terror groups has been noted above. It can be assumed that decision making on USSR policy supporting Palestinian terrorism is complicated by the Soviet Union's own problem with aircraft hijacking in the USSR and eastern Europe by citizens of these countries perceiving no other way of leaving their homelands. Reflecting its contradictory needs to extend tangible support to radical Arab groups and yet to dissuade Soviet citizens of any notions that Palestinian tactics constitute acceptable conduct for them, the Soviet response to the air terrorism problem is inconsistent.

The USSR suffered a rash of hijacking incidents in the early 1970s—eleven in 1971 alone[25]—but few of the perpetrators succeeded in reaching the West. Most of these actions, as well as scattered earlier attempts in the 1950s and 1960s, appear to have been foiled by Aeroflot crew members, sometimes with loss of life. In response to the increasing incidence of armed seizure of Soviet aircraft in the 1970s, security measures were tightened at Soviet airports and armed guards were carried on most Aeroflot flights near border regions. The Soviets forced mutual compulsory extradition agreements on its party-state allies and on Afghanistan, Iran, and Finland. Severe legal penalties for unlawful interference with aircraft were enacted in the Soviet Union. Foreign Minister Andrei Gromyko stated in the UN General Assembly in 1972 that the Soviet Union opposes:

> . . . acts of terrorism which disrupt the diplomatic activities of States and their representatives, transport communications between them and the normal course of international contacts and meetings, and it opposes acts of violence which serve no positive end and cause loss of human life.[26]

Also in 1972, articles in two major Soviet publications sharply castigated several Palestinian groups for terrorist acts, including hijackings and attacks on nonmilitary targets. Yet these articles and others were compromised by misrepresentation of Palestinian assaults as being directed primarily at Israeli conventional military targets, and by criticism of terrorist acts for the damage they did to Palestinian prestige rather than for their barbarity.[27] In later articles, the Soviet press has claimed that Israeli agents have perpetrated some of the bloodier Palestinian terror attacks.[28]

The major thrusts of Soviet participation in international debate on the air terrorism issue have been exertion of pressure for an agreement requiring mandatory extradition of hijackers and objection to any proposal requiring collective action by all states against other states unless the action is approved by the Security Council (in which the Soviet Union can exercise its veto power). Thus the Soviets oppose any provision requiring mandatory sanctions against countries failing to extradite or punish hijackers, a convention favored by many Western states. The Soviet Union is uneasy about being compelled to halt Aeroflot service to, say, Algeria, and is well aware that use of its veto power in the Security Council opposing application of compulsory sanctions against an offending country would reap political benefit from radical states.

The Soviet Union and other party-states have consistently supported the Palestinian position in international debates.[29] Yet it is doubtful that the Soviets would also support the Palestinian contention that terrorist attacks are acceptable means of fighting "misery, frustrations, grievance, and despair" if such a statement were applied to miserable, frustrated, aggrieved, and desperate Soviet citizens hijacking aircraft in efforts to leave the USSR.[30]

Summary

The inadequacy of the international response to the problem of unlawful interference with aircraft derives from the political circumstances described above. Six key reasons for the impasse can be discerned.

Politicization of the United Nations,
Its Agencies, and Conventions

As long as political manipulation remains an accepted method of diplomacy at the United Nations, attempts to effect a solution to the air terrorism problem through its auspices are fruitless. When the International Civil Aviation Organization, the U.N. specialized agency whose stated aims include the advancement of air transport safety, invited the Palestine Liberation Organization, a major perpetrator of unlawful interference with aircraft, to attend its meetings as an observer, it forfeited both moral and practical pretensions of acting on the issue.

State Support of Terrorist Groups

If only one state among the more than 150 countries of the world provides a haven to terrorists, unlawful interference with aircraft will still remain a menace to the safety of international air transportation. As the decade of the 1980s begins, four countries (Algeria, Libya, Iraq, South Yemen) offer a willing haven to terrorists and a number of other countries provide a less enthusiastic, but nonetheless real, sanctuary. Many more countries supply terrorist training, weapons, intelligence, and logistic and diplomatic assistance. Suppression of terrorism clearly does not receive worldwide support.

Influence of Petroleum-Wealthy States

The influence of petroleum-wealthy countries has increased apace with their riches and control over energy resources. Several of these states extend substantial support to terrorist groups on the basis of religious or ideological identity; others proffer aid in an attempt to purchase immunity from terrorist subversion in their own countries. Cognizant of their support for Palestinian terror movements, many purchasing countries are reticent to back strong antiterrorist measures for fear of offending producer states and losing oil supplies or jeopardizing foreign trade.

Appeasement of Terrorist Groups

Several countries (and their airlines) have adopted a policy of appeasement of terrorist groups, granting concessions to them in exchange for immunity from terrorist acts against their own countries or property. For some countries, such appeasement merely indicates agreement to a rapid release from prison for any terrorist who is apprehended. For others, it is a practice of preemptive capitulation, an acknowledgment in advance to look the other way when terrorist groups gather, build weapons stockpiles, or take other measures in support of terrorism. France, in the early 1970s, and Cyprus have followed such policies. The French arrangement foundered in the mid-1970s following several Arab attacks against targets in France, but the French remain cynically opposed to strong international measures aimed at curbing terrorism. Cyprus, torn by domestic ethnic strife, is probably too weak to force an end to terrorist exploitation. Both countries claim economic gain from their political appeasement—France in the form of preferential foreign trade with Arab countries, and Cyprus through vastly increased banking receipts from handling of funds belonging to terrorist groups, arms dealers, and radical Arab states. In narrow nationalist terms, the agreements struck by capitulationist states may be viewed by them as commercial exchanges; however perceived in mercantile terms, such arrangements have not proved useful in reducing terrorism.

Airlines too have made deals with terrorist groups in attempts to stave off terrorist attacks. Five carriers in particular are rumored to have deposited extortion funds in Swiss bank accounts for the PFLP and/or the PLO; only MEA of Lebanon admits to such payments.[31] Though buying off terrorism against their own aircraft, carriers submitting to protectionist demands have not proved that extortion is a credible tactic in diminishing the terrorist threat to the airline industry as a whole.

Conflict Between Policies of Political Asylum and Extradition

Less tainted by charges of expedience, the conflict between policies of political asylum for and extradition of terrorists is nonetheless a serious one for many countries. In the United States, Latin America, and in some west European states, the principle of political asylum for persons fleeing perceived repression is strongly held. Nonextradition of persons escaping political persecution is a key provision in many bilateral extradition treaties. Although the United States has supported proposed conventions requiring mandatory extradition of aircraft hijackers, it has shown no inclination to forcibly return Cuban hijackers who land in the United States or East German hijackers who land in the American sector of Berlin. Similarly, west European countries may impose modest prison sentences upon east European hijackers, but do not extradite them.

Some observers would argue that American refusal to extradite persons fleeing communist (or other repressive) regimes represents a double standard in comparison with statements favoring stricter policies toward

Arab terrorists. Defenders of the American view would cite experience of political repression and usual absence of actual or threatened violence among political refugees as mitigating factors. Further, many governments advocating mandatory extradition of hijackers approve of punishment, such as a prison term, in instances where extradition could endanger the subject's life. Sanctuary countries for terrorists neither extradite nor prosecute them.

An additional complication to mandatory extradition of hijackers is potential application of the death penalty to returned prisoners. Several Western governments have outlawed a death penalty in their own countries and are reluctant to extradite persons to states where a death sentence or imprisonment under particularly harsh conditions could be expected.

Lack of Enforcement Capability

Whatever international convention on unlawful inteference with aircraft might be enacted, the inability of the international community (for example, the United Nations or ICAO) to enforce it would seriously undermine its credibility. International sanctions applied against countries violating norms on other issues have proved notoriously ineffective. The reality posed by the fact that several countries frequently offering haven to and otherwise supporting terrorists are also major oil/gas producers further diminishes the likelihood of successful application of antiterrorist sanctions.

Notes

1. Paul Wilkinson, *Terrorism and the Liberal State* (London and Basingstoke: Macmillan Press Ltd., 1977), pp. 53-54.

2. An internationally known psychiatrist and authority on terror and terrorism uses this classification in the title and text of this book. See Frederick J. Hacker, *Crusaders, Criminals, Crazies* (New York: W.W. Norton & Co., 1976), especially pp. 8-34.

3. Drew Middleton, "1979 Terrorist Toll Put at a Record 587," *New York Times*, May 11, 1980, p. 14.

4. Timothy S. Robinson, "Croatian Group Says It Bombed Yugoslav Envoy's Home Here," *Washington Post*, June 5, 1980, p. A31.

5. See, for example, "Canada Ousts Yugoslav Diplomat," *Washington Post*, May 12, 1979, p. A21; "Croatian Community is Upset by Blasts," *New York Times*, June 9, 1979, p. 8; "FBI Investigating Yugoslavian Tie in L.A. Violence," *Washington Post*, June 10, 1979, p.

A15; Jack Anderson, "FBI Ignored Tito Links to U.S. Killing," *Washington Post*, August 16, 1979, p. D69; and Anderson, "Yugoslav Secret Agent Leaves U.S.," *Washington Post*, October 3, 1979, p. B17.

6. "East Germans Aid Nkomo," *Newsweek* XCIV:2 (July 9, 1979), p. 17.

7. Evidence of transnational collaboration in the execution of terrorist acts is overwhelming and has been reported in numerous publications of various orientations. A sampling of such presentations indicates the widespread belief in the involvement of numerous groups and states: U.S., Congress, Senate, Committee on the Judiciary, *Terroristic Activity: International Terrorism*, part 4, before a subcommittee of the Committee on the Judiciary, Senate, 94th Congress, 1st session, 1975; David B. Tinnin, "Terror, Inc.," *Playboy* 24:5 (May, 1977), pp. 153-154 + ; "The Tightening Links of Terrorism," *Time*, 110:18 (October 31, 1977), p. 45; "Terrorism: The World at Bay," Public Broadcasting System, March 21, 1978; "Terror International," *Newsweek* XCI:21 (May 22, 1978), pp. 36-37; Alan D. Buckley, ed., "International Terrorism," special issue of *Journal of International Affairs* [Columbia University] 32:1 (Spring/Summer, 1978); Claire Sterling, "The Terrorist Network," *The Atlantic* 242:5 (November, 1978), pp. 37-47; "Executives' Assassins Linked to Palestinians, Soviets," *Washington Post*, December 31, 1978, p. A1; Andrew Blake, "Secrets of an IRA Terrorist," *Boston Sunday Globe*, September 2, 1979, p. 1; and Charles Horner, "The Facts About Terrorism," *Commentary* 69:6 (June, 1980), pp. 40-45. See also the following books: Yonah Alexander, ed., *International Terrorism* (New York: Praeger Publishers, 1974); David Carlton and Carlo Schaerf, eds., *International Terrorism and World Security* (New York: John Wiley & Sons, 1975); Christopher Dobson and Ronald Payne, *The Terrorists* (New York: Facts on File, 1979); Walter Laqueur, *Terrorism* (Boston: Little, Brown & Co., 1977); Marius Livingston, ed., *International Terrorism in the Contemporary World* (Westport, Conn.: Greenwood Press, 1978); Albert Parry, *Terrorism* (New York: Vanguard Press, 1976); *Terrorism and the Liberal State*; Wilkinson, *Terrorism: International Dimensions*, Conflict Studies, 113 (London: Institute for the Study of Conflict, 1979). The book by Dobson and Payne includes a useful chapter on financing of terrorist activity.

8. Michael Getler, "West Says Yugoslavia Let Terrorist Visit, Leave," *Washington Post*, September 16, 1976, p. A16; "Hunted Terrorist Reported in Yugoslavia," *New York Times*, September 17, 1976, p. A3; "Exit Carlos," *Newsweek* LXXXVIII:13 (September 27, 1976), p. 54. For accounts of Soviet-bloc assistance to Arab terrorist groups, see the following: Ray S. Cline, "Terrorism: Seedbed for Soviet Influence," *Midstream*, XXVI:5 (May, 1980), pp. 5-8; Horner, "The Facts About Terrorism"; Herbert Krosney, "Soviets Aid, Train PLO Guerrillas,"

Boston Sunday Globe, September 23, 1979, p. 1; Krosney, "PLO Defector Tells of Soviet Links," *Boston Globe*, September 24, 1979, p. 3; Tinnin, "Terror, Inc."; and Sterling, "The Terrorist Network."

9. See "Happy Landings ?," *Newsweek*, XC:18 (October 31, 1977), p. 56.

10. See Paul Hoffman, "Germans Tighten Flight Security in Face of Threats to Lufthansa," *New York Times*, November 16, 1977, p. A3; Milton R. Benjamin, "Lufthansa Combats Terrorist Threats," *Washington Post*, November 16, 1977, p. A19; Michael Getler, "West Germans Uneasy About Flying Lufthansa," *Washington Post*, November 17, 1977, p. A35; "Lufthansa Profits Off," *Washington Post*, June 30, 1978, p. F3.

11. See "MEA Runs for Cover," *Flight* 110:3517 (August 7, 1976), p. 308; Asad Nasr, "Lebanese Air Transport After the Civil War of 1975-1976," *ITA Bulletin* 14 (April 11, 1977), pp. 323-328; Arthur Reed, "MEA: You Can't Keep a Good Airline Down," *Air Transport World*, 15:7 (July, 1978), pp. 62-64; and Derek Wood, "Middle East Airlines Survives and Prospers," *Interavia* XXXIV:10 (October 1979), pp. 951-952. A company account of MEA difficulties in 1975-1976, available from the airline, is: Reginald Turnhill, *Battle for Survival* (London: Maxclif Publishing Co., 1977).

12. Doug Richardson, "Can Airliners Be Protected from Missile Attack?", *Flight* 115:3651 (March 10, 1979), pp. 738-740; "El Al Counters SAM Threat," *Flight* 117:3702 (March 1, 1980), p. 622; and "El Al Equips Aircraft with Sensor Systems for Missile Diversion," *Aviation Week* 112:21 (May 26, 1980), p. 93.

13. For texts of these and other documents noted in this chapter, see Yonah Alexander, Marjorie Ann Browne, and Allan S. Nanes, *Control of Terrorism: International Documents* (New York: Crane, Russak & Co., 1979).

14. Ironically, the Somali government was an indirect participant in the Entebbe hijacking and hostage-taking. PFLP leader Wadi Haddad directed the entire operation from there.

15. Admission of the PLO to ICAO as an observer is discussed in chapter 4 of this book.

16. See the text of the European Civil Aviation Conference resolution on strengthening security measures in civil aviation, reprinted by *ITA Bulletin* 44 (December 26, 1977), pp. 1033-34.

17. The Bonn declaration is included in Alexander, Browne, and Nanes, *Control of Terrorism: International Documents*, p. 215.

18. European firms do not manufacture aircraft equivalent to the U.S. models now desired by Libya. For an account of the trade embargo sympathetic to Libya, see Thomas W. Lippman, "Trade Ban Irks Libyans," *Washington Post*, August 11, 1978, p. A20. See also

"Government Expected to Ban 747 Sale to Libya," *Aviation Daily* 243:22 (May 31, 1979), p. 182, and "Libyan 747s," *Aviation Week* 112:20 (May 19, 1980), p. 27.

19. See "Two Controversial Items in New Terrorism Bill," *Aviation Daily* 242:3 (March 5, 1979), p. 21, and "ALPA Organizes Lobbying Group for Anti-Hijack Bill," *Aviation Daily* 248:35 (April 18, 1980), p. 279.

20. See Philip Jacobson, "Terrorist at Large," *Washington Post*, November 6, 1977, p. C1.

21. The Palestinian was Abu Daoud, suspected of masterminding the massacre of Israeli athletes at the 1972 Munich Olympics and almost all other Black September attacks. See the *New York Times* and *Washington Post*, both of January 12, 1977; "French Arms Sales to Middle East," *Interavia Air Letter* 8672 (January 14, 1977), p. 2; "The French Justice that Was," *The Economist* 262:6959 (January 15, 1977), p. 43; "L'Affaire Daoud: Too Hot to Handle," *Time*, 10:4 (January 24, 1977); pp. 29-31; "A Terrorist Cross Fire," *Newsweek* LXXXIX:4 (January 24, 1977), pp. 43-46; and Sandra E. Rapoport, "Abu Daoud and the Law," *Commentary*, 63:3 (March, 1977), pp. 70-72.

22. General Vito Miceli in "L'Expresso," quoted in the *Jewish Telegraphic Agency Daily News Bulletin* LVIII:20 (January 29, 1980), p. 2.

23. The phrase is from introductions to UN Resolutions 31/102 (1976) and 32/147 (1977), both of which convey a sense of justification of terrorism. See above.

24. See, for example, "Arab States Praise Attack as 'Noble' and 'Courageous,' " *Washington Post*, March 13, 1978, p. A19.

25. "Hijackings in the Soviet Union," *Aviation Week* 97:18 (October 30, 1972), p. 24.

26. Address of Andrei Gromyko, UN General Assembly, 27th Session, Plenary Meetings, 2,040th Meeting, September 26, 1972, p. 10.

27. P. Demchenko, "Palistinskoye soprotivlenye i proiski reaktsii," *Pravda*, August 29, 1972, p. 4; and Y. Kornilov, "Meetings with the Fedayeen," *New Times* 42 (October 1972), pp. 24-25.

28. See especially Rishat Mametov, "Kuda vedyot sledi," *Literaturnaya gazeta* 52 (December 26, 1973), p. 9; and Vladimir Terekhov, "International Terrorism and the Fight Against It," *New Times* 11 (March 1974), pp. 20-22. Similar charges have appeared in the media of other party-states. See, for example, *Rude Pravo* (Prague), January 24, 1974. A Yugoslavian newspaper accused the United States of firing the rocket-propelled grenades that hit a JAT DC-9 at Orly airport in 1975; Fatah claimed responsibility for the assault which was aimed at a nearby El Al aircraft but missed its target. See *Vjesnik* (Belgrade), January 15, 1975.

29. In a 1979 booklet on Aeroflot the deputy director of the USSR

Ministry of Civil Aviation wrote that the admission of the PLO to ICAO as an observer was "fully legal." This statement appears in a section on unlawful interference with aircraft, but PLO involvement in air terrorism is not mentioned. See S.S. Pavlov, *Trassy mira i druzhby* (Moscow: Izdatel'stvo Znanye, 1979), p. 47.

30. For further consideration of the Soviet approach to the issue of unlawful interference with aircraft, see the author's *The Political and Economic Implications of the International Routes of Aeroflot*, pp. 241-257, and W. Scott Thompson, "Political Violence and the 'Correlation of Forces,' " *Orbis*, XIX:4 (Winter 1976), pp. 1270-1288.

31. "Boeing Commission Payments Used to Pay Off Terrorists, says MEA Chairman," *Flight*, 116:3693 (December 29, 1979), p. 2110.

Bibliography

Air Transport

Air Transport Association of America. *Airline Capital Requirements in the 1980's*. Washington, D.C.: Air Transport Association of America, 1979.

Allen, Roy. *Capital Financing and Re-Equipment of the World's Commercial Airline Fleets in the 1980s*. London: The Economist Intelligence Unit Ltd., 1979.

Brancker, J.W.S. *IATA and What It Does*. Leiden, The Netherlands: A.W. Sijthoff International Publishing, 1977.

Buergenthal, Thomas. *Law-Making in the International Civil Aviation Organization*. Syracuse: Syracuse University Press, 1969.

Bugayev, B.P. *K novym vysotam (To New Heights)*. Moscow: Izdatel'stvo Znanye, 1976.

Burkhardt, Robert A. *The Civil Aeronautics Board*. Dulles International Airport, Virginia: Green Hills Publishing Company, Inc., 1974.

Cheng, Bin. *The Law of International Air Transport*. London: Stevens & & Sons, 1962.

Chomentovsky, Victor. *Impact of Air Transport on the French Economy*. Paris: Institute of Air Transport, 1978.

Chuang, R.Y. *The International Air Transport Association*. Leiden, The Netherlands: A.W. Sijthoff International Publishing Company, 1971. 1971.

Cook, Don. *The Chicago Aviation Agreements: An Approach to World Policy*. New York: American Enterprise Association, Inc., 1945.

Cooper, John C. The *Right to Fly*. New York: Henry Holt and Co., 1947.

Corbett, David. *Politics and the Airlines*. London: George Allen & Unwin, 1965.

Daley, Robert. *An American Saga: Juan Trippe and His Pan American Empire*. New York: Random House, 1980.

Davies, R.E.G. *A History of the World's Airlines*. London: Oxford University Press, 1967.

Davies, R.E.G. *Airlines of the United States Since 1914*. London: Putnam & Company Ltd., 1972.

Friedman, Jesse J. *A New Air Transport Policy for the North Atlantic*. New York: Atheneum, 1976.

Gidwitz, Betsy. "The Political and Economic Implications of the International Routes of Aeroflot." Unpublished study, Massachusetts Institute of Technology, 1976.

Gordonov, Lazar Sh. *Vozdushnye puti zarubezhnykh stran (Air Routes of Foreign Countries)*. Moscow: Gosudarstvennoye Izdatel'stvo Geograficheskoy literaturi, 1961.

Haanappel, Peter P.C. *Ratemaking in International Air Transport*. Deventer, The Netherlands: Kluwer B.V., 1978.

Harbridge House, Inc. *U.S. International Aviation Policy at the Crossroads: A Study of Alternative Policies and Their Consequences*. Prepared for the Department of State, Department of Transportation, and the President's Council on International Economic Policy. Boston: Harbridge House, 1975.

Heymann, Hans, Jr. *The U.S.-Soviet Civil Air Agreement from Inception to Inauguration: A Case Study*. Santa Monica: Rand Corp., 1972.

International Civil Aviation Organization. *Handbook on Capacity Clauses in Bilateral Agreements*. Circular 72-AT/9, 1965.

_____. *Regulation of Capacity in International Air Transport Services*. Circular 137-AT/43, 1977.

Jackson, Ronald W. *China Clipper*. New York: Everest House, 1980.

Kane, Robert M. and Vose, Allan D. *Air Transportation*. Dubuque, Iowa: Wm. C. Brown Book Co., 1969.

Lauriac, Jacques. *Air Transport Policies Regarding Public and Private Airlines*. Paris: Institute of Air Transport, 1979.

Lowenfeld, Andreas F. *Aviation Law*. New York: Matthew Bender, 1972.

McWhinney, Edward, and Bradley, Martin, eds. *The Freedom of the Air*. Dobbs Ferry, N.Y.: Oceana Publications, Inc., 1968.

Miller, Georgette. *Liability in International Air Transport*. Deventer, The Netherlands: Kluwer B.V., 1977.

O'Connor, William E. *Economic Regulation of the World's Airlines*. New York: Praeger Publishers, 1971.

Pavlov, Sergei S. *Trassy mira i druzhby* [*Routes of Peace and Friendship*]. Moscow: Izdatel'stvo Znanye, 1979.

Pillai, K.G.J. *The Air Net*. New York: Grossman Publishers, 1969.

Robbins, Christopher. *Air America*. New York: G.P. Putnam's Sons, 1979.

Rumyantseva, Zinaida P. *Mirovoy vozdushnyy transport* [*World Air Transport*]. Moscow: Izdatel'stvo Znanye, 1971.

Sealy, Kenneth R. *The Geography of Air Transport*. Chicago: Aldine Publishing Co., 1968.

Straszheim, Mahlon. *The International Airline Industry*. Washington, D.C.: Brookings Institute, 1969.

Taaffe, Edward J., and Howard L. Gauthier, Jr. *Geography of Transportation*. Englewood Cliffs, N.J.: Prentice-Hall, Inc., 1973.

Taneja, Nawal. *The Commercial Airline Industry*. Lexington, Mass.: Lexington Books, 1976.

_____. *U.S. International Aviation Policy*. Lexington, Mass.: Lexington Books, 1980.

Thayer, Frederick C., Jr. *Air Transport Policy and National Security*. Chapel Hill: University of North Carolina Press, 1965.

Thornton, Robert L. *International Airlines and Politics*. Ann Arbor: Bureau of Business Research, Graduate School of Business Administration, University of Michigan, 1970.

U.S., Civil Aeronautics Board. *Aeronautical Statutes and Related Materials*, rev. ed. Washington, D.C., 1974.

_____. *Government Ownership, Subsidy, and Economic Assistance in International Commercial Aviation*. Washington, D.C., 1975.

_____. *Order to Show Cause: Agreements by the International Air Transport Association Relating to the Traffic Conferences*. Order 78-678. June 9, 1978.

_____. *Restrictive Practices Used by Foreign Countries to Favor Their National Carriers*. Washington, D.C., 1973.

U.S., Congress, House, Committee on Public Works and Transportation. *The Airline Deregulation Act of 1978*. Hearings before the Aviation Subcommittee. Washington, D.C., July 31, August 1-2, 1979.

U.S., Congress, Senate, Committee on Commerce, Science, and Transportation. *International Air Transportation Competition Act of 1979*. Hearings before Subcommittee on Aviation. Las Vegas, August 21-22, 1979.

_____. *International Aviation*. Hearings before Subcommittee on Aviation, 95th Congress, 1st Session. Washington, D.C.: Government Printing Office, 1978.

U.S., General Accounting Office. *The Critical Role of Government in International Air Transport*. Washington, D.C.: Government Printing Office, 1978.

Vereshchagin, Andrey N. *Mezhdunarodnoye vozdushnoye pravo* [*International Air Law*]. Moscow: Izdatel'stvo Mezhdunarodnoye otnoshenye, 1966.

Unlawful Interference with Aircraft

Agarwala, S.K. *Aircraft Hijacking and International Law*. Dobbs Ferry, N.Y.: Oceana Publications, 1973.

Alexander, Yonah, ed. *International Terrorism*. New York: Praeger Publishers, 1974.

Alexander, Yonah; Browne, Marjorie Ann; and Nanes, Allan S. *Terrorism: International Documents*. New York: Crane, Russak & Co., 1979.

Beaubois, H. *The Work Done by ICAO to Combat Acts of Unlawful Interference*. Paris: Institute of Air Transport, 1972.

Ben-Porat, Yeshayahu, et al. *Entebbe Rescue*. New York: Dell Publishing Co., 1977.

Carlton, David, and Schaerf, Carlo, eds. *International Terrorism and World Security*. New York: John Wiley & Sons, 1975.

Dobson, Christopher, and Payne, Ronald. *The Terrorists*. New York: Facts on File, 1979.

Hacker, Frederick J. *Crusaders, Criminals, Crazies*. New York: W.W. Norton & Co., 1976.

Joyner, Nancy Douglas. *Aerial Hijacking as an International Crime*. New York: Oceana Publications, 1974.

Laqueur, Walter. *Terrorism*. Boston: Little, Brown and Co., 1977.

Livingston, Marius H., ed. *International Terrorism in the Contemporary World*. Westport, Conn.: Greenwood Press, 1978.

Sobel, Lester A. *Political Terrorism*. New York: Facts on File, 1975.

_____. *Political Terrorism, Volume 2*. New York: Facts on File, 1978.

Stevenson, William. *90 Minutes at Entebbe*. New York: Bantam Books, 1976.

U.S., Congress, Senate, Committee on the Judiciary. *Terroristic Activity: International Terrorism*, Part 4. Hearings before a subcommittee of the Committee on the Judiciary, Senate, 94th Congress, 1st session, 1975.

Wilkinson, Paul. *Political Terrorism*. New York: John Wiley & Sons, 1974.

_____. *Terrorism and the Liberal State*. London and Basingstoke: Macmillan Press Ltd., 1977.

_____. *Terrorism: International Dimensions*. London: Institute for the Study of Conflict, 1979.

Index

ABA (Aktiebolaget Aerotransport; Sweden), wartime service, 45
Abidjan, 175-176
Administration, U.S., role in international air transport, 24-25, 120-121, 127
Aer Lingus: ownership, 7; transatlantic service, 148
Aeroflot: cooperation with Luft Hansa 1939, 41; espionage activity, 27-28; ethnic traffic, 162-163 history of, 22-23; IATA membership, 97; international service, 5; military routes, 166; postwar service, 55; prestige routes, 166; restrictive practices, 141; scope of operations, 2, 6; service to developing countries, 55-56; service to U.S., 147; service to West Germany, 147; strategic policy routes, 165-166; SST operations, 205-206; transsiberian route, 183
Aerolineas Argentinas: South Africa service, 172; U.S. service, 173
Aeromexico: Canada service, 174; international service, 67; Mid Atlantic service, 171; ownership, 8; U.S. service, 174
Aeroperu, U.S. service, 173
Aerospatiale, 197-198
Africa, 68-69, 175-177; international service in 176-177; U.S. carriers in, 59. *See also* African Airlines, Association of; African Civil Aviation Commission
Africa-Europe service, 175-176
African Airlines, Association of (AAFRA), 99
African Civil Aviation Commission (AFCAC), 90
Air Afrique, organization, 10-11, 68
Air America, 28
Air Asia, 28

Airbus, 197, 199, 210, 213
Air Canada: Caribbean service, 173; interest in other airlines, 8; international service, 3, 5; North Atlantic service 170; ownership, 7-8; route structure, 63-64; South America service, 173; U.S. service, 173
Aircraft Agreement, GATT, 1979, 213
aircraft manufacturers: as operators of airlines, 38; Brazil, 204; Britain, 196-197; Canada, 203-204; China, 203; Czechoslovakia, 202-203; France, 197-198; Italy, 199; Japan, 204; multinational Europe, 199-200; Netherlands, 198; Poland, 202; sales of aircraft, 20-21; Spain, 199; USSR, 200-202; U.S. 193-196
aircraft sales: bribery in, 213-214; factor in air-traffic negotiations, 149; financing of 208-215; protectionism of home industry, 212-213
Air France: aircraft purchasing, 21; At las membership, 14; Berlin air corridors, 185-188; Concorde service, 205-206; founding, 38; interest in other airlines, 8, 69; international service, 3, 5; Mid Atlantic service, 171; North Atlantic service, 170; ownership, 8, 39, 112; postwar service, 55; prewar history, 40; prestige routes, 166; South Atlantic service, 172; subsidy of,15, 112; transsiberian service, 183; wartime service, 44-45
Air-India: international service, 5; North Atlantic service, 170.
Air Inter, 3
Air Jamaica: Canada service, 173; Mid Atlantic service, 171; ownership, 8; U.S. service, 173
Airlift International, 6
Air Line Pilots Association, 129-130
Air Mail Act of 1934, 38

air mail contracts, historical role, 37, 39

Air New Zealand, 64, 160

Air Panama: ownership, 8; U.S. service, 174

Airport Associations Co-Ordinating Council (AACC), 101

airport authority, 119

Airport Development Program, 43

Air Tanzania, 13

Air Transport Association of America, 149-150

Airworthiness Directives (U.S., FAA), 118

Air Zaire, 176

Ala Littoria, 40, 44. See also Alitalia

Algeria, assistance to terrorist groups, 225, 229, 236

Alia Royal Jordania Airways, 69-70; safety record, 71

Alitalia: Africa service, 177; Atlas membership, 14; dispute with Pan Am, 140; dispute with TWA, 140; ethnic traffic, 162; interest in other airlines, 8; North Atlantic service, 170; origins, 52-53; South Atlantic service, 172. See also Ala Littoria

All Nippon Airways (ANA): bid for Taiwan service, 189; ownership, 7

All Red line, 48-49

American Airlines: Caribbean service, 173; exchange of route authorizations with Pan Am, 61; Mexico service, 174; purchase of Trans Caribbean, 59; route awards, 59; wartime service, 45

American Export Airlines (Amex): name changed to American Overseas Airlines, 56; ownership, 56; postwar route awards, 56-57. See also American Airlines.

American Export Lines shipping company, founder of American Export Airlines, 56

American Overseas Airlines (AOA): postwar route awards, 57; purchased by Pan American, 57. See

also American Export Airlines

ANA. See All Nippon Airways

Andean extension, 171

Ansett Airlines, 2

antitrust laws, U.S.: Department of Justice, 123; impact of IATA, 96, 98; regarding charter airline ownership, 2

Antonov, O.K., 200-201

Atwood, James, 155

Arab Air Carriers Organization (AACO), 99

Arab countries, 177-178, 220-234

Ariana (Afghanistan), 72

Arnold, Henry H. "Hap," 45

Asia, 178-179

Athens, gateway to Middle East, 163, 177-178

Atlas (consortium), 14

Australia: ethnic market, 162; postwar air-transport policy, 48, 64. See also Qantas

Austria: exclusion from Chicago Conference, 46; between East and West, 160; postwar air-transport policy, 53. See also Austrian Airlines

Austrian Airlines, 53

Avianca, 67; Mid Atlantic service, 171

Aviateca (Guatemala), U.S. service, 174

Aviation Week & Space Technology, 103

Azores, 136, 171

Bakhtiar (Afghanistan), 72

Balair (Switzerland), 2

Bangladesh Biman, 71-72

Bangkok-Hong Kong service, 179

Basque ETA, 220, 224

Beirut, 163, 177

Belairbus (Belgium), 199

Belize Airways, US service, 174

Berlin: air service manipulated by USSR, 146-147; Moscow service, 175; surface transport barriers, 164-165. See also Berlin air corridors

Berlin Agreeement, 100
Berlin air corridors, 185-188
Bermuda Agreement (Bermuda I), 51-52, 94, 135
Bermuda II, 61-62, 98
beyond rights, 136, 150
bilateral air-transport agreements, 152-154
Black September, air terrorism of, 220
Boeing Airplane Company, 38
Boeing Air Transport, 38
Boeing Company, 194
Bolivia, 42, 171, 174
Bonn Economic Summit Declaration, 231-232
Boston: ethnic market, 162; North Atlantic service, 167
Braathens, ownership, 9
Braniff Airways: acquisition of Panagra, 58-59; Caribbean service, 173; Central American service, 174; Mexico service, 174; 1969 route awards, 59; postwar route awards, 58; South America service, 173; transatlantic route award, 62
Brazil: aircraft industry, 204; air service, 172-174; prewar German service, 42-43
breakeven load factor, 140
bribery in aircraft industry, 213-214
Britain, Great: aircraft industry, 196-197; airline ownership, 8; negotiations with U.S., 51-52, 61-62; negotiations with USSR, 183; postwar air-transport policy, 48-50, 109, 149; subsidy to airlines, 21
British Aerospace Corporation, 197, 199
British Airways: Berlin air corridors, 185-188; Concorde service, 205-206; interest in other airlines, 8; international service, 3, 5; Mid Atlantic service, 171; North Atlantic service, 177; transsiberian service, 183. See also British European Airways, British Overseas Airways, Imperial Airways

British Caledonian Airways, 3; international service, 3, 5; ownership, 8, 9
British European Airways (BEA): aircraft purchase, 21; assistance to Lufthansa, 54; interest in Alitalia, 53. See also British Airways
British Midland Airways: aircraft leasing, 6; ownership, 8
British Overseas Airways Corporation (BOAC): postwar service, 55; wartime service, 44. See also British Airways
British West Indian Airways: Canada service 173; Mid Atlantic service, 171; U.S. service, 173
Browne, Secor, 87
Brzezinski, Zbigniew, 147
Buenos Aires, 172, 174
Bulgaria: exclusion from Chicago Conference, 46; assistance to terrorist groups, 225; joint stock airline in, 54-55
Burma Airways Corporation, 72
business class, 161
business routes, 161

CAAC, See Civil Aviation Administration of China
cabotage, 137, 138
Cairo: Middle East air hub, 177-178; wartime service, 44-45
Cairo-Tel Aviv service, 190
Cameroon Airlines, 176
Canada: aircraft industry, 203-204; airline ownership, 8; antiterrorism policy, 229, 231; Chicago Conference policy, 49; ethnic market, 162; negotiations with Greece, 148; postwar air transport policy, 63-64; surface transportation, 164. See also Air Canada, CP Air
Canada-U.S. service, 173
Canadian Pacific Airlines (CP Air): chosen instrument, 3; international service, 5; Mexico service, 174; North Atlantic service, 170; ownership, 7-8; route structure, 63-64,

U.S. service, 173
capacity, 51, 139-142
Capetown, 172
cargo airlines, 6
cargo, definition, 6
cargo, preferential direction of, 30
Caribbean-North America service, 173
CAT. *See* Civil Air Transport
Cathay Pacific Airways (CP Air; Hong Kong), 8, 65, 188
Central America-U.S. service, 173-174
Central Intelligence Agency, U.S. proprietary airlines, 28
charter airlines, 1-2
charter service, 1-2, 30, 167, 171, 172, 175
Chicago Conference, 1944, 46-51, 81
Chicago Convention, 81. *See also* International Civil Aviation Organization
China: prewar service, 41, 43; wartime service, 45
China, People's Republic of: aircraft industry, 203; air-transport policy, 65; assistance to terrorist groups, 225; bilateral negotiations with U.S., 145-146; German-managed service in 1930s and 1940s, 41; ICAO membership, 88; overflight rights, 179; transpacific service, 184; transsiberian service, 184; views on Taiwan service, 188-190
China, Republic of. *See* Taiwan
China Airlines (Taiwan): international network, 65-66; Japan service, 188-190;
chosen instrument, principle of 2-3, 139
Chosonminhang (North Korea), 65
Civil Aeronautics Board (CAB; U.S.): charter rate-setting for military use, 126; dissolution of, 115; international negotiations role, 24, 114, 127, 145, 147; organization of, 113-115; postal rate-setting, 125; postwar route awards, 56-60
Civil Air Transport (CAT; Taiwan), 28

Civil Aviation Administration of China (CAAC), 65; IATA membership, 97
Civil Aviation Council of Arab States (CACAS), 89
Clearing House, IATA, 92-93
CMA-Mexicana: ownership, 8; US service, 174
Colombia, prewar service, 42. *See also* Avianca, SCADTA
colonial routes, 166-167, 171
Common Market, air-transport regulation in, 89
Compagnie des Messageries Aériennes, 38
Concorde, 198, 204-206; in regotiations, 147, 149; prestige routes, 166. *See also* supersonic transport
Condor: charter airline, 2; ownership, 2
confidential memorandum of understanding, 148, 154
Copenhagen, 163
CP Air. *See* Canadian Pacific Airlines and Cathay Pacific Airways
Council for Mutual Economic Assistance (CMEA), air-transport regulation in, 90, 100
Croatia, *See* Ustashi
CSA (Ceskoslovenske Aerolinie): ethnic traffic, 163; postwar service, 54, 55
Cuba, assistance to terrorist groups, 221, 225. *See also* Cubana
Cubana, 67, 155; Mid Atlantic service, 171-172
currency conversion problem, 29
Curtiss Aeroplane & Motor Co., 38
Cyprus: gateway between Arab states and Israel, 178; impact of 1974 Turkish invasion on air transport, 70; role in terrorist activity, 225, 237
Cyprus Airways, 70
Cyprus Turkish Airlines, 70
Czechoslovakia: aircraft industry, 202-203; assitance to terrorist groups, 221, 225; charter member of ICAO,

48; ethnic market, 163; postwar air-transport policy, 54-55; use of Aeroflot in 1968 invasion, 28. *See also* CSA

Dakar, 172, 175-176
Dassault, 198
Delta Air Lines: Canada service, 173; IATA membership, 97; merger with Chicago & Southern, 1953, 58; North Atlantic route award, 62
Deruluft (Deutsche-Russische Luftver-kehr), 41
Deutsche Luft Hansa Aktien-Gesell-schaft (DLH), 38, 44, 53. *See also* Lufthansa
Deutsche Lufthansa Aktiengesellschaft, Köln. *See* Lufthansa
Deutsche Lufthansa, Berlin-Schönefeld, (East Germany), 53-55.
Deutscher Aero Lloyd, 37
developing countries: IATA member-ship of airlines, 97, ICAO member-ship of airlines, 86-87; problems in airline management, 20
diplomatic traffic, 164
discriminatory measures, against for-eign airlines, 28-32, 140-141, 151
DLH. *See* Deutsche Luft Hansa
Djakarta, 179
Dobrolet, 39
Dominicana, 173

East African Airways, 12-13, 17 n. 3
East African Common Services Organ-ization, 12
Eastern Airlines: Canada service, 3, 173; Caribbean service, 173; Mexico service, 174; takeover of Colonial, 58; wartime service, 45
Economic and Social Council (ECOSOC; United Nations), 101
economic instrument, airlines used as, 19-21
Ecuador, 173-174; wartime service, 42. *See also* Ecuatoriana
Ecuatoriana, 173
Egypt, 177-178. World War II wartime

service, 44. *See also* Egyptair, Nefertiti Aviation
Egyptair, 69; proposed Tel Aviv ser-vice, 190; safety record, 71
El Al Israel Airlines: Cairo service, 190; ethnic traffic, 162; impact of Middle East conflict, 25, 70; North Atlantic service, 170; route network, 70; safety record, 71; South Africa service, 177; terrorist acts against, 221-229, 233
enforcement: of antiterrorism agree-ments, 227-238; of bilateral air-transport agreements, 144
entry points, destinations, 150
environmental standards, 144, 196, 207-208
equivalent access, approach in bilateral negotiations, 152
espionage, airline industry used for, 27-28, 34-35 n. 19, 126-127
Ethiopian Airlines, 68-69, 176; Eritrean terror attacks against, 224
ethnic traffic, 162-163, 174, 177-178, 179
Eurasia air service, 41
Eurocontrol, 89-90
Europe, international service, 174
Europe-Africa service, 174-175
Europe-Japan service, 179-184
Europe-Middle East service, 177-178
European Airlines, Association of (AEA), 99
European Civil Aviation Conference, 89
Evergreen International Airlines, 28
executive branch of government, role in international air transport, 24-25, 120-121, 127
exclusive franchise, principle of, 3
Export-Import Bank, US, 209-210
extradition, 234, 237-238

FALN, *See* Fuerzas Armadas de Lib-eración
Far East-Middle East service, 177
Fatah, air terrorism of, 220-221

Fedayeen (Iran), 225
Federal Aviation Administration, 115-119, 120, 128
financing: of aircraft, 208-211; of airlines, 14-15
Finland: exclusion from Chicago Conference, 46; exclusion from SAS, 10
Flight International, 103
Flying Tiger: leasing of aircraft, 6; international network, 6. *See also* Seaboard World
Fokker Aircraft Corporation, 38, 198, 199
Ford Motor Co., 38
foreign affairs ministry, role in international air transport, 23-26, 120, 127-128, 145-148
foreign exchange, airlines as earners of, 20
foreign policy, airlines as instruments of, 22-26, 146-148
France: aircraft industry, 197-198; aircraft sales techniques, 149; airline designation, 3; airline ownership, 8; air-transport negotiating policy, 149; antiterrorism policy, 229, 231, 233, 237; subsidy to airlines, 15. *See also* Air France, UTA
Frankfurt: Berlin air corridor, 185-187; European service, 174-175; North Atlantic service, 167-170
freedoms of the air, 47, 49, 50, 136-137
freight: definition, 6; international, 4-5; on mixed loads, 6
freight carriers, 6. *See* Airlift International, Flying Tiger, Trans Mediterranean Airlines
Frontier Airlines, Canada service, 173
Fuerzas Armadas de Liberación (FALN), 225

Galapagos Islands, air service to, 42
Garuda (Indonesia), 72
gateway, gateway traffic, 136, 163-164
General Agreement on Tariffs and Trade, Aircraft Agreement, 213
General Electric, 196

Germany, Democratic Republic of (East Germany), 155; assistance to terrorist groups, 221, 224, 225; Berlin air corridors, 185-188. *See also* Interflug
Germany, Federal Republic of (West Germany), 19; aircraft industry, 199; antiterrorism policy, 231, 233; Berlin air corridors, 185-188; European service, 175; negotiations with East European countries, 155; negotiations with USSR, 25, 146-147; postwar air-transport policy, 53-54; *See also* Lufthansa
Germany, National Socialist, 41-44
Ghana, 22, 26
Ghana Airways, 22, 26
government financial support of airlines, 15, 143-144
Grace, W.R., & Co. *See* Panagra
Grazhdanskaya aviatsiya, 103
Greece: ethnic market, 162; Middle East gateway, 178; negotiations with Canada, 148
groundhandling of aircraft, 29-30
Gulf Air, organization, 11-12

Hague Convention, 228-229
Haj traffic, 163
Hapag-Lloyd, 9
hijacking of aircraft, 219-242
Hilton International, 151
Hong Kong, 179-184
Hong Kong-Bangkok service, 179
Hong Kong-Tokyo service, 179
Hungary: assistance to terrorist groups, 225; exclusion from Chicago Conference 46; joint-stock airline in, 54-55

Iberia
Mid Atlantic service, 171; North Atlantic service, 170; South Africa service, 177
Iceland, 146
Icelandair, 146
Ilyushin, S.V., 200-201

Imperial Airways, 38, 40. *See also*
British Airways
India: air-transport development in,
71; ties with Pakistan, 178-179; ties
with Sri Lanka, 179. *See also* Air-
India
Indian Airlines, 71
Institut du Transport Aérien, 102
Institute of Air and Space Law, McGill
University, 103
Interagency Group on International
Aviation (IGIA), 128
Intercontinental Hotels Corporation,
151
Interflug: East Berlin traffic, 187;
founding, 54; permits for routes,
155
Intermountain, 28
International Air Carrier Association,
99
International Air Services Transit
Agreement (IASTA), 47, 50, 136
International Air Traffic Association
(old IATA), 91
International Air Transport Associa-
tion (IATA): founding, 51;
organization, 91-99; politicization,
95-96; problems, 97-99; reforms, 98;
response to air terrorism, 230
International Civil Airports Association
(ICAA), 100-101
International Civil Aviation Organization (ICAO), 81-90; China-Taiwan
dispute, 88; economic policy advocate, 86-87; founding, 46-51; 81;
organization, 82-84; Palestine
Liberation Organization as
observer, 88-89; politicization,
84-89, 228-230; repository for
bilateral agreements, 154; response
to air terrorism, 88-89, 228-230,
236. *See also* Chicago Convention
International Federation of Airline
Pilots Associations (IFALPA), 102;
response to air terrorism, 230-231
Iran, 70, 77 n. 24, 225
Iranair, 70, 77 n. 24

Iraq: assistance to terrorist groups,
225, 236; negotiations with Japan,
24-25. *See also* Iraqi Airways
Iraqi Airways: espionage tool, 28;
safety record, 71; service to Japan,
24-25
Ireland: air-transport policy, 148;
ethnic traffic, 162. *See also* Aer
Lingus
Israel: aircraft industry, 204; Cairo service, 178; ethnic traffic, 162; European service, 178; Far East service,
178; 1978 bilateral agreement with
U.S., 62; negotiations with Japan,
25; negotiations with Netherlands,
148; North Atlantic service, 178;
political problems, 178; religious-
pilgrimage traffic, 163; South Africa
service, 178; surface transport barriers, 164-165. *See also* El Al Israel
Airlines
Italy: aircraft industry, 199, 210; antiterrorism policy, 231, 233; ethnic
market, 162; exclusion from
Chicago Conference, 46; postwar
air-transport policy, 52-53. *See also*
Ala Littoria, Alitalia

Japan: aircraft industry, 204, 210; exclusion from Chicago Conference,
46; aircraft purchases under
pressure, 26; antiterrorism policy,
231; negotiations with Arabs, 24-25;
postwar air service, 64; prewar air
service, 42-43; wartime air service,
44. *See also* Japan Air Lines, Japan
Asia Airways
Japan Air Lines: Europe-Japan service,
179-184; international service 5, 64;
ownership, 7; proposed Taiwan service, 188-190
Japan Asia Airways, 189-190
Japan-Europe service, 179-184
Japan-Taiwan service, 188-190
Japanese Red Army, 220, 221, 223, 224
Jedda, 177; pilgrimage traffic, 163
Johannesburg, 172, 175-177

joint operations, 141
joint-stock airlines, 54-55
Journal of Air Law and Commerce, 103
Journal of the Royal Aeronautical Society, 103
Jordan; negotiations with U.S., 24; surface transportation barriers, 164-165: *See also* Alia Royal Jordanian Airways
Jogoslovanski Aerotransport (JAT): postwar service, 55; Ustashi attacks on, 223
Junkers Aircraft Works, 38
Junkers Luftverkehr, 38, 41
Justice, Department of, U.S., role in international air transport, 123

Karachi, 178
Kelly Act (1925), 39
Kenya Airways, 68
KLM: assistance to Garuda, 72; founding, 39; international service, 5; Mid Atlantic service, 171; North Atlantic service, 170; postwar service, 55; prewar service, 40; relationship to Martinair, 2; South Africa service, 177; South Atlantic service, 172; wartime service, 44. *See also* Martinair
Korean Air Lines, 64-65
KSSU, 14
Kuala Lumpur, 179
Kuznetsov, N.D., 201, 205

LACSA (Costa Rica), U.S. service, 174
Lagos, 44, 175-176
LAN-Chile, U.S. service, 173
LANICA (Nicaragua), U.S. service, 174
Larnaca, 178
Latin America route awards, U.S., 1946, 58
Latin American Air Transport, Association of (AITAL), 99
Latin American Civil Aviation Commission (LACAC), 89
Lebanon: role in Middle East air transport, 69; role in terrorist activity, 225 *See also* Middle East Airlines, Trans Mediterranean Airways
legislative branch of government, role in international air transport, 121-122, 127
leasing aircraft, 5, 211-212
Libya, assistance to terrorist groups, 225, 232, 236. *See also* Libyan Arab Airlines
Libyan Arab Airlines, 69
Linee Aeree Italiane (LAI), 52-53
Lockhead Corp., 195-196
London: African service, 175-176; European service, 174-175; North Atlantic service, 167-170
lost opportunity, approach in bilateral negotiations, 152
LOT: ethnic market, 163; near-collision, 216 n. 8; postwar service, 54-55
Lufthansa: argument over name, 53-54; Atlas membership, 14; fleet, 194, 196; founding, 53-54; international service, 5; organization, 19; owner of Condor, 2; ownership, 7; Mid Atlantic service, 171; North Atlantic service, 170; South Africa service, 177; South Atlantic service, 172; terrorist activity against, 221, 226, 228
Luft Hansa. *See* Deutsche Luft Hansa
Luxembourg: destination for Icelandair, 146; negotiations with USSR, 147

McDonnell Douglas Corp. 193-195, 210-211
Maersk Air, ownership, 9
Malawi, South Africa service, 177
Malaysia, negotiating policy, 149. *See also* Malaysia-Singapore Airlines, Malaysian Airlines System
Malaysia-Singapore Airlines (MSA), history of, 13

Malaysian Airlines System (MAS): founding 13; Taiwan-Tokyo service, 188-190

Malev, as joint-stock airline, 55

Martinair: charter airline, 2; ownership, 9; relationship to KLM, 2, 9

market opportunity, 150-151

marketing and sales restrictions, 31, 151. See also protectionism

Massachusetts Institute of Technology, 85, 103

MBB (Messerschmitt-Bölkow-Blohm), 199

merchant carrier, 164

Mexico, 67, 173-174

Mexico-U.S. service, 173-174

Miami, 173, 174

Mid Atlantic route, 171-172

Middle East, regional traffic, 178

Middle East Airlines (MEA), 69; extortion of, 237; impact of Lebanese war on, 226; Israeli attack against, 226

Middle East-Europe service, 177-178

Middle East-Far East service, 177

Mid Pacific service, 184

military-defense routes, 166

military use of airlines, 26-27, 125-126, 166

Montoneros, 225

Montreal Convention, 228-229

Moscow, Europe service, 175

most favored nation, approach in bilateral negotiations, 152

Mozambique, South Africa service, 177

Nairobi, 176-177

Nairobi-Johannesburg service, 177

National Airlines: North Atlantic route awards, 58, 62; Caribbean route award, 58

National Arab Youth for the Liberation of Palestine, 222-223

National Transportation Safety Board, 115, 118-119, 128

Nefertiti Aviation, 190

negotiations, bilateral, 135-158

Nepal, 164

Netherlands, the: aircraft industry, 199; air-transport negotiating policy, 148. See also KLM

New Delhi, 178

New Zealand, postwar air-transport policy, 48. See also Air New Zealand

Nicosia, 163

Nigeria Airways, 176

Nkomo, Joshua, 224

Nkrumah, Kwame, 22

non aviation quid pro quo, 148, 152, 154

North American-Caribbean service, 173

North America-South America service, 173

North Atlantic route: characteristics, 167-171; postwar service, 54

North Atlantic route awards, U.S., 56-58

North Atlantic Treaty Organization (NATO), as issue in bilateral negotiations, 146, 148

Northeast Airlines, wartime service, 45

North Korea: assistance to terrorist groups, 221, 225; ICAO membership, 85. See also Chosonminhang

North Pacific route, 184

Northwest Orient Airlines: IATA membership, 97; route awards, 59; Taiwan-Japan service, 188; wartime service, 45

Norway, 164

Olympic Airways: ethnic traffic, 162; international service, 5; Middle East service, 178; South Africa service, 177

open skies policy, U.S., 47, 63

Orient Airlines Association (OAA), 99

overseas Chinese, 179

ownership of airlines: government, 6-8; multiple governments, 9-13; other airlines, 8-9; private, 6-8; shipping firms, 9

Pacific route awards, U.S., 59
Pakistan: air-transport development, 19-20, 71; ties with India, 178-179. *See also* Pakistan International Airlines
Pakistan International Airlines (PIA): history, 19-20, 71; service to India, 178-179
Palestine Liberation Army, 225
Palestine Liberation Organization (PLO): extortion of airlines, 237; observer status at ICAO, 88-89, 229
Palestinian organizations: Black September, 220; Fatah, 221; National Arab Youth for the Liberation of Palestine, 222-223; Palestine Liberation Organization, 88-89, 229; Popular Front for the Liberation of Palestine, 221; Popular Front for the Liberation of Palestine — General Command, 221-222
Panagra (Pan American-Grace Airways, Inc.): acquisition by Braniff, 58-59; prewar South American service, 43; postwar route awards, 58
Pan African Airlines, 28
Panama Canal, 42
Pan American World Airways: Africa service, 176; around the world service, 5; Bermuda II route awards, 62; Berlin air corridor service, 185-188; Central America service, 174; dispute with Alitalia, 140; end of monopoly on U.S. international service, 45, 56; Europe-Japan service, 179-184; exchange of route awards with American, 61; exchange of route awards with TWA, 60-61; IATA membership, 97; India-Pakistan service 178-179; Ireland service, 148; Latin America service in 1930s and 1940s, 43; military routes, 166; North Atlantic service, 170; USSR service, 24, 147-148, 165-166; wartime service, 45
Paris: Africa service, 175-176; Europe
service, 174-175; Mid Atlantic service, 171-172; North Atlantic service, 167-170; South Atlantic service, 172; transsiberian service, 183
PEFCO, *See* Private Export Funding Corp.
Peking, 184
permits, 154-155
personal traffic routes, 161-163
Peru, 42, 171, 173. *See also* Aero Peru
Poland: aircraft industry, 202; assistance to terrorist groups, 225; charter member of ICAO, 48; ethnic market, 162
polar route, 183, 184
political asylum, 237-238
political use of airlines, 21-26, 145-149
pooling, 141-142
postal service, in international air transport, 125. *See also* cargo
Popular Front for the Liberation of Palestine, air terrorism of, 221, 226, 229, 237
Popular Front for the Liberation of Palestine — General Command, air terrorism of, 221-222
Pratt & Whitney, 38, 196, 202
prestige routes, 166
pricing of tariffs, 142-143
Portugal: ethnic market, 162; European service, 175
Private Export Funding Corp. (PEFCO), 209
protectionism: aircraft industry, 212-213; airlines, 123-124, 141
Provisional International Civil Aviation Organization (PICAO), 50

Qadaffi, Muammer, 222
Qantas (Queensland and Northern Territory Aerial Services), 2; international service, 64

reciprocity, principle in bilateral negotiations, 151
regulation: bilateral, 135-158; conflicts

between agencies, 127-128; internal, 109-134; multinational, 79-107; regional, 89-90, 155

religious-pilgrimage traffic, 163

Red Army Faction (West Germany), 224, 226

Red Brigade (Italy), 224

Red Help (Netherlands), 224

Rengo Sekigun (Japan), 220, 221, 223, 224

Republic Airlines, Canada Service, 3

restrictive measures. See protectionism

revenue potential, 151

right of innocent passage (first freedom), 136

Rolls Royce, 197

Romania: aircraft industry, 202; exclusion from Chicago Conference, 46

routes: categories of traffic markets, 161-167; characteristics of major international routes, 167-184; structure, 159-161; unconventional international routes, 184-191

Royal Air Maroc, 69

Sabena: Atlas membership, 14; founding, 39; international service, 5; North Atlantic service, 170; organization, 111-113; postwar service, 55; prewar history, 40; South Atlantic service, 172; subsidy of, 15; wartime service, 45 sabotage of aircraft, 219-242

Safair (South Africa), 69, 177

safety, 117-119

Saiqa, 225

Sandinistas, 225

Saudi Arabia, 145; assitance to terrorist groups, 225

SCADTA (Sociedad Colombo-Alemana de Transportes Aeros), 42. See also Avianca

Scandinavian Airlines System (SAS): assistance to Thai Airways International, 72; ethnic traffic, 163; founding, 10, 54; KSSU membership, 14;

international service, 5; North Atlantic service, 170; organization, 10, 111-112, 113; ownership, 7; polar service, 183; postwar service, 55; sandwich war, 95; South Africa service, 177

Seaboard World Airlines, 60. See also Flying Tiger

security standards, 144-145. See terrorism

Shannon, 136, 148, 171

shipping lines: as organizers of airlines, 9; as owners of airlines, 37-38. See also American Export, Hapag-Lloyd, W.R. Grace Co.

show-cause order, U.S. CAB, 98-99

SILA (Svensk Interkontinental Lufttrafik), 46

silk route, 179-184

Singapore, 66, 179

Singapore Airlines (STA), 66; IATA membership, 97

SITA (Société Internationale de Télécommunications Aéronautiques), 100

SLM (Surinaamse Luchtvaart Maatschappij), Mid Atlantic service, 171

Soloviev P.A., 201

South Africa: ICAO membership, 88; South Atlantic service, 172; ties with black-governed African countries, 177. See also Safair, South African Airways

South African Airways, 69; South Atlantic service, 172

South America: air transport in 1930s and 1940s, 42-43; international service, 174; postwar air transport, 66-67

South America-North America service, 173

South Atlantic service 172

Southern Air Transport, 28

South Korea, 149. See also Korean Air Lines

South Moluccans, 224

South Pacific service, 184

South Yemen, assistance to terrorist groups, 225, 236
Soviet Union. *See* Union of Soviet Socialist Republics
Spain: aircraft industry, 199; European service, 175
State, Department of, U.S., 24, 120, 122, 127-128, 145-147, 165-166
strategic policy routes, 165-166
subsidy: to aircraft industry, 197-198; to airlines, 15, 21, 143-144, 166
surface transportation, as competition, 164
supersonic transport aircraft (SST), 112, 197, 204-207
Swissair: international service, 5; KSSU membership, 14; North Atlantic service, 170; ownership, 7; postwar service, 55; relationship with Balair, 2; South Africa service, 177; South Atlantic service, 172
Syria: assistance to terrorist groups, 222, 225; negotiations with U.S., 24

TABSO, as joint-stock airline, 55
Taipei, 179, 184, 189
Taiwan: ICAO membership, 88; international service, 179. See China Airlines
Taiwan-Japan service, 188-190
TAN (Honduras), U.S. service, 174
Tariff Conferences, IATA, 94-95, 142-143
Tarom, as joint-stock airline, 55; fleet, 106 n. 20, 197
Tata, J.R.D., 71
taxation, preferential, 30
TDA. TOA *See* Domestic Airlines
technical stop, 136
Tel Aviv, 177; Cairo route, 190
terminals, 139
terrorism, air, 219-242; issue in ICAO, 88-89, 228-230; issue in IFALPA, 102, 230-231; issue in U.S., 227-228; major perpetrators, 220-225; response of different countries, 231-235

Thai Airways International, 72
Thornton, Robert L., 46
THY (Turk Hava Yollari): interest in Cyprus Turkish Airlines, 70; route network, 70; safety record, 71
TMA, *See* Trans Mediterranean Airways cargo carrier, 6
TOA Domestic Airlines (TDA), 7
Tokyo, 179-184
Tokyo Convention, 228-229
tourism: government agencies of 123-125; international organizations of, 101-102
tourism-related traffic, 162
traffic rights, 135-139, 150-152
traffic stop, 136
transatlantic service, 168-169 (fig.)
Transatlantic Route Renewal Case, U.S., 57
Trans Australia Airways, 2
Transcontinental & Western Air, wartime service, 45. *See* TWA
transpacific service, 184
transsiberian service, 182-184
Transportation, Department of, U.S., 115-118, 128
Trans Mediterranean Airways (TMA; Lebanon), 69. around the world service, 5; cargo carrier, 6
Trans World Airlines (TWA): around the world service, 59; assistance to Ethiopian Airlines, 68-69; assistance to Lufthansa, 54; Bermuda II route awards, 62; dispute with Alitalia, 140; exchange of route authorizations with Pan Am, 60; interest in Iranian Airways, 70; interest in LAI, 53; Ireland service, 148; loss of around the world service, 61; North Atlantic service, 170; postwar route awards, 57-60
Trippe, Juan, 45, 56, 60
Truman, Harry, influence in postwar route awards, 58
Tupamaros, 225
Tupolev, A.N., 200-201, 204-206
Turbomeca, 198

Turkish People's Liberation group, 225
turnaround service, 137
TWA. *See* Trans World Airlines

Union of Soviet Socialist Republics:
    aircraft industry, 69, 200-202,
    205-206, 211; assistance to terrorist
    groups, 221, 225, 229, 234-235;
    Berlin air corridors, 185-188; cur-
    rency conversion policy, 29; ethnic
    market, 163; negotiations about
    Berlin service, 25; negotiations with
    the United States. 23-25, 146-148;
    negotiations with West Germany,
    25; postwar air-transport policy,
    46-48, 55; restrictive practices, 147,
    151; surface transportation, 164;
    transsiberian service, 182-184
unions. *See* Air Line Pilots Associa-
    tion, International Federation of
    Airline Pilots Associations
United Aircraft and Transport Corp.,
    38
United Air Lines; founding, 38; war-
    time service, 45
United Nations, response to terror-
    ism issue, 227-228
United Red Army (Japan), 220, 221,
    223
United States: aircraft industry,
    193-196, 209-210; antiterrorism
    policy, 229, 231, 232; ethnic
    market, 162; negotiations with Arab
    states, 145; negotiations with the
    People's Republic of China,
    145-146; negotiations with USSR,
    23-24, 146-148; postwar air-
    transport policy, 46-50, 56-63,
    145-149; prewar air-transport policy,
    38-39; route award policy, 3; war-
    time service, 45. *See also* Civil
    Aeronautics Board, Federal Avia-
    tion Administration, Department of
    State, Department of Transporta-
    tion, and listings for individual U.S.
    airlines

U.S.-Canada service, 173
U.S.-Central America service, 173-
    174
U.S.-Mexico service, 174
US. Air, Canada service, 3
user charges, 29, 144
USSR. *See* Union of Soviet Socialist
    Republics
Ustashi, 220, 223-224
UTA (Union de Transports Aerians;
    France): interest in other airlines, 8;
    international service, 3, 5; KSSU
    membership, 14; ownership, 8

Varig (Brazil): international service, 5,
    66-67; ownership, 7; South Atlantic
    service, 172; U.S. service, 173
VFW (Vereinigte Flugtechnische
    Werke), 199
Viasa (Venezuela): Mid Atlantic ser-
    vice, 171; U.S. service, 173
Vienna, 160, 163
visiting friends and relatives (VFR)
    traffic, 162-163
Vozdushniv transport, 103

Warsaw Convention, 123
Western Air Lines: Canada service, 3,
    173; Mexico service, 174
World Airways, leasing of aircraft, 6
World Tourism Organization (WTO),
    101
World War II, air transport in,
    43-46

Yakovlev, A.S., 200
Yugoslavia; assistance to terrorist
    groups, 225; European service, 175;
    joint-stock airline in, 55; Ustashi
    terrorist attacks against, 223-224.
    See also JAT

Zambia, South Africa service, 177
Zimbabwe, South Africa service, 177
Zimbabwe African People's Union
    (ZAPU), air terrorism of, 224

About the Author

Betsy Gidwitz holds a joint appointment at the Massachusetts Institute of Technology as a research associate in the Department of Political Science and a lecturer in the Flight Transportation Laboratory of the Department of Aeronautics and Astronautics. Her responsibilities at M.I.T. involve teaching graduate courses in and conducting research on political influences in the international commercial air-transport industry. She has published several articles on international affairs, including political aspects of international civil aviation.